Industrial Labor in the Republic of Senegal

PRAEGER SPECIAL STUDIES IN
INTERNATIONAL ECONOMICS AND DEVELOPMENT

Industrial Labor in the Republic of Senegal

Guy Pfeffermann

Foreword by Thomas Balogh

FREDERICK A. PRAEGER, Publishers
New York · Washington · London

The purpose of the Praeger Special Studies is to make specialized research monographs in U.S. and international economics and politics available to the academic, business, and government communities. For further information, write to the Special Projects Division, Frederick A. Praeger, Publishers, 111 Fourth Avenue, New York, N.Y. 10003.

FREDERICK A. PRAEGER, PUBLISHERS
111 Fourth Avenue, New York, N.Y. 10003, U.S.A.
77-79 Charlotte Street, London W.1, England

Published in the United States of America in 1968
by Frederick A. Praeger, Inc., Publishers

© 1968 by Frederick A. Praeger, Inc.

Library of Congress Catalog Card Number: 68-18926

Printed in the United States of America

To Irene

ACKNOWLEDGMENTS

I was able to undertake this study thanks to a three-year Besse scholarship to St. Antony's College, Oxford. A college travel grant enabled me to visit Senegal, where I enjoyed the kind hospitality of President Leopold Sedar Senghor.

I am indebted to many persons for help and constructive criticism. Among those I wish to thank in particular are E. F. Jackson, A. D. Flanders and R. B. Sutcliffe at Oxford, and C. F. Brun, P. H. Delmas, and J. B. Mas in Dakar.

I also wish to express my thanks to C. W. Newbury who read and criticized the historical parts of the book, and to M. Tondowski who helped me eliminate some of my most blatant misuses of the English language.

Last but not least, I wish to thank Mrs. M. Edwards, Mrs. L. Leach, and Mrs. C. Morris who had the patience to decipher my draft and put it into its present form.

Guy Pfeffermann

Washington, D.C.

FOREWORD

Mr. Pfeffermann has attempted to apply neo-classical methods of analysis to the fascinating problem of industrial development in Senegal, an excolonial, tropical area. While the result has been negative, the attempt, in my opinion, has been well worthwhile. Not only does it show the need for substantial modification of the assumptions on which that theory has been built up when it is applied to the harsh realities of the countries in the condition in which Senegal has found itself; the impact of the extremely complex interrelationships between the exmetropolitan with the excolonial area; the continuing institutional background which makes for automatic dominance and thus inhibits orderly development towards a more equal distribution of economic activity and income. Much the most fascinating role is played in this concatenation of affairs by the monetary and economic institutions of European origin in Africa which has been similar in the ex-British territories, on which I was working in the past. The translation into this queer excolonial atmosphere of North Atlantic arrangements for the protection of wage earners leads not to prosperity and equality, but stagnation and inequality, a fact of which the International Labor Office ought to take more note than it actually does in its well-meant but ill-fated proselytizing activities.

I hope that Mr. Pfeffermann will, at some time, carry forward his work and investigate how an adaptation of rural education to contemporary tropical requirements, a change in land tenure systems, and (especially in Senegal) an enlightened policy towards modifying the economic impact of certain religious sects can reverse the tendency to stagnation and injustice which Mr. Pfeffermann so clearly demonstrated. With his painstaking assemblage of data very difficult to come by, he has produced a work which will contribute to our knowledge of how the neo-imperialist system works in a fascinating part of the world.

Thomas Balogh

Balliol College
Oxford
April, 1968

CONTENTS Page

PART I

THE EQUILIBRIUM OF THE MARKET
UNDER COMPETITIVE CONDITIONS

PART II

IMPERFECTIONS OF THE LABOR MARKET: MULTIRACIAL
STRUCTURE, TRADE UNIONS AND GOVERNMENT

ix

LIST OF TABLES

xiv

LIST OF FIGURES

ABBREVIATIONS

AOF	Afrique Occidentale Française
BCEAO	Banque Centrale des Etats de l'Afrique de l'Ouest
BEI	Brevêt d'Enseignement Industriel
BEPC	Brevêt d'Etudes du Premier Cycle
CAP	Certificat d'Aptitude Professionnelle
CELPOM	Comité d'Etudes et de Liaison du Patronat pour l'Outre-Mer
CELPUF	Comité d'Etudes et de Liaison du Patronat de l'Union Française
CEP	Certificat d'Etudes Primaires Elémentaires
Cert.	Certificate
cfa	Communauté Financière Africaine (In colonial times: Comptoirs Français d'Afrique)
CNPF	Conseil National du Patronat Français
EEC	European Economic Community ("Common Market")
FENASYCOA	Fédération Nationale des Syndicats des Commerçants de l'Ouest Africain
FIDES	Fonds d'Investissement pour le Développement Economique et Social Outre-Mer
FOB	Free on Board
GDP	Gross Domestic Product
GNP	Gross National Product
IFC	International Finance Corporation (World Bank Group)
ILO	International Labor Organization
INSEE	Institut National de Statistiques et d'Etudes Economiques

MP	Member of Parliament
NNF	Nonnuclear Family
OEP	Oxford Economic Papers
PRA-S	Parti du Regroupement Africain -- Sénégal
PUF	Presses Universitaires de France
PW & C	Public Works and Construction Firms
QJE	Quarterly Journal of Economics
RIT	Rapport d'Inspection du Travail
SCYMPEX	Syndicat des Commerçants Importateurs et Exportateurs de l'Ouest Africain
Sit. Ec.	Situation Economique du Sénégal, Yearly Publication, Services de la Statistique, Dakar
smig	Salaire Minimum Interprofessionnel Garanti.
UNISYNDI	Union Intersyndicale d'Enterprises et d'Industries (de l'AOF)
UNTS	Union Nationale des Travailleurs du Sénégal
UPS	Union Progressiste Sénégalaise
UST	Union Sénégalaise du Travail

NOTE ON SOURCES AND CURRENCY

Sources

Data from interviews with industrial workers and employers were used for certain parts of this study. Interview schedules are shown with the answers and comments in Appendix G. References to interviews in the text consist in a letter and a number. W stands for workers' interviews and E for employers' interviews; each question has a number. An example: (W 17) refers to question 17 in the workers' interviews schedule; (E 8) refers to question 8 in the employers' interviews schedule.

Currency

The unit of currency usually used in this book is the cfa franc (Communauté Financière Africaine). The rate of exchange of the cfa franc is US $1 = cfa 246.85; i.e., cfa 100 = US $0.4051.

Industrial Labor in the Republic of Senegal

INTRODUCTION

OBJECT AND OUTLINE

Senegal shares its institutional background and much of its present institutional framework with the other tropical Franc-area countries of Africa. Problems of political economy in a post-colonial--some authors call it "neo-colonial"-- country are to a great extent common to all these developing countries.

This book examines the labor market of Senegal and analyzes the degree of compatibility between labor policies and the requirements of economic development:

- What are the features of the labor market?

- Are the labor policies pursued by industrial employers, trade unions and the government compatible with the requirements of economic development?

- If not, how can these policies be modified so as to permit faster growth?

In the first part, we shall analyze the features of the labor market "under competitive conditions" (without government, trade union and racial imperfections) in the light of economic theory and of the factors specific to Senegal: What form would supply and demand curves take in the absence of market imperfections?

In the second part, we will examine market imperfections due to racial factors, to trade-unionism and to government labor policies influencing the equilibrium "under competitive conditions."

Having determined the respective influences of racial factors, trade union and government policies on the labor market, we will, in the third part, ask what effects present features of the labor market have on economic development; first, we shall examine the effects of market imperfections on variables that are significant for economic growth, then we shall analyze changes in present labor policies which might favor faster economic development.

1

One of the central issues raised in this book is that
of the choice of techniques: What are the determinants of
the choice of factor-proportions in industry? Empirical
evidence, rather than economic theory, will be analyzed in
this respect. The question of "balanced growth" will also
be dealt with.

The theoretical aspects of the problems of economic
development will not be stressed; the book attempts to
show how social factors, such as those deriving from the
colonial and post-colonial situation, from the political
position of trade unions, and from traditional family solidarities, complicate economic choices.

The scarcity of literature on industrial development
in French West Africa and in the successor-States is well
known; apart from official publications, a few newspaper
articles and socio-economic studies by the University of
Dakar, very little has been published on these problems.
Much of this regrettable situation is due to the reticence
of private businessmen to disclose detailed information on
industry; the traditional reserved attitude of French businessmen towards outside enquiry is found in Senegal,
amplified by the peculiar political situation of foreign
entrepreneurs; during the colonial time private employers
were suspicious of enquiries because these might have been
used politically against them by trade unions, African parties, and the left wing of the colonial administration;
independence reinforced suspicion. Local governments back
foreign enterprises because (i) it is indispensable for industrial development and (ii) agreements were signed between
African governments and France; expatriate--mostly French--
industrial employers remain largely their own masters in the
private sector of the economy. This exposes the local governments to various attacks by trade unions and opposition
parties which threaten to disrupt the present equilibrium in
which governments have abandoned part of the exercise of their
sovereignty in the private sector.

As no previous work has been done in this field, it is
necessary to give an account of the underlying features of
Senegalese industry. Although similarities can be observed
between imperfections of the labor market in Senegal and in
other African economies--notably in matters such as trade-
unionism and wage policies--the situation of Senegal has
particular features which need to be stressed.

Unless otherwise specified, the words "industry" and
"industrial" will be used in a broad sense (justified by
the country's state of development); "industry" includes

manufacturing, energy, mining, public works, construction and
modern transportation; it embraces the whole "modern sector"
minus services other than transportation; the words "labor,"
"labor force" and "manpower" will refer to Africans; this
includes non-Senegalese Africans working in Senegal but excludes Senegalese workers abroad; the term "expatriate" will
be used mainly to refer to the French community working in
Senegal; sometimes (when pointed out) it will include Syro-
Lebanese living in Senegal.

In order to understand the relationship between industrial labor and economic growth, we will first describe
Senegal's industrial background and conditions for economic
growth in Senegal.

INDUSTRIAL BACKGROUND

Senegal has always been the most heavily industrialized
French territory in Africa south of the Sahara (including
Madagascar). Groundnut oil, jute and sisal textiles, soap
and other products were already manufactured in Senegal before
World War II. During the war, communications between Senegal
and Europe were interrupted and industrial investment was encouraged by the local administration which remained under the
authority of the Vichy Government; between 1942 and 1945,
thirty licenses for establishing industrial enterprises were
granted by the administration of Senegal. After the war,
Dakar remained the main industrial center of the Federation
of French West Africa (Afrique Occidentale Française, or AOF).
Since the mid-fifties, the rise of the Ivory Coast's economy has
affected Senegal's industries adversely.

The colonial system of AOF began to disintegrate in
1958, when Guinea withdrew from AOF and left the Monetary
Union of West Africa; Senegalese industrialists lost most
of the Guinean market. In 1960, the Federation of Mali
(made up of Senegal and the former French Sudan) broke up and
trade relations between Senegal and Soudan (called Mali since
1960) suffered; much of Mali's foreign trade was diverted
through the Ivory Coast instead of being carried by rail to
and from the Dakar harbor.

The Senegalese industries had to rely more and more on
the narrow domestic market; nonetheless, in 1964 Senegal
was still, of all former French colonies in tropical Africa,
the most heavily industrialized and the one in which social
overhead was most developed.

The industrial sector of Senegal in the broad sense accounts for about 20 percent of the Gross Domestic Product;[1]
this percentage is high in comparison with most other African
economies.

There are more than 70 industrial firms employing over
50 workers, including 26 employing over 200 workers according to a recent private survey.[2] This figure excludes
transportation, energy, construction, and oil storage and
distribution; it can be taken as a minimum estimate. The
following table gives an idea of the structure of industry:

TABLE 1

Estimate of Senegal's Industrial Firms
(excluding transportation, energy and construction)

Industry	Number of Firms		
	Under 50 employees	51 to 199 employees	200 employees and more
Extractive	1	4	2
Petroleum*	?	?	8
Food	16	11	3
Groundnut Processing	–	3	4
Textile & Footwear	7	6	6
Woodware & Packaging	3	3	1
Chemical Industries	2	4	1
Metal Engineering	8	12	2
Construction Materials	2	3	1
Public Works	?	1	8
Total	39+	47+	36

* Oil storage and distribution, oil refinery.

Source: ISEA, Inventaire des Etablissements Industriels du
         Sénégal (Dakar: ISEA, 1963).

There are about 100 industrial enterprises employing over 50
employees; the structure of industrial employment in 1962
complements the description of the structure of Senegal's
industry:

Industrial Employment (1962)[3]

Manufacturing and Energy	36.5%
Public Works and Construction	34.5%
Transport	24.5%
Mining	4.5%

Most Senegalese industries are located in and around
Dakar, on the Cap Vert peninsula--Africa's foremost Western
cape; the geographical concentration of industry results
from lack of integration of that sector into the economy as
a whole: Import and export facilities are more important in
determining the location of industries than the site of raw
materials.

The administrative and commercial functions of Dakar
make it an important market for consumer goods; Dakar is the
largest city in French-speaking West Africa--about 525,000
inhabitants--and one of the wealthiest in terms of purchasing
power, partly because of the existence of its large European
population (of over 30,000). Moreover, external economies
are available in and around the city which do not exist in
other parts of Senegal.

Attempts by the Senegalese government to decentralize
industry have not been successful. Industrialists were discouraged from setting up plants "in the bush" because of high
costs (transportation of imported inputs, of marketable out-
puts, setting-up social overhead facilities for the labor
force, etc.). Few factories are to be found outside the Cap
Vert area.

Most industrial firms were established after World War
II; there have been four main waves of industrial investment. A first set of factories was set up around 1928-30;
the World Depression prevented the process of industrialization from following a continually rising course; there was
no significant investment until shortly before, and during,
World War II; this constituted an autarchic effect on the
part of Senegal to survive the war blockade. The third--and
most important--phase of industrial development took place
when public works firms and related industries were established in Senegal for implementing French economic and social
development plans (FIDES programs); 1948-51 was the first
phase of FIDES investments; consumer goods industries were
also established at that time, with the entire AOF market
(some 17 million people) in mind. A fourth phase of industrialization started after the setting-up of an African

government (1957-58). Few industrial firms were established in Senegal after independence (1960), despite the
existence of an "Investment Code"--in contrast to what hap-
pened in the Ivory Coast.

TABLE 2

Types of Industrial Investment: Number of New Firms

Phase	(a)	(b)	(c)	(d)	(e)	(f)	(g)	(h)
pre = 1925	1	-	-	-	-	-	-	1
1926-30	2	2	1	-	1	-	-	6
1931-35	-	-	1	-	-	-	-	1
1936-40	1	-	-	2	-	1	1	5
1941-45	2	-	2	-	1	1	-	6
1946-50	-	5	-	1	2	2	5	15
1951-55	1	1	2	2	-	2	2	10
1956-60	-	-	5	3	-	2	1	11
1961-65	-	-	2	1	1	2	-	6
Total								61

(a) Fats & Oils (Groundnuts)   (b) Public Works
(c) Food (excl. Groundnuts)   (d) Textile & Footwear
(e) Chemical Ind. (other than (a)) (f) Metal Engineering
(g) Other Ind. (incl. Mining)   (h) Total number of
                                        firms

Source: ISEA, Inventaire des Etablissements Industriels du
          Sénégal (Dakar: ISEA, 1963).

TABLE 3

Industrial Investment (1956-65)

Year	Number of New Firms	Product
1956	3	Tuna Canning Biscuits Tins and Barrels
1957 (first year of "semi-autonomy")	4	Calcium Phosphate Mining Noodles and Semolina Blankets Confection
1958	2	Soft Drinks Textile Printing
1959	2	Tuna Canning Metallic Beds
1960 (independence)	nil	
1961	2	Shirts and Raincoats Agricultural Machinery
1962	2	Soft Drinks Doors and Window Frames
1963	2	Oil Refinery Tuna Refrigeration Plant
1964	nil	
1965	nil	

Sources: BCEAO, Notes d'Information et Statistiques (Paris:
BCEAO, Monthly); ISEA, Inventaire des Etablissements Industriels du Sénégal (Dakar: ISEA, 1963).

Three facts should be kept in mind concerning industrialization in Senegal: (i) Many industrial ventures have a
somewhat artificial character: They came as a result of subsidies (by the colonial administration) during and after

World War II; the role of the government in industrialization has also been strong in public works and construction
where firms were introduced into Senegal as a result of public investment programs; political circumstance and government intervention played an important role in industrialization. (ii) Because of political factors and because of increasing industrialization in countries which formerly purchased Senegalese manufactured products, Senegal is at
present over-equipped; there is excess capacity in textile
and food industries; public works firms have reduced their activities since 1963 while expanding operations in other
African areas. (iii) There has been less industrial investment in Senegal between independence and 1965 than between
1956 and independence.

Most of Senegal's manufacturing sector consists of light
industry. "Heavy industry" in Senegal consists merely of
(a) one oil refinery which has refined imported inputs since
1964; it operates at considerably less than full capacity;
(b) one cement plant which produces about 200,000 tons per
year; and (c) one plant producing agricultural machinery.
Other manufacturing industries produce--almost exclusively--
light consumer goods.

With the development of industrial, commercial and administrative activities, the urban population of Senegal
increased; the population of Dakar rose at a much faster
rate than the Senegalese population as a whole as a result
of migration to town:

Index of Population

Year	Senegal	Dakar
1936	100	100
1966	190	565

Sources: For 1936: Annuaire Statistique AOF, Tome I (Dakar;
          1949). For 1966: Marchés Tropicaux, (Paris; 1966),
          March 26.

Private employment rose until the end of the colonial
period (about 1957), declined during the phase of "semi-
autonomy" (1957-59) and levelled off in the sixties. Present figures of employment are not known with precision;
government statistics for 1962 indicate about 65,000 private
employees; public employment amounted to about 35,000 in
1964. Total employment is about 100,000, including

expatriate employees. Grave deficiencies in the government's statistical services--particularly in matters of
employment--are the main cause of this lack of precision.

Migration to Dakar persisted after the late 1950's,
when employment began to decline; traditional solidarities
between urban wage-earners and their rural relatives ("extended family system") allowed migration to continue despite
the absence of new employment opportunities; relatives ar-
rive in town and find it possible to live at a wage-earner's
expense.

                    *   *   *

A diversified industrial labor force existed long before World War II. In 1943,

...workers could be found in all occupations
(metal workers, construction workers, machine and
vehicle drivers, textile mill workers, leather
workers, printers, workers in the food industries,
etc.).4

Occupational breakdowns have less meaning in Africa
than in industrialized countries because of a low degree of
specialization; it is more relevant for this study to divide wage-earners into unskilled workers--mostly illiterate--
skilled workers, and foremen.

Qualification of Labor Force

Year	Percentage of unskilled workers in total labor force
1947	about 60%
1962	about 44%

The multiracial character of the Senegalese labor force
must also be pointed out. Many unskilled Frenchmen migrated
to West Africa without having secured a job; these petits
blancs often competed for jobs with African labor, slowing
down the latter's training and promotion. In 1947, all foremen and nearly 20 percent of skilled workers employed in
industry were expatriates. The colonial, and later the Senegalese
administration sought to discourage unskilled Frenchmen from
remaining in Africa; the proportion of unskilled expatriates
eventually declined. Since independence there is no more
actual competition between Africans and Europeans for jobs

other than supervisory, technical or clerical. Now, even
when Europeans are hired as "workers" (according to their
wage-grade, or administrative job description), they perform supervisory tasks. The present racial structure of
industrial employment is shown in the following table:

TABLE 4

Industrial Employment (1962)

Senegalese	28,221	87.0%
Non-Senegalese Africans	1,524	4.7%
French	2,376)	
Non-French Expatriates	262)	8.3%
Total	32,373	100.0%

Source: Ministère du Travail, Statistiques de la Sécurité
          Sociale (Dakar: roneoed, 1964).

     The industrial sector of Senegal must now be placed in-
to the broader context of national economic development.
What are the conditions for economic development in Senegal?

THE BACKGROUND TO ECONOMIC GROWTH

     The first question to be asked is whether the concept
of economic dualism is relevant in the case of Senegal: If
so, the analysis of growth policies will be possible in
terms of inter-sectoral relationships. Once we have established whether an analysis in terms of economic dualism is
meaningful, we can examine very briefly past and present
policies for economic growth in Senegal and ask whether
these succeeded in stimulating growth, and if not so, why.

Dualism and Economic Growth in Senegal

     The structure of Senegal's economy and its evolution have
been described in publications the scope of which is beyond
that of this book.[5] Some of the essential features of the
economy are (i) extreme scarcity of resources, (ii) the resulting narrowness of the domestic market.

     If the concept of dualism is relevant, Senegal's econ-
omy could be divided into (a) an agricultural sector that
includes about 87 percent of the working population; it

produces most of Senegal's exports--groundnuts--and is unable
to feed the Senegalese population adequately at present, and
(b) a modern sector in many ways closer to Europe than to
Senegal's traditional sector; this includes industry, public administration and modern services.

In a recent article on Latin America, Keith B. Griffin
questioned and largely denied the relevance of the concept
of social dualism in the case of Latin America.[6] His argument is based on a denial of the fact that European society
was superimposed upon an indigenous social structure which
continued its existence "essentially undisturbed and unchanged"[7]; instead, according to Griffin, colonialism has
not isolated but destroyed the indigenous social structure
and re-integrated it into a capitalist-colonialist (international) economic system. Therefore, development should not
be viewed as "merging non-integrated societies so that their
common interest becomes apparent" but on the contrary,
society ought to be viewed "as composed of various groups
with opposing interests."[8]

Griffin does not go as far as denying the relevance of
the concept of economic dualism in a static sense (discrepancy between income per head in the modern, versus the traditional, sector) but argues that the interests of social
groups in each of the sectors and between the sectors are
likely to conflict, so that each group tries to maximize
its own advantage against the interests of other groups.

There is no question about the existence of two sectors
in a static economic sense in Senegal. The Dakar area includes almost all industrial resources, energy, modern services and élite in Senegal, although it only comprises 16.2
percent of the country's population. Similarly, over 75
percent of the expatriate population of Senegal lives in and
around Dakar.

Apart from the Cap Vert area, there are only eight
towns of over 10,000 inhabitants in Senegal, three of these of
over 45,000; the largest centers of urban population outside the Cap Vert area are Kaolack (69,560), Thiès (69,140)
and Saint Louis--former capital of Senegal--(48,840). The
rest of the population lives scattered in about 13,000
villages which makes provision of overhead capital a tremendously arduous and costly task.

The rate of illiteracy is much higher in the rural
areas (over 95 percent among the adult population) than in
Dakar (about 75 percent for men and 97 percent for women).

The rate of school attendance is rank-correlated to the dis-
persion of the population (with the exception of Senegal
Oriental--but the departure is very slight):

TABLE 5

Regional Rates of School Attendance

	(a)	(b)	(c)	(d)
Administrative Regions	% of Population living in villa- ges of less than 500 inhabitants	Invert rank *	% of school attendance	Rank *
Cap Vert	1.6	1	75.0	1
Fleuve (Saint Louis)	37.0	2	41.5	2
Thiès	44.5	3	36.6	3
Casamance	57.2	4	33.9	4
Sine-Saloum (Kaolack)	58.5	5 /5/	22.2	6 /5/
Diourbel	72.0	6 /6/	16.2	7 /6/
Sénégal Oriental	74.5	7	25.1	5

* In brackets: Without Senegal Oriental.
Sources: Services de la Statistique, Repertoire des Villages
           (Dakar: roneoed, 1964); Services de la Statistique,
           Situation Economique du Sénégal 1963 (Dakar,
           1964), p. 17.

The over-all rate of school attendance of about 35.3 percent
in fact means that most urban children attend school, while
most rural children do not.

Moreover, a phenomenon of "élite migration" common to
most developing countries can be found in Senegal. That minority of slightly educated rural children severs its links
with the villages and goes to town, trying to find administrative employment.[9] This deprives the worst-off sector of the
economy of its badly needed potential leadership.

Because of desertion of agriculture by its educated
minority, the task of bridging the gap between the two sectors is largely carried out by technical assistants; these
face "cultural dualism": The very concept of "development"
is not easily accessible to illiterate Senegalese peasants:

"African dialects do not include abstract terms.
For instance, in Wolof, the most widespread language

in Senegal, "there are at least ten verbs (all
phonetically different from each other) meaning
'tearing off,' each of them meaning one specific
way of tearing off, or one specific torn-off object ...
education must give /Senegalese peasants7 a channel
for thought at the elementary stage; the will to
develop can only come at a second stage."[10]

It is not necessary to point out the striking contrast between the mental state of Senegalese peasants and that of
the highly sophisticated élite among urbanized French-
speaking Africans.

Some of the features of colonization in Latin America,
and some of that continent's social and political realities
are also irrelevant in the case of Senegal (as well as of
much of tropical Africa): (i) The main difference is that
there is no foreign appropriation of land; in a system of
shifting agriculture land is res nullius. The right to cul-
tivate is allocated every year to farmers by traditional
village authorities; land is nobody's good. Therefore there
can be no conflict of interest between latifundia owners and
tenants, etc. (ii) In the cities there is no conflict between a minority of unionized workers and a majority of non-
organized ones, as is the case in Latin America. Collective
bargaining and national minimum wage rates have eliminated
gross discrepancies among African wage-earners. (iii) A
further and most important difference between the two cases
is that there is no "urban-based middle class party"[11] in
Senegal. The economic functions of the middle class are
largely performed by expatriates; these do not exert direct
political incluence; the dominant political party is mostly
rural-based, and relies on the votes of peasants rather
than on support from the small African "urban middle class."

Moreover, the interests of the urban and of the traditional sectors coincide to a very large extent: The urban
part of the economy is very tightly related to production of
cash crop; any declines in agricultural production affect
industrial output adversely.

Thus, in contrast with Griffin's analysis of Latin
America, it seems legitimate to say that there is economic
and social dualism in Senegal, and no basic conflicts of
interest between the different social groups. In an economic
and social sense, an analysis of the Senegalese economy in
terms of dualism appears to be adequate for the purpose of

this book;   the Senegalese peasants continued, after colonization, their "essentially undisturbed and unchanged"
existence.[12]

What, then, are the main features of the traditional
sector, and how are the two sectors geared to each other?

Cultivated land is distributed almost evenly between
cash crop and food crop:

TABLE 6

Agricultural Area and Output

Crop	Cultivated Area (in 1,000 hectars)	Estimated Output (in 1,000 tons)
Groundnuts	1,055	1,019
Millet	1,011	532
Other (food)	241	
Total	2,307	

Source: Services de la Statistique, Situation Economique
         du Sénégal 1965 (Dakar, 1966), pp. 29-32.

The quantity of cash crop produced and its price determine the monetary purchasing power of the rural population;   at present, cash crop is purchased by government
agencies at about 22 cfa francs per kilo.

Groundnut products constitute about three-quarters of
Senegal's exports in value (1964);   minerals represent about
8.5 percent. Other exports consist mainly of tuna fish,
flour and footwear. Imports of equipment represent only
about 12 percent to 13 percent of total imports. Because
of stagnation of agricultural productivity and rise in imports, Senegal suffers from a balance of trade deficit.
Industrial exports do not show a rising trend: It is
Senegal's agricultural sector that basically determines the
level of export earnings.

The structure of the economy can be shown in a breakdown of Gross Domestic Product. Agriculture and commerce
are the two largest contributors to GDP--a traditional feature of colonial-type economies.

TABLE 7

Structure of GDP (1965)

	Percent
Agriculture (including subsistence)	35.4
Industry and Crafts	11.3
Public Works and Construction	4.3
Transport	4.9
Services	5.3
Commerce	35.5
Production of Public Administration	1.3
Production of Households	2.0
Total	100.0

Source: Services de la Statistique, Situation Economique
du Sénégal 1965, (Dakar, 1966).

In 1965 GDP amounted to 148.82 billion cfa francs (about
US $585 million).

The expenditure of the Senegalese government amounts to
over 50 billion cfa francs[13]--a very large fraction of GDP.
Public expenditure increased about fivefold between 1959 and
1964 and has remained fairly stable since then. State revenue
only amounts to about 34 billion cfa francs; the deficit is
financed by foreign aid and--up to exhaustion--by running
down public reserves.

The crucial factor that emerges from an analysis of the
Senegalese economy is the interrelation between the agricultural and the modern sectors. Senegalese Statistical Services calculated that there is some correlation between
agricultural output and GNP per head for the economy as a
whole (coefficient of correlation +0.7); although production of groundnuts and derived products makes up only 23 percent of GDP, its real importance is much greater: It is the
main "leading" sector of the economy.[14]

Groundnut output influences (i) rural demand for manufactured consumer goods, (ii) rural demand for agricultural
machinery and fertilizers, (iii) the level of activity in
the groundnut-processing industry and in industries linked
to the latter (manufacture of sacks, barrels, energy, etc.).

In the short run, the relationship between the traditional sector and the modern one is not symmetrical: While
changes in agricultural output influence industrial activity
very deeply, changes in industrial output have little or no
effect on agricultural production. In the long run, it may
be argued that changes in the manufacture of agricultural
machinery and fertilizers will influence output in the traditional sector; but at present there is only one plant
producing agricultural machinery in Senegal and most of its
inputs are imported and have therefore no growth-inducing
effects on other Senegalese industries. A fertilizer plant
will start operating in 1968 (including IFC capital).

It seems that any long-term program of economic development aiming at increasing GNP per head might start by focusing on agricultural development. Did past development policies and post-independence plans succeed in raising GDP per
head?

DEVELOPMENT POLICIES PAST AND PRESENT

Many attempts were made by the French and later by the
Senegalese to increase GNP per head. Senegal received a
large share of French public investment overseas; after independence, aid replaced direct investment but the order of
magnitude remained the same.

After World War II, the FIDES program was started,
which ran from 1948 to 1958.

Yearly Value of French Public Investment in AOF
(In million 1956 pounds sterling)

from 1931 to 1937	4.0
from 1947 to 1948	4.3
from 1949 to 1956	25.4

Source: AOF 1957, Service Statistiques du Gouvernment
          Général (Dakar, 1958), p. 339.

The FIDES program emphasized nondirectly productive investment:

FIDES Program for Senegal

	Percentage of Overhead on Total Investment
1948-53 (First Plan)	79.0
1953-58 (Second Plan)	78.0

Source: Ministère de la Coopération, République du Sénégal--
Economie et Plan de Développement (Paris, 1964),
p. 73.

It was said by the French administration itself that "public
investment has principally increased the activities of public
works and construction" firms.[15] The standard of living of
the Senegalese population was barely affected by the Plan's
implementation. "This Plan favored development in the cities
while the 'bush' remained in its century-old immobility and
poverty."[16] Indeed, it was clear already in 1951 that the
implementation of the Plan did "not have any marked effect on
the standard of living of the masses ... Groundnut farmers,
unskilled workers ... and their families do not eat better or
more food than before World War II; they are not housed more
decently; they do not dress better ...."[17]

FIDES operations were carried out by large expatriate
firms using capital-intensive methods of production; they
paid very few wages to local employees[18] and recruited teams
of specialized workers which "followed" the works throughout
the country, providing little employment opportunities for
inhabitants of the regions in which works were carried out.

The Senegalese government took the relay from French
planning in 1960. The government's aim, as expressed in the
First National Plan and in statements on policy, is to raise
GNP per head through développement harmonisé. What exactly
is meant by this expression is unclear, since there is no
effort in the Plan at a theoretical approach. It seems,
however, that développement harmonisé has much in common
with a broader version of "balanced growth" as expressed by
W. Arthur Lewis and Hla Myint, according to which, economic
development requires uniform coordinated progress on all
fronts including agriculture, social overhead and directly
productive investment.

The difficulties encountered in increasing agricultural
productivity are beyond the scope of this book; it must

simply be noted that they are tremendous; a huge gap must be
bridged between the technology and above all the mental structures of the modern sector (public administration) and those
of a scattered population whose productivity is lower than
that of the Egyptian fellah. However, part of the reason why the
government failed to raise agricultural productivity--
stagnated since World War II--is undoubtedly due to the inefficiency of the administration and its lack of contact with
the world of peasants; the engineering firm in charge of
preparing the First National Plan (1961-64) sorted out
positive and negative human factors of development and put
"the behavior of public employees--notably in rural areas--
among the negative factors."[19]

Finally, for an over-all appraisal of economic stagnation in Senegal, the following series was worked out that represents the evolution of GDP deflated by population growth
(adopting a "low" hypothesis of 2 percent per annum) and
weighted by the evolution of wholesale prices:

TABLE 8

Estimated Index of GDP per Head in Real Terms

Year	Index
1956	100.0
1957	94.61
1958	86.56
1959	80.19
1960	79.05
1961	78.38
1962	77.59
1963	72.24
1964	74.20
1965	71.98

Sources: Services de la Statistique, Comptes Economiques du
          Sénégal 1959-1962 (Dakar, 1964); BCEAO, Notes
          d'Information et Statistiques (Paris: BCEAO, No.
          141).

Past and present policies did not lead to economic
growth in terms of GDP per head. We can now turn our attention to labor problems, and their relation to economic
growth.

Excluding imperfections due to trade unions, government
policy and the multiracial structure of employment for the
moment, the first problem will be to analyze--in the light of
economic theory as well as of specific features of the Senegalese economy--demand for and supply of labor "under competitive conditions."

Notes to Introduction

1. Services de la Statistique, Situation Economique du
   Sénégal en 1964, (Dakar, 1965), p. 79.

2. ISEA, Inventaire des Etablissements Industriels du
   Sénégal (Dakar: ISEA, 1963); On public works firms,
   Africa (January-February, 1964).

3. Ministère du Travail, Statistiques de la Sécurité
   Sociale (Dakar: roneoed, 1964).

4. RIT Dakar 1943 (Dakar: Labor Administration, 1943).

5. Hubert Deschamps, Le Sénégal et la Gambie (Paris: PUF,
   1964); Marcel Massé, A Study of Manufacturing in Senegal (Oxford, B.Phil. Thesis, 1966); Jean Barbier,
   L'Economie de l'Arachide au Sénégal (Lille, Doctorate
   Thesis, Faculty of Law, 1960).

6. Keith B. Griffin, "Reflections on Latin American Development," Oxford Economic Papers (March, 1966).

7. Ibid.

8. Ibid.

9. Mirielle Bouthier, "La Diversification des Cultures et
   ses Problèmes au Sénégal," Tiers Monde, Vol. VI, No. 24,
   1965.

10. Ibid.

11. Keith B. Griffin, op. cit.

12. Ibid.

13. Ministère des Finances, Rapport au Conseil National de
     l'UPS (Dakar: roneoed, 1964).

14. J.B. Mas, Le Rôle de l'Arachide dans la Croissance
     Economique du Sénégal, (Dakar: Services de la Statis-
     tique, 1964);   Comptes Economiques du Sénégal 1959-1962
     (Dakar: Services de la Statistique, 1964).

15. Annuaire Statistique de l'AOF, Vol. V, Tome 3   (Dakar:
     Services de la Statistique, 1957), p. 181.

16. Jean Rous, Chronique de la Décolonisation (Paris:
     Présence Africaine, 1965), p. 237.

17. RIT Sud Sénégal 1951 (Kaolack: Labor Inspectorate,
     roneoed, 1952).

18. A public works firm interviewed in 1964--one of the
     firms which worked for FIDES plans--stated that labor
     costs amounted to less than 15 percent of retail price.
     Two-thirds of labor costs are for African employees.

19. COGERAF Rapport sur les Structures des Administrations
     Centrales de la République du Sénégal (Paris: COGERAF,
     1960).

PART   **I**   THE EQUILIBRIUM OF
THE MARKET UNDER
COMPETITIVE CONDITIONS

Our purpose is to analyze the effects of policies on
the labor market. In order to be able to show the respective influences of trade union and government policies, and
of imperfections due to the multiracial composition of the
labor market on demand, supply, wages and employment, we
must isolate these variables from such influences. In the
first chapter, we shall turn to economic theory. In the
second chapter, the specific features of the Senegalese economy will be introduced. Both approaches complement each
other and lead to a hypothetical analysis of equilibrium
"under competitive conditions."

CHAPTER **1** A THEORETICAL

APPROACH

This chapter does not attempt to discuss economic theories, but to find theoretical guidelines which will be needed for a later analysis of trade union and government policies.

What does economic theory teach concerning demand for and supply of industrial labor in developing countries? How are supply and demand determined? What are the theoretical limits to wages and employment?

During the nineteenth century, labor was primarily viewed as a factor of production bought and sold under conditions of perfect competition; the "cost of production" and "productivity" of labor governing its supply and demand were analyzed by classical and neoclassical economists. Alfred Marshall expanded the "marginal productivity theory of labor" and broadened the perspective of the analysis, stating that "wages are not governed by demand-prices, nor by supply-prices, but by the whole set of causes which govern demand and supply."[1]

Later economists gave political and institutional factors increasing importance in the theory of wages and employment. Attention focused on a "set of causes": Conventional forces, market forces--in conditions of perfect and imperfect competition--collective bargaining, public regulations;[2] the general level of productivity and the bargaining power of trade unions, and the regulatory action of the state were in the center of analysis.

Labor problems attracted the attention of economists dealing with backward areas at an early stage; at first, the problem confronting these was to create a suitable supply of labor for new colonial plantations, mines and industries. In the sparsely populated areas of Africa, demographic problems and migrations were carefully studied; methods for increasing the supply of labor were analyzed: Forced labor, "recruitment agents," head taxes, etc.

Attention later focused on micro-economic problems such
as the workers' reactions during the process of urbanization:
The existence of backward-sloping supply curves of labor was
in the center of debate. The stabilizing effect of various
wage policies was analyzed for the benefit of the colonial
administration and employers.

Only since World War II has emphasis shifted from the
interests of colonial administrations and firms to more general problems of economic growth (i.e., increasing the national
product per head); classical theories of wages were rejected
by many modern economists because of the obvious absence of a
market economy in most developing countries: The influence of
governments and of foreign investors on economic conditions is
so strong that theories largely based on "pure and perfect
competition" are unsatisfactory tools. Problems such as the
determination, evolution and distribution of wages are deeply
influenced by political factors; this is especially the case
in former colonial territories which have become politically
independent without, however, enjoying full economic independence: The former French colonies of tropical Africa provide
good examples.

Modern economic theory has devoted a great deal of attention
to supply and demand schedules of industrial labor, since it
affects not only present conditions but prospects of economic
development.

DEMAND FOR INDUSTRIAL LABOR

How are industrial wage rates determined in developing
economies and what are the limits set to their determination?

In the short run, the volume of industrial employment
depends on the evolution of demand in the product market; in
the long run, it also depends on changes in the techniques of
production.

In theory, sociological factors might prevent the level
of industrial wages from being set below a certain rate:
"Wage rates may not fall to the point where the community
feels that the employer is 'exploiting' his workers."[3] In
colonial or post-colonial dualistic economies in which the
majority of industrial firms are foreign-owned and foreign-
managed, this rule does not necessarily apply: There is no
single "community"; expatriate employers do not belong to the
same community as their personnel and are therefore indifferent, up to a point, to moral pressure from the indigenous

society. Moreover, in small developing countries there are few standards with which the indigenous community is able to compare industrial wage rates.

Apart from social pressure, the floor to industrial wages is set by earnings in the subsistence sector; minimum wages must be slightly higher than agricultural earnings so as to attract labor and to compensate for the costs of transfer and of life in the cities. Supply schedules of labor depend on the average productivity in agriculture: The lower the latter, the lower the minimum wage rate sufficient to attract labor from the agricultural into the modern sector. W. Arthur Lewis estimated that there is usually "a gap of 30 percent or more between the capitalist wages and subsistence earnings."[4] If whole families join the modern sector, the wage rate will have to be higher than would be the case if only individual members of rural families were to be transferred.[5]

Since average productivity in developing countries is low--by definition--industrial wages should be, in the absence of trade unions and governments, set at a much lower level than in industrialized countries.

If the wage rate is determined by reference to marginal productivity of labor in the industrial sector, the firms' demand curve for labor should be identical with the marginal revenue productivity of labor to these firms; wages would still be lower than in industrialized countries because of the low initial productivity of untrained workers entering the modern sector of the economy.

It is the low productivity of indigenous labor which creates the need to keep up an expensive expatriate labor force, thus of maintaining a dualistic labor market: Indigenous and foreign labor constitute, in the extreme theoretical case, two noncompeting groups on the labor market. Indigenous labor is hired for unskilled jobs; the highest level of qualification of indigenous workers may often not exceed that of skilled workers' jobs.

In the long run, demand for labor is determined by the evolution of the product market and by the choice of capital-intensity; the question of factor-proportions is essential in planning economic growth. Labor in developing countries is cheaper than in developed ones; at a naive level neo-classical economic theory suggests that labor-intensive methods of production should be favored in backward countries. However, evidence seems to show that there is a trend in many developing

economies toward more capital-intensive methods of production:
In many African economies there has been, since independence,
a rise in GNP and a rise in industrial production, but stagnation (in some cases contraction) of industrial employment.

This paradox will be analyzed in detail at a later stage.
At this point it is important to show that part of the inadequacy of economic theory to account for actual trends in
factor-proportions comes from the simplified view that the
choice of techniques depends on two homogeneous factors,
capital and labor. This view is misleading: In fact, labor
is heterogeneous--in developing countries there is usually
abundance of unskilled labor but an acute shortage of supervisory labor; training facilities likely to convert the former
into the latter are often inadequate. In fact, the main
scarcity, in most developing economies, may not so much be
capital as certain types of labor.

Theory shows that in countries with low agricultural and
industrial productivity of labor, industrial wages are most
likely to be low (slightly above agricultural earnings). Uneconomic use of unskilled labor leaves room for increasing
productivity without modifying employment.

While sociological factors have little impact on setting
limits to wage-determination in multiracial economies, the demand schedule for industrial labor is influenced by agricultural earnings (and productivity), the marginal productivity of
industrial workers and, of course, the workers' diet; in the
long run, the crucial determinants are demand on the product
market and choice of techniques of production.

SUPPLY OF INDUSTRIAL LABOR

What is the theoretical shape of the supply curve of industrial labor in developing countries? How far is the theory
of "unlimited supplies of labor" relevant to tropical Africa?
What are the factors influencing the slope of the curve?

Simplified growth models based on Lewis' article of 1954[6]
basically consist of two sectors: A "traditional" sector
(primitive technology, few purchased inputs, no salaried employment, limited use of credit) and a "modern" one (industry,
modern services). There is a "fundamental relationship between
the two sectors": "When the capitalist sector expands, it
draws upon labor from the subsistence sector."[7] The supply
elasticity of labor is usually determined by the marginal product of labor in the traditional sector and by the micro-

economic calculus of individuals: The marginal product of labor contributes in determining the possibility of, the individual calculus the willingness for, farmers to enter the modern sector (part time or full time).

Unlimited Supplies of Labor?

Lewis' first model rests on the assumption that unlimited supplies of labor are available in certain developing countries. In these, there are sectors in which the marginal product of labor is near zero, possibly even negative.[8] Labor can thus be withdrawn from the traditional sector and transferred into the modern one without, ceteris paribus, affecting the volume of agricultural output in any way. The theory implies that in addition to possible overt unemployment, there is a reservoir of disguised unemployment that constitutes--if mobilized--a concealed source of savings; such reservoirs can exist in agriculture, in the tertiary sector of activity and even in industry, when employers treat their employees like retainers. It is commonly agreed that agriculture should provide the largest reservoir of disguised unemployment.

There are conceptual and practical difficulties involved in the theory of disguised unemployment; Lewis himself points out that his analysis is primarily relevant to heavily over-populated areas in Asia;[9] nowhere in Lewis' presentation of the model is there a specific reference to relatively sparsely populated African economies. Moreover, Lewis confined the unlimited character of labor to supplies of unskilled manpower; in the long run, this reservation may be lifted at the cost of setting up an adequate manpower-training scheme, but in the short run it deprives the theory of some of its appeal.

The seasonal character of agricultural work is pointed out by Colin Clark and Margaret Haswell: "Any plans for the permanent diversion of this rural labor surplus into other employments come up against the fact that it is not available throughout the year."[10] The authors provide ample statistical evidence supporting their view.

The possibility of maintaining agricultural production at a constant level, while withdrawing labor from the land, has also been questioned by Professors Schultz and Viner who deny that the marginal product of labor in primitive agricultural societies is zero. Their view is that primitive agricultural systems usually make an efficient use of the available factors of production. Given the low level of technology and existing opportunities in such systems, there is a satisfactory allocation of resources, however low the level of equilibrium may appear to be in comparison with more advanced systems of pro-

duction.   Professor Schultz finds (although his evidence is
not as broad as Clark and Haswell's) that there is "no evidence ... that a transfer of some small fraction, say five per
cent, of the existing labor force out of agriculture, with
other things being equal could be made without reducing ...
production."[11]

Professor Myint sees a weakness of the theory in its
failure to distinguish clearly between the product of a unit
of labor (man/hour) and that of a worker; the number of people
employed in agriculture can only be diminished without affecting the level of output if the supply of labor in terms of
hours worked--productivity being constant--increases.   "The
amount of 'disguised unemployment' depends on what ... /̅is
considered 7̅ to be a full day's work for each."[12]   It is possible to withdraw a fraction of the labor force from the
traditional sector without reducing output but this can only
be done at the cost of the remaining farmers putting in more
work.   The supply elasticity of labor depends on the latter's
willingness to work longer hours or harder.

Labor can be removed from the land at the cost of (a) a
reduction in agricultural output, or (b) the farmers left on
the land working harder than before the departure of the
migrants.   Unless the second condition is fulfilled, removing
labor from the land will reduce the quantity of food per head
and/or--in the case of export crops--of export earnings (i.e.,
the capacity to import food).

Positive or Negative Slope?

Individual responses to changes in prices and/or wages
affect the supply of labor; the latter depends on the farmers'
willingness to leave their traditional occupations to enter
the modern sector of the economy.   In a transitory phase the
labor force can be partially committed to both sectors on a
seasonal basis.

Until the end of the colonial period, the view was
accepted by many experts in tropical dependencies that "the
people of the underdeveloped countries /̅ do not 7̅ ... respond
to economic incentives and prospects of material improvement":[13]   Negative measures were used by the colonial administrations and by private employers, rather than positive
economic incentives.   This assumption led the colonial administration to impose head taxes and other fiscal measures in
order to force farmers to join the modern sector of the
economy.   Private employers justified low wages in the same

way, arguing that indigenous workers reacted negatively to economic incentive (i.e., that their preference for leisure increased as income rose).

It was commonly believed in the colonies that income-effects predominated over substitution-effects in the behavior of workers: "Wage earners ... are alleged to have relatively low want schedules or high preference for leisure as against income, so that they work less at higher wage rates and more at lower ones."[14] The supply curve of labor was believed to be positively inclined only up to a certain level--corresponding to a "target" of consumer goods commanded at that level; above that level, the curve was believed to slope backward.

The backward-bending supply curve of labor theory rests on the assumption that individual economic calculations by Africans do not obey the same rules as those of workers in advanced economies: "Nonindustrial workers are reluctant to enter industrial employment because of a lack of appreciation of the new status system in terms of the old."[15] According to W. E. Moore "There is little room for notions of individual 'utility' maximization--economic behavior is guided by traditional factors and community norms."[16]

If the backward-bending supply curve of labor theory is shown to be right, two consequences follow: (i) Since changes in the marginal rate of remuneration do not affect the quantity of labor offered on the market above a certain income-level, migrations from agriculture into industry would cease--above a certain level of agricultural income--to be influenced by changes in prices for crops or changes in quantity produced (e.g., as a consequence of favorable climatic conditions); (ii) a departure from low wage policies in industry might reduce the supply of labor; economic incentives such as premiums linked to individual productivity would be unlikely to have positive effects on the quantity of labor offered. The theory of the backward-bending supply curve of labor provides a basis for "cheap labor" policies.

Elliot Berg throws some doubt upon the validity of the theory, in the case of Africa.[17] He emphasizes the universality of economic rationality: "In contemporary Africa the target income concept is losing its applicability as wants increase in size and flexibility"; according to Berg's study which is based on evidence from various parts of Africa, the individual's offer of labor is largely determined by economic factors: (i) By the intensity of preference for money income as against "leisure" in the village, (ii) by the level of

income from village production; (iii) by the "effort-price of
income" earnable in the village, and (iv) by the "effort-price
of income" earnable outside the village. The supply of labor
to the economy as a whole was found to be inversely related to
village income: The rate of migration to town increases when
harvests have been bad; likewise, if prices for cash crops fall,
village income decreases, and the "effort-price of income"
earned in the village increases, thus favoring an increase of
the migratory flow to town.

In the case of urbanized workers, Berg found that the
supply of labor was positively correlated to the level of
industrial wages: For the modern sector as a whole "the aggregate supply curve of labor ... is positively sloped throughout most of its length."[18]

This conclusion implies that (i) the rate of migration to
town is inversely related to village income; thus, policies
increasing agricultural productivity (and income) might slow
down the rate of migration to town; (ii) in the modern sector
of the economy, a departure from "cheap labor" policies might
increase the supply of labor.

It is not clear why positive individual responses to
economic incentives should be incompatible with traditional
cultural patterns; it is conceivable that individuals moved by
the desire to maximize community utility might respond positively to economic incentives. This could be achieved by
transfers of money from the towns into the agricultural sector
and by institutions such as "extended families" based on traditional solidarities, which imply that urbanized workers
maintain part of their family as retainers.

*   *   *

The quantity of labor supplied in the modern sector of
the economy depends on (a) the farmers' willingness to put in
extra work (if farmers are unwilling to increase their effort,
migration reduces agricultural output--assuming constant pro-
ductivity--and/or export earnings); (b) the response to
changes in income on the part of would-be migrants; the latter
depends mainly on the relationship between marginal preferences
for income and marginal preferences for leisure.

How does the Senegalese labor market fit into this
theoretical framework?

Notes To Chapter 1

1. Alfred Marshall, Principles (8th ed.; London: Macmillan, 1961), p. 532.

2. E. H. Phelps Brown, The Economics of Labor (Yale, 1962).

3. P. T. Bauer and B. S. Yamey, The Economics of Underdeveloped Countries (Cambridge, 1959), p. 78.

4. W. A. Lewis, "Economic Development with Unlimited Supplies of Labor," The Manchester School (May, 1954).

5. Dipak Mazumdar, "Underemployment in Agriculture and the Industrial Wage-Rate," Economica (November, 1959), p. 328.

6. W. A. Lewis, op.cit.

7. Gerald M. Meier, Leading Issues in Development Economics (Oxford: OUP, 1964), p. 85.

8. W. A. Lewis, op.cit.

9. Ibid.

10. Colin Clark and Margaret Haswell, The Economics of Subsistence Agriculture (London: Macmillan, 1964), p. 130.

11. T. Schultz, "The Role of Government in Promoting Economic Growth," in Agriculture in Economic Development, Eicher and Witt, eds. (New York: McGraw-Hill, 1964), p. 375.

12. Hla Myint, The Economics of the Developing Countries (London: Hutchinson, 1965), p. 87.

13. Ibid.

14. E. J. Berg, "Backward-sloping Labor Supply Functions in Dual Economies - The African Case," QJE (August, 1961), p. 468.

15. W. E. Moore, Industrialization and Labor (Ithaca, N.Y.: Cornell University Press, 1951), pp. 35 ff.

16. W. E. Moore, "Labor Attitudes Towards Industrialization in Underdeveloped Countries," American Economic Review (May, 1955).

17. E. J. Berg, op.cit., p. 487.

18. Loc.cit.

CHAPTER **2** THE SENEGALESE
LABOR MARKET

Insofar as it is possible to remove the influence of trade unions and government, as well as certain market imperfections due to the multiracial structure of employment, this chapter will attempt to determine at what level of equilibrium demand and supply curves of labor intersect in Senegal. Much of the evidence is based on interview-schedules used with Senegalese workers and employers in 1964 and 1965.

What determines the level of demand for labor in Senegalese industry? Is the concept of "cheap labor policies" relevant in an analysis of private industry in Senegal? Can the attitude of expatriate employers be said to be "paternalistic" towards their African labor force?

On the supply side, the existing reservoirs of industrial labor will be examined; (in agriculture and outside agriculture) we will also describe some of the features of labor supply in Senegal (mobility, background, slope of supply curve).

In conclusion, the equilibrium "under competitive conditions" will be analyzed in the light of theory and of the specific features of the Senegalese economy.

DETERMINANTS OF DEMAND

In few industrial firms interviewed did the level of employment rise since 1957 (E 16); recruitment has been very sluggish in recent years: Only about 40 percent of firms hired any additional labor during the period 1963-64 (E 17). Present and future needs for additional labor mainly focus on specialized workers and on primary school-leavers without vocational training.

According to industrial employers, the level of employment varies mainly according to trends of the product market (E 18). There does not seem to be a close relationship between changes in wages and the level of employment; in 1953,

32

employment decreased and nominal wages rose by 20 percent but demand on the product market also receded, so that it is difficult to draw conclusions from evidence: In 1961, nominal legal minimum wages rose by 10 percent in spite of the government "wage freeze" policy; this increase had no effect on decisions to recruit and on the level of employment.

In an economy in which wages are determined to a large extent by the government and show great stability, the employer's attention focuses on the evolution of the product market; the latter is the most important variable determining employment levels. Moreover, the low absolute level of wages for unskilled labor leaves room for adjustment without repercussions on the level of employment.

Entrepreneurs show great pessimism as to the future evolution of the product market; an official survey of 1964 shows that a mere 8 percent of industrial employers anticipated expansion at that time; 62 percent of them expected a decline. For most firms there has been stagnation in the Senegalese industry since 1957 (E 9).

Interviews confirm the existence of a relationship between the evolution of the product market and employment: None of the firms having experienced a declining market recruited labor in 1963-64,   among firms having experienced stagnating or slowly progressing markets (less than 3 percent per year), the majority did not hire any extra labor; recruitment is linked to expansion of the market.

Industrial employers' attitudes towards their labor force may be of great significance in determining the level of equilibrium on the labor market. Is the concept of "cheap labor policies" useful in a study of Senegal? And can the behavior of managers be said to be "paternalistic"?

"CHEAP LABOR" POLICIES OF PRIVATE EMPLOYERS AND PATERNALISM

The analysis of "cheap labor" policies relies heavily on Professor Myint's examination of the question.[1] There should be no confusion between the concept of "cheap labor" policies, which refers to attitudes of private employers, and of "wage freeze" policies which refers to government policy of keeping legal minimum wages at a constant level over a period of time.

What does the concept of "cheap labor policies" mean? What is its significance for economic development? Are

symptoms of "cheap labor policies" and/or paternalism to be
found among expatriate employers in Senegal?

The Concept of "Cheap Labor Policies"
and Its Significance

Professor Myint distinguishes three sets of factors that
are characteristic of "cheap labor policies": Quantitative,
qualitative, and psychological factors. All three concern
policies of expatriate employers.

(a) Historically, during the initial phases of industrialization in backward countries,

> wages tended to stick at their initial level in
> spite of the rapid expansion of the mining and
> plantation exports.[2]

(b) The owners of the mines and plantations $\underline{/}$ and industrial
firms_7 usually explained this situation in terms of
the very poor quality of labor ... According to them
the ... low level of wages ... merely reflected the
uniformly low level of labor productivity ... Some
would complain that even at the low wages paid, the
indigenous labor was "expensive" because its productivity was lower still.[3]

(c) Professor Myint adds a third set of factors which affected
the type of wage economy that developed in the developing
countries. These factors include

> the employers' conventional beliefs that, in general,
> indigenous labor not only had low productivity but
> had limited capacity for improvement; and that it
> was used to the customarily low material standard
> of living and would not respond positively to the
> incentive of higher wages. This crystallized into
> the convention of maintaining low wages ...[4]

The consequences of these attitudes were important to the
development of the countries:

> in the early stages of entry into the wage economy,
> the quality of the raw indigenous labor just emerging
> out of the subsistence economy was undoubtedly very
> poor.

But: Had the $\underline{/}$ foreign enterprises_7 ... adopted the
policy of raising wages to attract more labor, the
gap between the wages and the short-run productivity

of the raw labor would have induced them to adopt
various further policies of economizing labor and
raising its productivity--say by more careful
selection, gradation and training[5] ... then the
mines and plantations would have performed their
expected role as the "leading sector" raising
productivity in the rest of the economies in which
they operated. As it was, their low wage policy
induced them to use labor extravagantly, merely as
an undifferentiated mass of "cheap" or "expendable"
brawn-power. So through the vicious circle of
low wages and low productivity, the productivity of
the indigenous labor ... was fossilized at its very
low initial level.[6]

As other observers of developing countries put it, "low
wages tend to make management profligate with a cheap labor
resource"[7] and "the basic assumption /‾of industrial employers ‾7 is that workers must somehow or other train themselves."[8]

Moreover, the level of industrial wages is usually
assessed on the basis of an appraisal of the productivity of
labor. It is very difficult to measure the productivity of
one worker in industrialized economies; the same difficulty
arises in developing countries, but psychological factors
magnify it: The majority of managers and foremen being expatriate, their appraisal of productivity is often influenced
by prejudice. In Africa, "performance is measured almost
exclusively by the /‾expatriate‾7 foreman's opinion or appraisal of the worker,"[9] thus the level of wages tends to remain low
even if the productivity of certain workers increases in the
course of time.

"Cheap labor policies" keep the level of productivity
down and hinder the emergence of a highly qualified indigenous
labor force. How does the Senegalese situation fit into the
analysis of "cheap labor policies"? The quantitative aspect
of "cheap labor policies" will not be examined at this point,
because of the need for a norm of reference to measure wages
and standards of living; the question which will be asked is:
Are the qualitative and psychological factors of "cheap labor
policies" to be found with industrial employers? If so, the
fact that wages may have risen as a result of government and
trade union policy does not deprive the concept of "cheap
labor policies" of its relevance: Unless attitudes and beliefs
of industrial managers concerning indigenous labor change,
higher wages imposed by government and trade unions do not

necessarily lead employers to raise the level of productivity
of their labor force (at great initial expense). In a develop-
mental perspective, attitudes and beliefs of industrial employers are more important than the actual level of wages imposed
by government and trade union policies.

Private Employers' Labor Policies in Senegal

Recruitment and Training

Methods of selecting the labor force among candidates pre-
senting themselves at the factory gates are generally pragmatic;
only one-fifth of industrial firms interviewed had tests for all
potential employees (E 21); most firms take candidates on trial
for one month; the decision to recruit is then taken on the
basis of the workers' foremen.

Over 40 percent of workers interviewed (W 31) said that
they had found their present jobs with the help of some "rela-
ative" already employed in the firms. Workers often press
their employers to recruit members of their extended family.
Such recruitment methods are unsystematic.

Likewise, the majority of workers interviewed had undergone
no systematic training (W 27). A breakdown of statistics according to the workers' occupational status reveals that three-
quarters of African foremen and four-fifths of skilled workers
had not learned their trade in a training course; most of them
were promoted for reasons of seniority rather than because of
improvement in their skills:

Training of Industrial Workers by Occupational Status

	On the Job	Apprenticeship	Technical School
	%	%	%
Unskilled	88.0	12.0	nil
Skilled	49.0	31.0	20.0
Foremen	62.5	12.5	25.0

Nearly 60 percent of the firms interviewed did not have a
manpower-training scheme of their own (E 22), however limited
in scope; the main reason given for this is the short-term
planning horizon due to political risk in the longer run.

Appraisal of Productivity

Half the employers interviewed claimed to have serious
labor problems in their firms. Criticism of performance is

frequent with industrial managers in former French colonies. Criteria used for appraising performance are very subjective: Only 27 percent of managers interviewed stated that productivity of labor could be measured by reference to objective data; in all other cases, employers based their appraisal on judgement by expatriate foremen (E 38). This is likely to give a biased image of productivity, since promotion of African workers is not necessarily in the interest of expatriate foremen.

Supervision and authority are also crucial problems in Senegal; they are characteristic of a transitory phase during which there is no more abundant supply of cheap expatriate labor, while firms have not yet trained their African labor force adequately (E 31). Few firms, however, thought it relevant to set up manpower-training schemes for supervisors, thus perpetuating low productivity and inefficiency.

Response to Marginal Changes in Remuneration

Industrial employers' wage policies vary according to their past experience and to their appraisal of African workers' response to economic incentives in the form of premiums linked to some index of productivity.

Most industrial employers doubt the efficacy of monetary incentives; they do not think that workers do react positively to them; at best, workers' reactions are judged to be neutral, sometimes negative. Less than one-third of employers interviewed believed that even a well worked-out system of premiums might have a favorable effect on productivity of labor (E 55).

Entrepreneurs who deny the efficacy of monetary incentives give two kinds of reasons in support of their opinions. The first reason is economic: It rests on the assumption that the size of the "extended family" living at the workers' expense varies according to the latters' wages; increasing wages is likely to induce marginal members of the "extended families" to settle down in town for good at the expense of industrial workers. The workers, it is said, are aware of this fact, and know that increases in wages would be absorbed by extra expenditures for marginal relatives; therefore, the incentive effect of premiums is considerably reduced--or suppressed--since premiums do not offer any real advantage to the wage-earners. This line of argument was often used by colonial employers to justify low wages as an optimum solution. The relationship between remuneration and the size of the "extended family" will be discussed at a later point.

A second line of argument condemns the system of monetary
incentives on psychological grounds: (a) Employers find it
very difficult to explain the principle of premiums linked to
one or several variables to African workers whose attitude is
often one of distrust: These see no reason why part of their
remuneration should depend on factors which they often cannot
control individually. The lower the level of skill and the
higher the degree of mechanization, the less workers feel in
a position to influence productivity, especially at the
individual level and the harder it is to determine each worker's contribution to productivity. (b) A "ratchet effect"
comes into play: Once a worker has been paid out a premium in
excess of his average wage, he is likely to consider this
supplement as an acquired right (droit acquis); to reduce or
suppress this supplement in the next period leaves workers and
their families with a sense of frustration. This affects the
social climate in the firm adversely. Many employers therefore refrained from establishing a premium system, or eventually disconnected the premiums from objective variables, thus
transforming them into gratuities.

Both lines of argument merely reflect opinions; however,
it is on the basis of such opinions that policies of industrial firms are worked out.

Promotion Policies

Promotion often tends, in the absence of objective standards of productivity, to become a privilege, and wage-grades
become scales for paternal reward. Few factories worked out a
systematic promotion policy: Less than one-third of the firms
interviewed established some system whereby wage-grades are
periodically checked for each employee (E 24); likewise, only
slightly over one-third of firms have a system for revision of
wages (E 47); other firms wait for workers to submit grievances
to the management.

Credit to Workers

The bargaining power of employers vis à vis their personnel is greatly reinforced by the workers' difficulty in planning their domestic budget. The periodicity of the workers'
expenditure is not always adjusted to that of their income;
in other words, in the absence of savings, some sort of credit
is needed. General poverty among workers rules out mutual
assistance and makes it unlikely that commercial banks might
step in. As a result, workers turn towards their own employers and quite large debts are incurred. As many as 83 percent

of industrial employers declared that they acted as bankers
towards their personnel (E 49). There are, in all, over fifteen usual reasons for workers asking for credit (religious
feasts, hire-purchase, family celebrations, medical expenses,
etc.).

The disadvantages of liberal credit policies to the management are managerial and psychological. Managerial difficulties arise in larger firms, when it comes to administering
the credit system. The permanent presence of an expatriate
accountant is often thought necessary to avoid tribal solidarity leading to fraud and discrimination in the allocation of
credit.

Psychological difficulties are less easy to solve:
Credit has the effect of reducing the amount of money paid out
fortnightly to the workers. Shifting part of their responsibility for organizing their domestic budget to their employers, workers are often discouraged by the actual wage they
receive; this discouragement is combined with a feeling of
dependence towards the employer--a feeling of resignation or
resentment results, which constitutes a handicap to efficient
manpower management and keeps productivity of labor low.

A minority of employers ceased giving credit to their
personnel completely from one day to the next. Discontent
grew among the workers after such measures were taken. Policies aimed at reducing credit without suppressing it completely failed.[10]

Industrial workers' debts constitute a very powerful
(although double-edged) tool for employers to exert their
bargaining power. They establish "paternal" ties between
themselves and their employees.

                    *   *   *

Colonial habits have not left the industrial scene in
French-speaking Africa. In Senegal, methods for recruiting
and screening labor are haphazard; few manpower-training
schemes are operated by industrial firms; productivity of
labor is usually appraised on the basis of subjective judgements by expatriate foremen--the quality of African labor is
thought to be poor by most industrial employers. Policies of
fringe benefits and promotion are unsystematic and rest on the
employers' belief in the validity of the backward-sloping
supply curve of labor theory; credit policies greatly increase
employers' bargaining power over their personnel; workers depend on employers for organizing their domestic budgets; the

majority of employers are forced to or are willing to perform
a paternal role towards African employees.

The qualitative and psychological factors of "cheap labor
policies" are to be found in Senegalese industry; they tend to
depress the level of wages and to favor uneconomic use of
labor.

SUPPLY OF INDUSTRIAL LABOR IN SENEGAL

How elastic is supply of industrial labor in Senegal?
What are the main features of supply of labor?

Agriculture as a Reservoir of Industrial Labor

Agricultural productivity in Senegal is low and stagnating.

There is extreme scarcity of capital and a system of
shifting agriculture in Senegal; unused cultivatable land is
plentiful for the country as a whole. In 1964, total land
cultivated amounted to 2.225 million hectars (about 0.9 hectar
per head of agricultural population). A total of 47 percent
of the surface is devoted to the cultivation of groundnuts
(cash crop), 43 percent to millet (food crop), the rest to
various food crops (cassava, paddy rice, etc.).

Productivity per hectar is low and varies considerably
from one region to another, according to rainfall (less than
400 mm. per year in the Fleuve area, over 1,500 mm. in the
southern province of Casamance):

TABLE 9

Agricultural Productivity (1962-63)*

	Yield per Cultivated Hectar	Annual Production per Man
Groundnuts	880 kg.	370 kg.
Millet	494 kg.	180 kg.
Rice	1,290 kg.	36.5 kg
Cassava	4,311 kg.	62 kg.
Other		36 kg.

* Average 1962-63.

Source: Services de la Statistique, Situation Economique du
         Sénégal 1964 (Dakar, 1965).

Total value of agricultural output (excluding cattle-raising and fishing) is about 31 billion cfa francs (average 1962 and 1963), or about 12,400 cfa francs (US $50) per head of rural population; adding the value of fishing and cattle-raising, the per head output is about 15,200 cfa francs (US $61).

Large quantities of food have to be imported into Senegal:

Imports of Food, 1964

Total imports of food:	15.8 billion cfa francs
of which=Imports of cereals:	5 billion cfa francs +
Imports of food as percent of total imports:	37
Domestic food crop production:	about 15 billion cfa francs

Agricultural productivity stagnates. Fairly accurate population figures are available for 1948 and 1962-63:

TABLE 10

Agricultural Productivity (1948-63)

Rural population:	1948:	1.650 million
	1963:	2.5 million +
Output:		
Groundnuts:	1948:	596,000 tons
	1962-63 average	923,000 tons
Millet:	1948:	303,000 tons
	1962-63 average	451,000 tons
Output per head:		
Groundnuts:	1948:	360 kg.
	1962-63 average	370 kg.
Millet:	1948:	184 kg.
	1962-63 average	180 kg.

Sources: Gouvernement Général de l'AOF, Annuaire Statistique de l'AOF (Dakar, 1951); Services de la Statistique, Situation Economique du Sénégal 1964 (Dakar, 1965).

Increases in output are due almost exclusively to cultivation
of larger surfaces; technology remained constant since 1948 despite the government's attempts at increasing productivity.

As regards labor, there is strong evidence that no significant number of peasants can be removed from agriculture
without affecting production adversely. Agricultural work is
seasonal: Senegal's climate is such that agricultural operations must take place within about 120 days (rainy season);
during these four months, the entire rural labor force available is required and fully employed, including women and
children.

During the colonial period, young men used to migrate
from Soudan, Guinea, and Upper Volta to supplement the Senegalese labor force during the rainy season; they worked on a
share-crop basis. The colonial administrations encouraged
this type of migration and facilitated it by chartering
special trains from the Niger River to the Senegalese groundnut basin; these seasonal migrants were called navetanes.

According to former Governor General Hubert Deschamps,[11]
Senegal's supply of labor "is not sufficient for agriculture.
There is need, during the time of the crop, for forty to
seventy thousand navetanes from Soudan." Since independence
there are no more statistics concerning seasonal migration of
agricultural labor; it is commonly agreed that migration fell
off sharply as a consequence of the break-up of the Federation
of French West Africa.

Thus it appears that the marginal product of labor in
agriculture during the season of agricultural activity is far
from zero; supplies of fully committed industrial labor imply
a reduction in agricultural output and need for increased
imports of food, if no extra effort is put in by the labor
force that remains on the land.

Reservoirs of Industrial Labor
Other Than Agriculture

There are two main reservoirs of nonagricultural labor
for Senegalese industry: (a) Unemployed workers, and (b)
Senegalese workers abroad.

A government survey of 1960 estimates that there were
about 11,000 wage-earners who had lost their jobs, in 1958-
59.[12] Other more recent sources indicate 50-60,000 unemployed; most of these live in and around Dakar; they take

advantage of "extended family" solidarities and form part of
the pool of "hangers-on" who live on their relatives' wages.
A large pool of "near-unemployed" petty traders, shoe-cleaners
occasional beggers, etc., can be added to unemployment
figures. Many Senegalese serving for the French Army found
themselves unemployed when the latter withdrew after 1961.
The total figure of potential labor force available in Senegal
is about 100,000 (i.e., of the same order of magnitude as
total employment).

Indirect confirmation of these figures can be found on
the basis of population figures: The male population aged
fifteen to sixty-nine represents 56 percent of the total male
population of Senegal (1960);[13] the urban population of Senegal is about 800,000; that of Dakar and Rufisque alone
575,000. Assuming that 50 percent of the population is male,
the following figures can be obtained:

- Male population, Dakar and Rufisque (1966): 288,000
- Of which between 15 and 69 years of age: 162,000
- Nonemployed male urban population: 125,000 +
- Total urban unemployment (male and female): 350,000 +

Part of the "nonemployed urban population" consists of
farmers residing in town and of self-employed traders and arti-
sans; it is, however, not unreasonable to assume that there is
a pool of about 100,000 unemployed men in Senegal; this confirms direct evaluation of unemployment figures.

The quality of the unemployed is also indicated by the
government survey of 1960; half the unemployed registered were
unskilled; about 35 percent were medium-skilled workers, most
of these in public works; the rest consisted of clerical
staff. The qualitative standard of the pool of urban unemployed as a whole seems to be inferior to that indicated in
the survey.

A number of Senegalese are employed in African states
other than Senegal; their number cannot be appraised in the
absence of statistics.

There is also a migratory flow of Senegalese workers to
France; before 1964, there were no administrative or legal restrictions to immigration into France. Since then, agreements
were concluded between France and Senegal; migration is only
legal for workers who have secured employment before migrating; the aim of the agreements is to raise the level of qualification of Senegalese workers in France.

The stream of migration to France was initiated after 1918 and continued between the two World Wars; most of the migrants were navy employees working their passage to Europe; later, demobilized Senegalese soldiers who served with French troops in Indo-China settled in France. Since 1959-60 certain tribal groups organized systematic migration to France. It follows a uniform pattern: Community savings finance the voyage of a small number of young men to France; these compete with North African and other Mediterranean job-seekers for unskilled work; the vast majority of Senegalese working in France are illiterate and do not acquire any qualification (they work as street-cleaners, in public works and roadbuilding, etc.). The African system of social organization is preserved in France: Workers re-group themselves by tribe, renting rooms in common; 75 percent of the wages earned are put into common funds that serve four purposes: (i) Boarding expenditures; (ii) money sent home to the community in Africa; (iii) clothing and pocket money for the workers; (iv) savings to be spent once the workers return to Africa. Workers are expected to return to Africa after a maximum of three years.[14]

There are no reliable statistics on the number of Senegalese workers in France; it seems to exceed 20,000. Very few Senegalese workers settle in France for over five years.

The total amount of nonagricultural reservoirs of male labor exceeds total present wage employment in Senegal by over 20 percent.

*   *   *

After these quantitative factors, we shall turn to qualitative ones: What are the main characteristics of the Senegalese supply of labor?

Characteristics of Supply of Labor

What is the background, the level of education, the degree of stability of the Senegalese labor force? How do Senegalese workers react to economic incentive?

Workers are usually recruited in Dakar itself; job-seekers wander from factory-gate to factory-gate; the government set up a labor exchange, but this has not yet modified traditional patterns of job-seeking. Provincial firms sometimes find unskilled workers in the provinces but usually recruit their skilled manpower in Dakar.

The process of urbanization has been gradual in Senegal (W 10). Only 6.6 percent of workers interviewed were born in Dakar (W 2), while three-quarters were working in that city. Data collected on the workers' parents and grandparents show that, in the vast majority of cases, the transition from the traditional to the modern sector took place during the present-day workers' lifetime:

TABLE 11

Occupation of Workers' Father and Paternal
Grandfather (W 5 & W 6)

	Occupation of Father %	Occupation of Grandfather %
Agriculture & Fishing	73.5	94.0
Commerce	12.5	4.0
Transport & Industry	8.0	1.5
Other	6.0	0.5

Sources: Interviews: W 5, W 6.

Less than half the present labor force had any industrial experience before starting on their present job; nearly 40 percent came straight from agriculture (W 25).

Close contacts are kept between the traditional and the industrial sector. Nearly half the workers spend their yearly paid holiday (three weeks) in their home village (or provincial town); many workers pay even more frequent visits home (W 11). There is a constant flow of money and goods between the villages and the industrial area: Workers send money and goods bought cheaply in town (e.g., rice, oil, clothing, etc.) to relatives in the provinces; peasants come to town, bringing foodstuffs (e.g., poultry) with them.

Over one-third of the workers interviewed said that they intended to return to their home villages once they reach pensioning age (W 20); this represents about three-quarters of all workers born in villages. Economic reasons appear to encourage workers to retire in villages rather than to remain in town;[15] this can be explained by the fact that old people can still work in their villages, whereas they could no longer earn their life in town; food is also judged to be cheaper in the villages where it is grown, than in town.

The educational level of industrial workers is very poor; none of the workers interviewed attended secondary school; 54.5 percent of them never went to school at all. Of those interviewed, 89.7 percent did not hold any school certificates; only 3.8 percent held a <u>certificat d'aptitude profess-ionnelle</u>, the lowest vocational degree.

French remains a foreign language to many Senegalese workers; the workers' degree of literacy is low even in the case of skilled and supervisory labor:

<u>Degree of Literacy</u> (W 18 and W 19)

			%
(a)	all workers:	can read French	42.9
		can write in French	39.1
		cannot read French	47.1
		cannot write in French	60.9
(b)	skilled workers:	cannot write in French	55.0
(c)	supervisory labor:	cannot write in French	26.0

These facts must be borne in mind when analyzing the relationship between African and European labor.

The Senegalese labor force is extremely stable: No industrial employer interviewed (E 25) complained about high rates of labor turnover; the problem of instability was never acute in Senegal (E 26).

The short-term situation is not much different: Absenteeism is low in most firms (E 27 and E 28). A study carried out by the University of Dakar[16] concludes that "in most firms absenteeism is not negligible: It is of the same order of magnitude as in the more industrialized countries." The trend of absenteeism during the last ten years (1954-1964) was judged satisfactory by half the employers interviewed; most of the others had not noticed any change. However, in developing countries, absenteeism poses much greater problems than in industrialized ones: Since there is scarcity of supply of skilled labor in the short term, the momentary absence of skilled workers has detrimental repercussions on output--while in Europe it is possible to replace absent skilled workers without significant loss of efficiency. Therefore, although the rate of absenteeism in Senegal is low, this does not mean that no efforts should be made to reduce it even further.[17]

A high degree of competition among unskilled job-seekers is the major cause of stability: Success in finding a job-- with all the prerogatives attached to it by labor legisla- tion--is considered by workers to be a fortunate privilege worth being safeguarded. Pressures from the "extended family" also favor stability; responsibilities accumulate on the wage- earners as more and more "relatives" come to live on their wages; it becomes increasingly difficult for workers to abandon their jobs, thereby curtailing family income.

*   *   *

Finally, data relating to response to incentive must be examined.

Workers, when asked why they had changed jobs in the past usually answered (whenever the change had been an effect of their will) that they were prompted by economic reasons:

<u>Motive for changing job in the past</u> (W 26)

Economic reasons: 72.5% Dismissal: 21.6% Other: 5.9%

Asked whether they would leave their present job, if another one was offered to them, the majority of workers answered that they would be prepared to change; most of those unwilling to contemplate a change belonged to the upper-age group (over forty):

<u>Would you change job for a higher wage?</u> (W 36)

Yes	60.9%
No	34.4%
Does not know	4.7%

Among workers answering "yes", 46 percent mentioned a specific sum for which they would be prepared to change jobs (W 37). The lower the income the larger the proportion who indicated a specific sum:

TABLE 12

Workers' Response to Economic Incentive by Income Groups

Workers' monthly wage	Workers indicating a specific wage-differential for which they are prepared to leave their present job
cfa francs	%
Under 10,000	69.5
" 11,000	74.0
" 12,000	69.5
" 13,000	52.0
" 14,000	44.5
" 15,000	38.5
" 16,000	41.5

Source: W 36, W 37.

Specific sums mentioned by poorer workers represent smaller fractions of their wage than those mentioned by the better-off ones:

Wage-Differential Mentioned by Workers cfa francs	Percent of Wage (average)	Wage (average)
500	4.0	12,500
1,000	7.0	14,000
over 1,000	17.0	26,000

Over half the workers are prepared to leave their jobs for an increment of 5 percent or less in their present wage.

Qualification also influences response to incentive; there are eight wage-grades in Senegal, which correspond to various qualifications: I-IV for unskilled labor (by European standards), V to VI for skilled labor, and M (for maîtrise) for supervisory labor. Higher skills reduce willingness to change jobs for economic reasons.

TABLE 13

Workers' Response to Economic Incentive by Wage-Grade

Wage-grade	Workers indicating a specific wage-differential for which they are prepared to leave their present job
	%
Unskilled	
I	59.0
II	49.0
III	30.0
IV	36.0
Skilled	
V	22.0
VI	31.0
VII	25.0
M	12.0

Source: Interviews: W 37.

There is no sign of lack of response to economic incentive in the choice of occupation: Thus the remarkable stability of Senegalese labor does not result from lack of sensitivity to economic opportunities, but from lack of employment opportunities. Stability is caused by the position of the demand curve rather than by the shape of the supply curve.

It is now possible to determine the equilibrium on the Sengalese labor market "under competitive conditions."

THE EQUILIBRIUM "UNDER COMPETITIVE CONDITIONS"

In dualistic economies, notably in Africa, employers commonly share the view that the supply curve of labor is backward-sloped; since fairly capital-intensive methods of production are favored by expatriate industrialists, the quantity of labor demanded on the market is likely to be low; the wasteful use of unskilled labor further reduces the likelihood of increases in demand for labor. Industrial wages tend to be low and the quantity of labor demanded is likely to be minimal, unless the product market expands at a rapid pace.

Supply of labor from the traditional sector may or may not depend on the relationship between agricultural and urban earnings; if it is assumed that it does not, migrations are

mainly motivated by noneconomic forces such as religion, tradition, etc. It is therefore impossible to predict the amount
of labor offered on the market on a purely economic basis.

If there is a negative correlation, however, between
agricultural earnings and the rate of migration (i.e., if the
supply curve of labor is positively inclined), there will be
abundant supplies of unskilled labor for industry as long as
urban wages exceed agricultural earnings.

In the absence of market imperfections, the equilibrium
on the labor market appears to be found at a low level of
wages (slightly above agricultural earnings) and at a low
volume of manpower demanded, if the supply curve is positively
inclined.

Urban wages are likely to exceed agricultural earnings so
as to attract extra manpower from the villages.

In Senegal, wages are largely determined by government
intervention; the latter pursues a policy of "wage freeze" in
the framework of its doctrine of "African socialism." Industrial wages remained fairly stable during the last five years.
In the eyes of industrial employers, the crucial variable is
the evolution of the product market; the domestic market stagnated since 1957 while export markets declined--except in the
case of groundnut products and minerals--as a result of
political and economic change in competing African countries.

The quantity of labor demanded by industrial employers is
low; uneconomic use of unskilled labor (regarded as a "cheap
commodity") leaves room for adjusting to slight changes in the
market trend or in the legal minimum wage without affecting
demand for labor.

Most industrial employers have not departed yet from
their "colonial" attitudes towards indigenous labor; they do
not seriously try to train their labor force, doubt the
latter's capacity for improvement and rely on expatriates for
certain skilled jobs and supervision. They believe that the
supply curve of labor is vertical or backward-bending; therefore, they see no need to maintain the level of wages above
the minimum required by the economy.

The demand curve for industrial labor in Senegal is likely to express inelasticity; the amount of labor demanded is
small and variations in wages do not have a great influence on
it.

                          *   *   *

Agricultural productivity is extremely low in Senegal and agricultural work highly seasonal--there is need for foreign manpower during the rainy season. The marginal productivity of labor is far from zero in Senegalese villages. Migration increases the strain on Senegal's balance of payments by making additional imports of food necessary so as to keep food consumption per head at a constant level if no extra work is put in by farmers remaining on the land.

On the basis of workers' interviews, it seems that the supply curve of labor is positively sloped within the region of existing wage rates: Workers do react to economic opportunities in changing their occupation; they are eager to maximize income in order to better cope with the financial weight of the "extended family."

There is a very large pool of unemployed unskilled men in Senegal--of the same order of magnitude as total employment; job-seekers wander from factory to factory in quest of employment.

Supply of unskilled labor is abundant but represents a strain on Senegal's balance of trade because of the added need for food imports it involves; present wages attract more job-seekers than can be employed in the next ten years.

In the absence of major market imperfections, we can try to represent supply and demand curves on Figure 1. If wages are represented on the vertical axis and employment on the horizontal one, let OA be the level of agricultural earnings,[18] and AS the margin by which the minimum wage level likely to attract labor exceeds that of agricultural earnings. There are no indications as to actual supply elasticity: It seems that the curve is fairly elastic (migration into town has continued for years at a regular rate); but it must be borne in mind that should Senegal attempt to solve its balance of trade difficulties by producing more food as well as more cash crop for export, supply of labor would then become very inelastic indeed. The graph represents supply as it is now, rather elastic. By contrast the demand curve is inelastic in its lower portion: Changes in wage rates hardly affect employment; however, it is likely that at higher wage rates, employment might be affected by changes in the rate of remuneration; therefore, the curve shows more elasticity in the higher than in the lower wage-rate ranges. SS' is the supply curve, DD' the demand curve.

FIGURE 1

Equilibrium of the Labor Market under "Competitive Conditions"

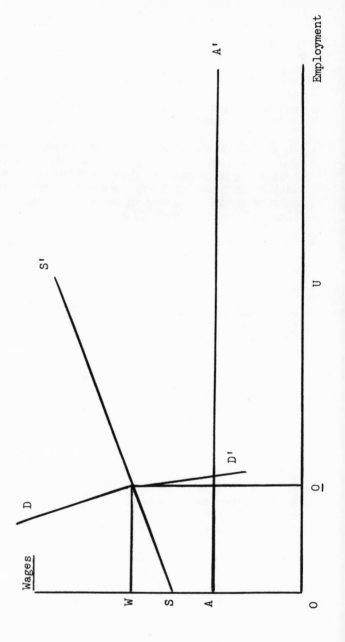

The point of intersection of the two curves determines the "equilibrium wage rate" W likely to be rather close to S because of the very strong bargaining power of industrial employers. It also determines industrial employment "under competitive conditions" which is shown in $\underline{O}$: $O\underline{O}$ represents industrial employment; unemployment is represented by $\underline{O}U$ that prolongs $O\underline{O}$.

Under "competitive conditions" wages are likely to be low and unemployment high.

Notes to Chapter 2

1. Hla Myint, The Economics of the Developing Countries (London: Hutchinson, 1965).

2. Ibid., p. 54.

3. Ibid.

4. Ibid.

5. Ibid., p. 56.

6. Ibid., pp. 56-57.

7. W. D. Weatherford, Jr., "Pakistan", in Labor in Developing Economies, Walter Galenson, ed. (Berkeley: University of California Press, 1962), p. 52.

8. Frederick H. Harbison, "Egypt", in Labor and Economic Development, Walter Galenson, ed. (New York: John Wiley and Sons, Inc., 1959), p. 155.

9. Ibid.

10. One firm organized a system of voluntary savings for its workers; overtime payments and other fringe benefits were transferred to savings accounts with the consent of shop delegates. After four months, only 20 percent of the workers who had participated in the scheme had refrained from withdrawing their accounts. None of the shop delegates was among these 20 percent.

11. Hubert Deschamps, Le Sénégal et la Gambie, (Paris: PUF, 1964), p. 74

12. Ministère du Travail, "Rapport de Synthèse sur les
     Travaux de la Commission sur le Chômage" (Dakar:
     roneoed, 1959).

13. Services de la Statistique, Situation Economique du
     Sénégal 1963 (Dakar, 1964) p. 13.

14. "Les Travailleurs Noirs en France," Réalités Africaines
     (May-June, 1963).

15. Reasons given by workers who desire to retire in their
     home villages:
     - Because their family lives there: 52%
     - Because life is "more pleasant":   19%
     - For economic reasons: 29%
     Reasons given by workers who desire to retire in
        town:
     - Because their family lives there: 55%
     - Because life is "more pleasant":   30%
     - For economic reasons: 15%

16. André Hauser, "L'absentéisme et la Mobilité des Travaill-
     eurs des Industries Manufacturières de la Région de Dakar"
     (Dakar: Université de Dakar, roneoed, undated), p. 40.

17. A textile factory illustrated this type of problem
     quantitatively: A worker had to be replaced by the
     "second best" substitute available for operating a
     machine. Daily output of that machine fell from 401
     kilo per day (average of absent worker) to 298 kilo.

18. AA' is parallel to OU in its relevant portion since
     evidence shows that despite immigration to town agri-
     cultural productivity remained roughly constant since
     World War II.

PART **II** IMPERFECTIONS OF THE LABOR
MARKET: MULTIRACIAL
STRUCTURE, TRADE UNIONS
AND GOVERNMENT

Actual conditions of industrial activity are far removed
from "competitive conditions" assumed above. Before analyzing the respective share of responsibility of expatriate employers, trade unions and government in creating market imperfections, we must briefly describe conditions of industrial activity in Chapter 3. Having introduced the basic structural and institutional imperfections that are independent of
labor policies, we will turn our attention to the three main
factors influencing Senegal's labor market: The multiracial
structure of employment, trade-union policies, and government
labor policies.

Once the ways in which labor policies distort the labor
market have been shown, the relationship between the labor
market and economic development will be discussed in Part
III.

CHAPTER **3** CONDITIONS OF

INDUSTRIAL ACTIVITY

The Senegalese market is exposed to little competition: Capital and management are largely foreign, "natural" or deliberate monopolies are very frequent in manufacturing; tariffs and price controls further remove Senegalese enterprises from competition; these imperfections will be briefly analyzed in this chapter, so as to provide a background to the effect of labor policies on the labor market, and to give a partial explanation for Senegal's lack of international competitiveness and the low level of activity in Senegalese industry.

The majority of industrial enterprises operating in former French colonies in Africa were set up by the French during the colonial period; they benefited from advantageous tax measures as well as from tariff protection against non-Franc zone exports. Half the enterprises in the sample (E 5) were established between 1940 and 1957, at a time when French sovereignty was regarded as a stable factor by investors. One-fifth of the firms started operating after 1957, when political insecurity had become an element in economic anticipations. The rest of the establishments considered are older: They started functioning before World War II.

Most industrial firms are under French management; senior executives in charge of technical and economic matters are almost all expatriates, most of them French. A few Senegalese executives can be found in some enterprises, usually in charge of commercial departments or as personnel managers.

The capital of industrial firms is entirely French in two-thirds of firms interviewed (E 3), international--but excluding Senegalese capital--in one-eighth of firms; a share of Senegalese (public) capital is included in about one-fifth of the firms interviewed (including two public transport companies).

The degree of dependence of Senegalese firms on foreign
headquarters in matters of employment and wage policy varies:

Degree of Dependence on (Foreign) Headquarters in
        Matters of Employment and Wages (E 4)

Entire independence   62.5% of Firms
Independence for indigenous
     labor only   25.0%
Dependence   12.5%

One quarter of the firms said they were independent in regard
to their Senegalese labor force, but not for decisions concerning expatriates; the latter were hired, and their wages determined in France.

              *   *   *

Senegal is both a poor and a small country; the market
for industrial goods is very narrow at the present level of
prices. As African states pursue increasingly nationalistic
tariff policies, Senegalese industry has to rely more and more
on the domestic market. One medium-sized industrial firm can
supply the entire domestic market for each of the main consumer goods; thus, there is very little room for additional firms.
The very smallness of the market explains the high degree of
industrial concentration: Small African countries tend to
constitute "natural" monopolies as far as the domestic market
is concerned; the bulk of industrial production is generated
in a handful of modern expatriate factories for each industry.[1]

Groundnut-processing industries, that form the largest
industry in Senegal, are composed of three big producers and
some smaller ones; all belong to a Syndicat des Huiliers--an
association that coordinates the policies of its members. The
groundnut-oil industry constitutes a coordinated oligopoly
acting in the same way as a monopoly, when taken as a whole.

Over 50 percent of firms interviewed said that there was
no domestic competition, but competition from imported goods
(E 10); only 26 percent of the firms admitted that there was
any form of competition for their products on the Senegalese
market from local firms or imports, given tariff protection.
The rest of the firms belong to a coordinated oligopoly.
Figure 2 shows the firms' share of total domestic production,

FIGURE 2

Share of Domestic Production for Industrial Firms

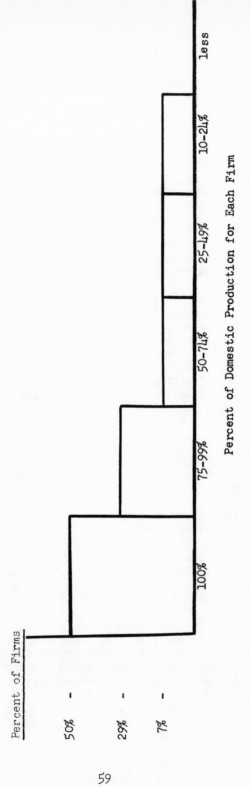

Percent of Domestic Production for Each Firm

Source: Interviews.

59

for each firm's respective product (excluding groundnut and mining industries).

Employers' associations also enable industrialists to achieve a great degree of coordination (only 24 percent of private employers interviewed do not belong to an employers' association (E 48 and E 60)). Coordination is aimed as far as possible at ironing out differentials--e.g., wage-differentials --which might harm certain industries. This increases stability of African labor. Employers' associations are all members of a central organization: UNISYNDI[2] competent for the whole of French-speaking West Africa; the main attraction of employers' associations is economic information--for small- er firms, associations constitute a useful link between them- selves and the administration (E 61).

Protection of Senegalese manufacturing industries against imported goods is well developed: "The role of the government in the manufacturing industry is mainly seen as protecting the local market for the existing industries."[3] The bulk of State revenue comes from import duties; the interests of Senegalese manufacturers and of the administra- tion coincide in raising high tariff protection. In addi- tion to tariff protection stricto sensu, the Senegalese govern- ment inherited a comprehensive system of price control for imported goods, from its colonial predecessor; discrimination plays against "cheap labor exporters" such as Japan, Hong Kong, India, etc.,[4] and in favor of EEC countries; there are no custom duties for imports from Franc zone countries but this principle is not respected by all African countries in inter- African trade.

Protection of "infant industries" exists for several Senegalese products including textiles; in these cases, protec- tion also extends to France (although protection against imports from France is in any case lower than protection against other countries). The ratio of retail prices in Dakar to FOB prices (Marseille) for clothes is about 1.60 : 1, ex- cluding the retailers' profit margin.[5]

Having been protected from foreign competition since their creation and enjoying a near-monopoly situation on the domestic market, Senegalese manufacturers of consumer goods are not, generally, competitive abroad. Exports represent only a small fraction, and a decreasing fraction at that, of total sales by Senegalese manufacturers.

TABLE 14

Textile Industry: Share of Exports on
Total Sales (1958-64)

1958	46%
1959	47%
1960	43%
1961	41%
1962	38%
1963	23%
1964 (10 months)	23%

Source: Interview with manager of largest textile plant in
Senegal.

Only export industries processing local raw materials export almost all their output. The curve representing the percentage of exported output by firm reflects the structure of
Senegalese industry: There are two groups of firms--those
that cater to export markets and those that manufacture light
consumer goods for the domestic market. The export-orientated
group comprises fewer firms than the domestic market-orientat-
ed group.

TABLE 15

Industrial Firms' Dependence on Exports

Percent of firms that exported the following percent of sales:	
- 0% of sales	19.0
- 0 to 25%	33.0
- 26 to 50%	14.0
- 51 to 75%	9.5
- 76 to 99%	19.0
- 100%	5.5

Source: Interviews: E 6.

The colonial structure of international trade has not yet
been significantly modified: Only a very small fraction of
Senegal's exports go to non-Franc zone countries; half the
exporting firms did not export at all outside the Franc zone;
for half of the other exporting firms, non-Franc zone exports
were marginal (E 7).

Traditional Franc zone markets decline as industrialization progresses in countries which formerly imported manufactured goods from Senegal; political factors closed the Guinean
and Malian markets almost entirely to Senegalese exporters.[6]
The smallness of exports to non-Franc zone countries (including Gambia) suggests lack of competitiveness (price rather
than quality handicap) and traditionalism with French industrial management in Senegal. Owing to the decline in traditional markets, the industrial sector is working to an increasing degree for the highly protected domestic market.

The level of activity in manufacturing industries is
rather low:

TABLE 16

Level of Industrial Activity in Percent of
Maximum Capacity* (E 13)

Percent of capacity used	Percent of firms
Over 90%	nil
76 to 90%	31%
51 to 75%	50%
0 to 50%	19%

* Employment and capital being constant.
Source: Interviews: E 13.

Loss of some of the traditional markets of AOF resulted
in industrial overequipment in Senegal, for many industries.

*   *   *

About one-quarter of industrialists interviewed did not
contemplate investing at all in the foreseeable future (E 14);
only one-quarter planned to invest for periods exceeding five
years; the rest had short-term planning horizons (less than
five years, usually two or three years).

The expatriate firms' policy is essentially one of profit-
maximization in the short run; lack of profitable investment
opportunities due to a stagnating domestic market as well as
prospects of political insecurity in the long run lead industrial firms to transfer re-investible profits out of Senegal.

Protection and monopoly situation on the domestic product
market ensure high rates of profit and fast amortization of
capital; most industrial firms are unwilling to plan their
investments ahead for periods exceeding three years.

There is virtually no competition in Senegalese industry.
Industrialists are under no strong market pressure to reduce
costs of production (notably through more efficient use of
African labor). Most profits are sent abroad.

The main source of imperfection in the labor market can
now be analyzed: The multiracial structure of employment.
Most trade union and government imperfections are direct or
indirect consequences of the latter.

Notes to Chapter 3

1. See Marcel Massé, A Study in Manufacturing in Senegal
    (Oxford: B. Phil. Thesis, 1966).

2. Employers' associations of the Franc zone are described
    in Appendix A.

3. Marcel Massé, op.cit., p. 105.

4. SCYMPEX, "Régime des Importations dans la République du
    Sénégal" (Dakar: SCYMPEX, roneoed, 1964); Chambre de
    Commerce de Dakar, "Réglementation Relative a l'Importa-
    tion des Marchandises au Sénégal" (Dakar: Chambre de
    Commerce, roneoed, 1964).

5. The case of men's shirts is mentioned in the Bulletin de
    la Chambre de Commerce de Dakar (August,1961), pp. 182-83:

        Price Marseille FOB   1,500 cfa francs
        Retailer's Cost, Dakar   2,400 cfa francs
        Retail Price, Dakar   3,600 cfa francs (assuming
                                        33 percent profit)

    Most of the difference between FOB price and cost in Dakar
    is due to taxation; domestic shirts are sold in Dakar
    shops from 1,700 cfa francs to over 2,000 cfa francs (see
    on that point: Bulletin de la Chambre de Commerce de
    Dakar, VI (1962) 136. On high prices in the
    Franc zone, see Gaston Leduc, "Les Prix et leur Formation
    dans les Economies Africaines." Cahiers de l'ISEA,
    Supplement to No. 145, 1964.

6. Mali devalued its currency in 1967 and joined the Franc
    area again.   This is expected to have favorable effects
    on Senegal's exports to Mali.

CHAPTER **4** EXPATRIATE LABOR

AND AFRICANIZATION

This chapter attempts to answer the following questions:
What are the problems posed to industry by the multiracial
structure of the market? How do private employers attempt to
solve these problems? If they do not succeed in solving them,
how does this failure influence the labor market?

THE STRUCTURE OF EMPLOYMENT AND THE
INCENTIVE TO AFRICANIZE

There are two distinct labor markets in the former French
colonies in Africa: One for African and one for expatriate
labor; the first is governed by supply and demand in the
countries in which industrial firms are located, the second by
supply and demand in Europe.

Technical and managerial skills are among the scarcest
factors in former French colonies in Africa; Senegalese indus-
try--one which has reached a higher degree of Africanization
than that of any other former French colony in tropical
Africa--depends critically on the presence of a large expatriate labor force:

TABLE 17

Expatriate Manpower in Percent of
Total Employment (E 33)

	Percent of Firms
- 3% or less	31.0
- 4 to 6%	31.0
- 7 to 9%	25.5
- 10 to 15%	nil
- over 15%	12.5

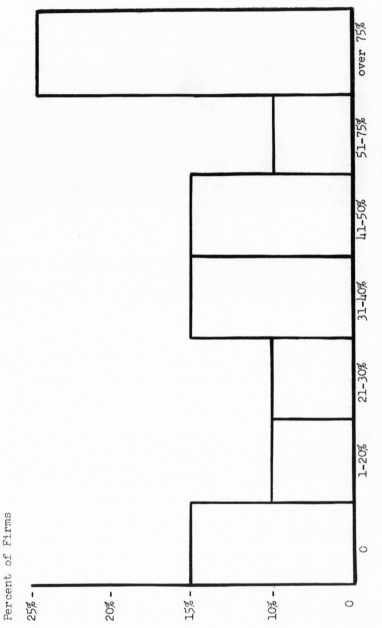

FIGURE 3

Africanization at the Foreman Level

Percent of Firms

Expatriate foremen in percent of all foremen

Source: Interviews.

66

The percentage of expatriates was not found to be related
to any single factor; it seems to depend on technical factors
and on the Africanization policy of the firms.

The process of Africanization usually starts at the
foreman level; the progress of Africanization can best be
measured in terms of proportion of expatriate foremen (E 34).

In more than one-third of enterprises interviewed, over
half the foremen are expatriates. Technical competence,
experience and, above all, undisputed authority over African
workers, are the main factors which entrepreneurs put forward
to justify the presence of such considerable expatriate labor
force.

*   *   *

The cost of expatriate labor is quite considerable.
Labor legislation, although egalitarian in spirit, allows many
fringe benefits to be attached to expatriates' wages: Free
housing, water, gas, electricity, medical insurance, sometimes
cars and servants, are provided by many industrial employers to
their expatriate staff and to their families. Employers must
also finance home leaves for expatriate employees and their
families once every twenty months (at a cost of about $400 per
adult and $200 per child) and one day of paid holiday per five
working days (as opposed to 1.5 days per month for African
labor). Gratuities including payment of a thirteenth month
wage are in current practice.

Despite the provisions of labor legislation the basic
wages of expatriates are usually higher than those of African
labor; expatriates are ranked higher in the hierarchy of wage-
grades than Africans (especially in smaller firms) or work
under an employment contract signed abroad--therefore not subject to comparison with Senegalese contracts.

The cost-differential between expatriate and African
labor (in comparable jobs) is much larger than a comparison
of basic wages suggests. Entrepreneurs were reluctant to
answer questions concerning this particular point; 42 percent refused to answer the question;[1] however, the answers
obtained are indicative of a large wage-differential (E 35):

TABLE 18

Ratio: Cost of Expatriate/Cost
of African Employee[*]

Cost-differential	Percent of firms
1.5 to 2 : 1	23
2 to 3 : 1	39
3 to 4 : 1	15
4 to 5 : 1	23
over 5 : 1	nil

[*] The sample includes 665 expatriate employees; most of these
are foremen, secretarial personnel, technical supervisors
and highly skilled workers; some of them are managers.
There are 525 African foremen in the sample. Comparisons
between the cost of African and European employees are
relevant for (a) foremen, (b) highly skilled workers, and
(c) secretarial staff.

In actual fact, it is usually the case that expatriate
workers--even when their wage-grade is the same as that of
an African worker--are heads of small departments within
industrial firms; in so far as highly skilled workers are
concerned, there is no competition between African and
expatriate labor, since the latter alone has functions of
supervision which wage-grades do not suggest. However,
competition does exist in the case of foremen and of
secretarial staff, which account for the majority of
expatriate labor in the sample.

It seems that a ratio of between 2.5 : 1 and 3 : 1 constitutes
a conservative estimate of average cost-differential (including fringe benefits) between African and expatriate labor in
the same rank if not necessarily for the same actual qualification.

*   *   *

There has been a gradual change in the types of expatriates employed in Senegal. When the first French came to
Africa in search of employment, their bargaining power was
very weak; many of them left Europe without proper qualifications, because unemployment was widespread; some of them left
for political reasons after the Liberation. Before 1952,

French employees were not protected from colonial employers by
a Labor Code: The latter often treated them very arbitrarily,
indeed.   Later, the rise of the EEC and the expansion of the
French economy created a strong demand for labor in France;
high wages and good living conditions were offered to industrial job-seekers in France; employment opportunities existed
there for their wives, which was not any more the case in
Senegal. Many Europeans left Africa, finding it more advantageous and more secure to take up employment in France. Simultaneously, a new type of expatriates started to come to
Africa; contrary to the initial petits blancs who came to
Africa willing to settle for the rest of their active life,
the new type of expatriate employees are highly specialized
technicians hired under short-term contracts (usually two
years). The average age of the latter is lower than that of
the formerly predominant type of French employee: The
average age of expatriates declined in recent years from
about forty years to about thirty-three (E 40).[2] The
mobility of the expatriate labor force increased as a
result (E 39); as younger technicians replace the petits
blancs their bargaining power increases and the cost-
differential between African and expatriate wages widens.
The gradual replacement of petits blancs by young technicians is still in progress.

*   *   *

An argument often put forward in the mid-fifties to
justify the size of the expatriate labor force must also be
examined.[3] This argument rests on the assumption that expatriates, unlike most Africans, are "strike-proof." Expatriate workers keep working when African workers go on strike.
It seems most doubtful whether this consideration still plays
a role today. It is true that some industrial enterprises
were able to operate while the entire African labor force was
on strike in the past; however, since then, the size of the
expatriate labor force has been reduced; this deprives the
"strike insurance" argument of much of its relevance. Indeed,
none of the firms interviewed (E 41) stated that it could
function normally without its African labor force; a few stated that production could continue "at slow pace" in the event
of an African strike; the majority of managers categorically
stated that production would be paralyzed in the event. While
practical advantages of the "strike insurance" decreased, the
assumption on which it rests was and still is correct: All
industrial employers confirmed that no expatriate ever joined
a strike (E 36); racial solidarity, and the likelihood of dismissal may be the causes of this attitude on the part of
expatriate employees.

*   *   *

It appears that economic incentive to Africanize and to
train the African labor force adequately is very strong. How
do private industrialists react to this incentive?

AFRICANIZATION IN PRIVATE INDUSTRY

For industrial managers desirous to find a suitable supply
of labor (semi-skilled or skilled)[4], two main sources are
available: The first is external to the firms and consists in
hiring pupils holding industrial certificates (CAP or BEI); the
second source is internal to the private sector and consists
of setting up manpower-training schemes independently from or
supplementary to external facilities.

In the case of workers without supervisory responsibilities most industrialists draw their manpower from vocational
schools, despite the oft-expressed criticism that these
schools give pupils a "bureaucratic outlook" on industrial
work. Alternatively, firms can set up training schemes of
their own. These function at two levels: (a) Alphabetization
of illiterate workers already employed, and (b) vocational
training of little-skilled but literate workers. The main
motivation for industrialists as regards setting up schemes
for nonsupervisory labor is that, with the increasing degree
of Africanization at the foreman level, it becomes more and
more important to improve the efficiency of the staff placed
under newly promoted African supervisors.

The crucial stage in manpower training is that of foremen:
Placed between expatriate managers--whose number is kept down
for reasons of economy--and a pool of workers with a low educational level, foremen carry very heavy responsibilities in
production. The low educational level of industrial workers
placed under them prevents foremen from delegating some of
their responsibilities to the workers as would be the case
in industrialized countries.

Most industrial firms are not satisfied with industrial
certificate holders leaving vocational schools as supervisors: Even more so than in the case of workers, the "bureaucratic" (or "civil servant") outlook is a common feature
among vocational school certificate holders, who often think
well of themselves because they attended vocational training
schools.

Moreover, the youthfulness of school-leavers often reduces their authority over elder workers.

Consequently, employers follow one of two policies:
Either they train their foremen among their own personnel
(selecting the more promising workers--but these are few and
rapidly creamed off), or they set up common institutions for
training African foremen: Two such institutions were set up
in Senegal; the main problem with them is that of financing.[5]

Most firms found that they obtained the best results in
training skilled workers and foremen on the job; schemes based
on Training Within Industry principles were introduced very
late into Senegal--from 1961 onwards--and results seem to be
satisfactory. However, the cost of a well-organized program
is high and many firms try to obtain financial assistance from
public authorities and international organizations for sharing
the cost of training their own personnel. Many industrial
firms hesitate between meeting the cost of Africanization and
that of keeping expatriate foremen.

But the main obstacles to Africanization are not financial but psychological; the difficulties arise (a) from
African workers and foremen trained by the firm, (b) from
other African employees, and (c) from expatriate labor.

Very often, as is the case in most of tropical Africa,
Africans trained to take over supervisory responsibilities
from expatriate employees do not possess all the nontechnical
qualities required for making efficient foremen; technical
skills are often found among workers who lack a general educational background and/or authority and/or adaptability to
overcome unforeseen and (for them) unprecedented difficulties
arising in production; any of these shortcomings hinders
efficiency in the firms and is likely to have detrimental
effects on human relations between workers and foremen.
Strengthening the expatriate management staff--numerically and
qualitatively--is often a conditio sine qua non for firms that
wish to operate efficiently in the first stages of Africanization. Moreover, social pressure may be extremely strong: It
often makes it very difficult for recently promoted Africans
to impose production norms and a certain discipline to other
Africans; they run the risk of being socially excluded outside
the factory; social pressure increases with the size of the
extended family. Redistribution of wages to numerous hangers-
on also attenuates the authority of foremen: In the absence
of traditional solidarities, the foremen's standard of living
might be much higher than that of the workers over whom they

exert authority, and their style of life different; pressure
of the extended family reduces the scope for such economic and
social differentiation.

Two situations very often arise in practice: Either a
young school-leaver is appointed foreman and elder workers re-
fuse to accept his authority, or an older worker who followed
a training course is promoted foreman; in that case, workers
of the foreman's age-group usually dispute his authority, considering him as a primus inter pares rather than as a
superior.

In both cases it is necessary to rely on expatriates for
backing the authority of newly promoted Africans, when needed;
the intervention of expatriates poses delicate psychological
problems; these may, in the case of inconsistent management,
render the whole idea of training manpower pointless.

But the basic problem facing industrialists operating in
the former French colonies of tropical Africa is neither one
of cost nor one of African psychology; it is that of the expatriates' own attitude toward manpower training and of their
reactions to Africanization.

Most industrialists find it inadequate to train skilled
workers and foremen in external establishments alone; these
establishments turn out specialized workers on the French
pattern, in an economy in which specialization of labor is
much less developed than in advanced economies. Lack of specialization and inadequacy of training lead most industrial
managers to consider that the only satisfactory method to
train skilled and supervisory labor, in the light of the
actual tasks to be performed, is to do so on the job.

This shifts responsibility for success of the training
process from State schools to the firms themselves; it also
brings the very raison d'être of external training facilities
based on the French pattern into question. Within industrial
firms, the only persons able to train Africans are expatriate
foremen and skilled workers: Neither expatriate managers nor
African foremen, already employed, have nearly as much experience of the practical aspects of the jobs as expatriate foremen and skilled workers, many of whom came to Africa fifteen
or twenty years ago and remained in the same firm.

When the top management of industrial firms (often
located in France) decides to Africanize one or several of
its plants, the order is channeled to the local management,

which in turn, addresses it to expatriate foremen. The first problem which arises is that of capacity: Most expatriate foremen are not capable at present of providing satisfactory training. Up to now, expatriate foremen were often absolute masters in their own department; they exercised a paternalistic authority over their African staff and had powers to dismiss their subordinates. There was no incentive for expatriate foremen to raise the technical abilities of their African teams; indeed, the very authority of French foremen (often of mediocre ability) rested on the incapacity of their African subordinates. Very few expatriate foremen were versed in the art of teaching. A sociologist noted in 1958 (before the idea of Africanization became an issue in French-speaking Africa) that "European employees have not been trained to perform the role of educator which should be theirs."[6]

This obstacle can be overcome by hiring specialists in training problems and in re-organizing industrial firms (animateurs). Within two or three years such specialists, if they can be found on the labor market, can train expatriate manpower to perform educational tasks. Good specialists are excessively rare and the cost of the procedure is high. Many firms dispense with it and obtain poor results. Moreover, a specialist's work can only be effective if he has direct authority from the top manager over the heads of the chiefs of departments. Only such authority can enable him to implement the re-education of expatriate foremen.

But there is a more fundamental question than that of capacity--that of willingness. Unless the top management of industrial firms succeeds in creating a psychological climate favorable to manpower training, expatriate foremen are likely to perform their educational tasks to the worst of their abilities. To them, the logical conclusion of the process of Africanization appears to be the loss of their own jobs. Training African foremen in such an atmosphere is bound to fail. Failures of this type are very common in Senegal, in the Ivory Coast, in Madagascar, and in other industrializing countries of French-speaking Africa. Failures discourage those industrial firms that have not yet decided whether to Africanize from doing so; they also may exert strong moral pressure on governments which, after some years, may well give up the idea of pressing for Africanization, sincerely believing that this would hamper industrial growth.

Three types of industrial firms must be distinguished in this respect: (a) Local firms with an expanding market; (b) branch factories of international firms; (c) local firms suffering from a stagnating or declining market.

In firms with an expanding market, Africanization can be carried out satisfactorily, given competent and consistent management. There is room in the future in these firms for expatriate as well as for African skilled workers and foremen. Provided training is planned in accordance with the expansion of the firm's output, investment program and recruitment plans, only financial problems stand in the way of successful Africanization.[7]

In branch factories of international firms, similar psychological conditions can be created by able management. In these plants (notably in oil companies, big shoe companies, etc.) decisions to "regionalize" the staff are usually taken at the very top. Even when Africanization is complete in branch factories, authority rests with "expatriates" in foreign headquarters; this makes the decision to Africanize far less difficult. Such decisions cannot easily and for long periods be resisted by petits blancs. The authority of foreign headquarters partly rests on interchangeability of local top managers at the will of the central office; this increases the chances of decisions to Africanize being actually implemented. Large firms can also, in many cases, offer alternative employment opportunities to their expatriate staff. Jobs can be reserved in France or in other local branch factories expanding at a faster rate than the Senegalese. Expatriate staff can be attracted by better working conditions (notably by the possibility for their wives to find jobs) and/or be forced to give up their Senegalese job. For international firms whose market is expanding, stagnation of one particular market such as the Senegalese is no hindrance to regionalizing their staff.

The most difficult case is that of local factories lacking both an expanding market and the possibility of transferring the staff to another country. This is a common case in former French colonies of Africa. Only in very few instances has the problem been solved in these firms. A few very efficient firms found an answer by gradually replacing their elder petits blancs by young technicians hired in France for periods of about two years. These are more mobile than elder expatriates, more willing to train Africans; elder expatriates retire or sometimes find a job in France. However, basically the problem of replacing the old staff remains unsolved. Closer contacts between African and French industrial employers' associations may facilitate coordination of manpower training with re-settling expatriates in expanding industries in Europe.

In most medium-sized plants of French-speaking Africa
(under 500 employees) attempts to train Africans meet the
active or, at best, the passive resistance of expatriate foremen. The local top management itself is more often than not
half-hearted in organizing training schemes. Its aim often
seems to be to prove to the government that Africanization is
bound to fail. These managers believe that cost-differentials
between expatriates and Africans are justified by differences
in productivity (short-term and long-term). This perpetuates
the colonial pattern of "cheap labor" attitudes.

*   *   *

In fact, it does not seem that there is any relationship
between cost-differential between African and expatriate
labor, and the degree of Africanization in the firms; there is
no relationship between percentage of expatriate foremen and
cost-differential in the different firms interviewed; nor is
there a relationship between over-all percentage of expatriate
personnel and cost-differential.[8]

In the case of Africanization at the foreman level it
appears that noneconomic factors are much stronger than
economic ones in influencing decisions of the management to
train Africans to replace expatriates.

In the case of the over-all percentage of expatriates employed, noneconomic factors also play a certain role, but the
main reason for lack of correlation lies in the supply inelasticity of Senegalese managers (inelasticity which no foreign
firm has yet seriously tried to remedy); whatever the cost-
differential, there is no alternative to expatriate management:
A nucleus of expatriate executives exists in every foreign-
owned plant. The majority of industrialists doubt whether this
situation will change during the next ten years: Africanization at the managerial level is expected to be extremely slow.

The only justification for maintaining a large expatriate
labor force at the supervisory level is the present productivity-
differential, itself a result of widespread unwillingness
to train the labor force adequately and also of race prejudice:
These two reasons influence each other.

It should be noted that the majority of African workers
interviewed said that they were indifferent to their foreman's
race (W 32): Most of them judge the latter individually.
Slightly over one-third of the workers said that they would
rather work under African supervision, usually for reasons of

language; 15.6 percent of workers said they preferred to work
under expatriate supervision. Thus, there is little pressure
on the part of industrial workers themselves for employers to
Africanize at the foreman level at a faster rate than hence-
forward. Trade unions have stated their will to press for
fast Africanization but have contributed in no way to solving
training problems.

                    *   *   *

     In the private sector "elements of inertia, race pre-
judice ... and /the7 frequent genuine belief that Africans ...
/are7 less productive and less trustworthy"[9] still exist with
expatriate managers and foremen. The need to Africanize became clearer much later in former French than in former British
colonies of tropical Africa. In many former French colonies
this need has not yet been recognized by most private firms
(Ivory Coast, Gabon, Madagascar, etc.). Deterioration of
Senegal's internal economic situation at the very time when
top managers became aware of the need to Africanize (1963-64)
rendered the process even more difficult by exacerbating
psychological resistance.

     How would Africanization affect the demand schedule of
industrial firms?

                EFFECTS OF AFRICANIZATION ON
                    EMPLOYMENT IN SENEGAL

     Assuming industrial output remained at its present level,
potential demand for Senegalese labor consists in the expatriate labor force that may eventually be replaced by Senegalese
labor. The analysis is based on the latest detailed labor
statistics, that concern 1962.[10]

     The industrial labor force of Senegal is about 32,373
(not including transport). The expatriate labor force employed in industry is about 2,638 or 8.3 percent of total industrial employment.

     During a transitory phase, productivity of Senegalese
labor will be lower than that of expatriates as a result of
inadequate training and lack of practical experience:

          Potential demand for
               African labor = Expatriate labor

                              . Ratio of European productivity
                                         African productivity

Effects of Africanization of Supervisory and Managerial Jobs on Employment

OK = capital input
OL = labor input

P = slope before Africanization
P' = slope after Africanization

AA' = induced demand for African labor

77

Potential demand for industrial labor is shown in Table 19
that represents the racial structure of industrial employment
in Senegal:

TABLE 19

Scope for Africanization

Type of Labor	Employment	Expatriates	Scope for Africanization %
Managerial	889	829	93
Supervisory & Technical	1,919	1,309	68
Clerical	3,378	500	15
Workers & Apprentices	26,187	nil	nil

Source: Ministère du Travail, Statistiques de la Sécurité
          Sociale (Dakar: roneoed, 1964).

        Taking productivity-differentials into account, potential
demand for Senegalese labor is over 2,638. Africanization
would reduce the cost of management and supervision since
expatriate labor costs about 2.5 to 3 times more than African
labor. The shift in relative prices of labor and capital due to
the lowering of total labor costs by Africanization would--if
employers tried to attain a neo-classical optimum--make the
use of more labor-intensive methods of production economic.
Figure 4 illustrates this point.

        Cost justifies Africanization. The most crucial problem
in the near future is to Africanize at the foreman level; most
firms do not possess a staff capable of training African foremen adequately and are not in a position to do so because of
psychological factors. Africanization would increase employment, lower costs of production, and make increasing use of
labor-intensive methods of production more economic. This
point will be discussed further in Chapter 11.

                        *   *   *

The next chapter examines how trade-unionism affects the Senegalese labor market.

Notes to Chapter 4

1. An extreme example encountered in Senegal: Three expatriate workers were employed in a flour mill in 1964; one of them was in the VIth wage-grade; African workers in that grade earn 28,000 cfa francs per month; the expatriate worker in the same wage-grade earned 160,000 cfa francs.

2. Relies also on conversations with industrial managers.

3. E. J. Berg, "French West Africa," in Labor and Economic Development, Walter Galenson, ed. (New York: John Wiley and Sons, Inc., 1959); E. J. Berg, "The Economic Basis of Political Choice in French West Africa," The American Political Science Review, Vol. LIV (June, 1960).

4. The question of training Senegalese managers is left out; there is an urgent need for business administration schools in Africa; the problem of training higher executives and managers has not yet been faced by Senegalese industry.

5. Two such institutions were set up in Senegal since independence; one was set up in accordance with modern principles of management laying emphasis on techniques of authority for supervisors, etc. Some 125 Senegalese followed the course; results were disappointing to most industrial managers who had invested in training their staff in this way. This was partly due to the fact that the techniques taught had been initially developed for workers in Western countries who have a much higher general education than Senegalese workers. Trainees were left frustrated, and no significant increase in productivity was noted by employers who financed training. A second institution avoided these difficulties and confined its tuition to "tailor-made" training in accordance with actual job-descriptions. This method proved cheaper and better suited to the needs of Senegalese firms. However, few firms have access to this institution which is financed by a handful of firms.

6. André Hauser, "Les Industries de Transformation de la
    Région de Dakar et leur Main d'Oeuvre" (Dakar: University
    of Dakar, roneoed, 1958), p. 11.

7. An example of what is generally considered to be a suc-
    cess in Africanization is described in Appendix B.

8. See details in Appendix G.

9. E. J. Berg, "The Economic Basis of Political Choice in
    French West Africa," op. cit., p. 397.

10. Ministère du Travail, Statistiques de la Sécurité Sociale
    (Dakar: roneoed, 1964).

CHAPTER **5** THE INFLUENCE OF SENEGALESE
TRADE UNIONS ON THE
LABOR MARKET

Quite a number of studies have been made in recent years
about the political role of West African trade unions; but
very little has been written so far on the industrial role of
these organizations. Trade-unionism started in Senegal well
before World War II and by 1956 there were about 50,000 members in that territory; since then, the number of unionized
employees declined slightly.[1] Workers elect shop delegates
in the plants who channel grievances to union officials and
to the management; these delegates are elected on lists submitted by trade unions.

What influence do trade unions exert on Senegal's labor
market? How do enduring features and industrial policies of
the unions influence the market?

POLITICAL BACKGROUND TO UNIONISM

Present industrial policies must be viewed against the
background of political evolution in Senegal.

Political traditions developed long before trade unions
reached a stage where they played a significant role; one
of the consequences of this time lag is that there has been
little if any competition for political posts of responsibility between trade-unionists and political leaders; the
former were, on the whole, about twenty years younger than
the latter. The latter were firmly installed at the head of
organized political parties as trade unions emerged, between
1936 and 1948. Trade unions have therefore not benefited
directly from the experience and skill of political leaders,
and union leaders had no "obvious" claim to sharing political
leadership.

The constitution of 1946 created the French Union; it
was based "on equality of rights and responsibilities": Assimilation of the overseas territories to metropolitan French
standards in all respects became a constitutional principle.

81

Public offices were opened to Africans and Frenchmen from the
métropole alike. Between 1946 and 1956, political parties
and trade unions mainly focused on the implementation of the
new egalitarian principles in everyday life: Forced labor
was expressly abolished in 1946; a law of 1950 defined conditions of equality between African and French public employees in great detail; a large economic and social development
plan was launched in 1948-49. The last monument of egalitarian legislation was the Labor Code for overseas territories,
passed in December 1952, which rested on the principles of
"equal pay for equal work" regardless of "origin, sex, age
and statute." Later, attention of African politicians turned
away from implementing egalitarian principles and focused on
establishing a new relationship between African territories
and France. They also devoted a great deal of effort to con-
solidating their domestic basis for power.

African cabinets were set up in each of the territories
in 1956-57. No federal executive body was set up in AOF contrary to the wishes of most Senegalese politicians;[2] the
federal ideal defended by Leopold Sedar Senghor failed to
prevail: This meant "balkanization" of French West Africa.

In 1960, Sengal and Mali became independent as a result
of bilateral negotiations with France. Political parties of
Senegal adjusted to the national framework, soon to be followed by the labor movements.

The dominant party of Senegal is President Senghor's
Union Progressiste Sénégalaise (UPS). It controls Parlia-
ment and Government; it is a mass party solidly established
in the rural as well as in the urban parts of Senegal.

Political evolution influenced trade unions very deeply
in their policies. During the French Union period (1946-58),
the assimilationist policy of the government   reflected
itself in the use by trade unions of what has been called the
Equality Lever.[3] Trade unions were led primarily by civil
servants; industrial workers merely constituted a rank and
file to African public employees. Therefore, the union's industrial policies focused primarily on defending economic
interests of public employees. The Equality Lever was based
upon the 1946 constitution's expressed egalitarian principles.
The use of the Lever consisted in demanding alignments in
wages and conditions of employment between (i) African civil
servants and French ones, (ii) auxiliary and temporary public
employees with permanent ones, (iii) employees in the private
and the public sector. In this way, unions tried to extend
wage increases for French public employees in France to
African workers.

The Equality Lever was far more efficient than open
anti-colonialism because of the official policy of **assimi**-
lation: As long as the welfare of the colonies depended
largely on the metropolitan budget, political opposition on
the part of the unions yielded less than pressure from within
aimed at hastening the process of assimilation. The main
consequence was that "revolutionary" doctrines were never
successful in rallying the majority of Senegalese trade-union
leaders and rank and file; unions that called themselves
"revolutionary" also used the Equality Lever. Trade unions
did contribute much to Senegal's political independence which
was a matter of negotiation between political leaders rather
than of "struggle."

After independence, most trade unions were re-grouped,
in accordance with the wishes of the UPS, into a "national
union" sharing the party's labor doctrine. Only one major
nonpolitical industrial union remained outside the "national union."

ENDURING FEATURES OF SENEGALESE UNIONISM

Contrary to what is found in industrialized countries,
the "African working class" constitutes a small minority of
the population. African workers never had to sacrifice part
of their income, for generations, for making capital formation possible: Capital flowed into the colonies and there
was little or no relationship between the level of wages and
the rate of capital formation. These two fundamental differences between Europe and Africa deprive African unions of
some of the moral support enjoyed by trade unions in Europe
since the industrial revolution. Instead, in many former
colonies, trade unions found some basis for moral support in
their "struggle for independence"; in Senegal, no trade
union can seriously claim to have played such a role. This
explains why trade unions were relatively easily subordinated
to political parties. But the unions themselves show intrinsic weaknesses.

First, they have at all times been extremely poor.
Unions were in most cases unable to pay their own officials
sufficiently and regularly--this is one of the main causes of
inefficient leadership; poverty also exposes unions to the
influence of the government by way of subsidies and favors
corruption of union officials by employers; also, unions are
unable to assist workers on strike financially. This deprives their industrial action of some of its "credibility."

Trade-union officials can be divided into three groups:
At the bottom are the shop delegates; they do not necessarily differ from the rest of the workers by their education,
skill or income and do not have any special training in
trade-unionism and labor legislation, unless a trade union or
the Labor Administration took over part of their education as
unionists. The shop delegates' autonomy of action within the
unions depends mainly upon the extent to which labor leaders
remain in touch with everyday problems; whenever top leaders
lose touch with the rank and file (as their own political involvement grows), shop delegates have to act on their own
behalf; many strikes started at the plant level on the sole
initiative of shop delegates. Turnover of shop delegates in
the plants tends to be low; suitable candidates are scarce
and experience in labor relations takes some years to
acquire: Stability increases the shop delegates' authority
over industrial workers.

The second layer of unionists is found with the sécré-
taires de syndicat (permanent union officials) who are members of the executive bodies of the various regional unions
and occupational federations; they are usually "petty
clerks," some of whom gave up their jobs and devote all
their efforts to unionism; few attended secondary school;
their knowledge of labor problems derives from reading the
Labor Code and from daily contacts with the Labor Administration. Union officials keep in touch with shop delegates:
They tour enterprises, collecting membership dues, bargain
with management and advise shop delegates. The character of
union officials is a key factor that often determines the
social climate within an industry: A great number of strikes
can be accounted for by the union official's personal ambi-
tions. Union officials are particularly exposed to corruption by industrial employers; few union officials are industrial workers themselves.

The third layer consists of "top leaders": They are
members of the executive body of national labor organizations. Their number has never exceeded two or three dozen in
Senegal since 1946. Their authority rests on traditional
as well as on a unionist basis; their relationship with
lower officials is that of clan leaders to members of a clan;
the relationship between top leaders, shop delegates and
workers is usually confined to occasional public meetings and
demonstrations.

In order to give a realistic image of the Senegalese
unions' functioning we must show how, despite their formal

structures resembling that of French trade unions, Senegalese
unions are part of the traditional social and political pattern.

The traditional political system of Senegal is based on
clans and caste divisions;[4] a clan is a group of people
among whom there is a "patron" of higher caste with "clients"
--in the Roman sense--of inferior caste: A man of noble
caste and some financial means "is responsible for the support of an informal household of hangers-on."[5] This system
is based on a man-to-man allegiance on the part of the dependent members of the clan; these accept to share the political fortunes of their chosen patron, expecting to benefit materially from his possible successes. In return for
the clan leader's obligation to redistribute much of the
material advantages gained, the clients back their patron
against rival clan leaders. The personal following of a clan
leader is the first element in electoral and unionist support; when it comes to conflicts between two clan leaders,
the respective sizes of the followings often determine which
of the leaders carries the day. Allegiances are very stable;
this explains how labor leaders were able to change their
ideology quite frequently without losing the support of
their followers: The leader of a "tendency" (within the
"national union" or outside) is above all the head of a clan:
He controls lower officials who bring in "their" shop delegates.

Being essentially a nonideological organization, vertical alignments can be kept fluid. Basic clan quarrels at
the lower level can remain unaffected by modifications,
alliances, break-ups at the top; if a backcountry trade-
union leader X allies himself with national top leader A,
his rival clan leader Y can be expected to ally himself with
national leader A's rival B. Should X shift his allegiance
to B, Y would probably discover one reason or another for
shifting his allegiance to A. The essential character of the
system is that it rests on duality at all levels: The clan
system cannot function when all the clans are unified within
one single hierarchy; a constant competition between two
groups is necessary for the very existence of the system.

This goes a long way to explaining why, despite many
attempts at unifying Senegal's trade unions under one leadership, no "national union" has ever proved workable. It is
also one of the basic reasons for the unions' incapacity--
especially since independence--to pursue coordinated policies
for raising wages or pursuing development policies.

INDUSTRIAL POLICIES AND EFFECTS ON
THE LABOR MARKET SINCE INDEPENDENCE

Industrial policies of the unions developed before and
immediately after World War II. There were many strikes during these periods. Material gains from early industrial
action increased the popularity of labor leaders with the
workers.

By 1947, Senegalese union leaders had proved capable of
pursuing short strikes and of negotiating collective agreements with industrial and commercial employers. By 1959,
most industries were ruled by collective agreements (see
Appendix D). However, the three main enduring features of
Senegalese unionism: Poverty, poorly qualified intermediary
leadership and clan quarrels worked against effective industrial policies being enforced.

Poverty of the unions is a consequence of the poverty
of their members; this profoundly influences the rank and
file's attitude towards their unions' industrial policies.
The most important and usually sole concern of the workers
is with immediate economic gains; all other considerations
(ideology, workers' education, etc.) fade into the background.

Two examples of this constraint show how carrying out
long-term policies can be prevented: (a) Senegalese trade
unions exercised their influence to encourage employers to
satisfy the workers' needs for credit--notably for religious
feasts. Thereby, short-term satisfactions were given to the
workers while re-inforcing the employers' already very strong
bargaining power towards their personnel in the longer run;
(b) While trying to pursue a policy of "increasing industrial
employment," trade unions often encourage workers to slow
down their work during normal working hours so as to maximize
overtime earnings; this depresses average productivity and
contributes towards creating a tense social climate in the
plants. In the long run, the result of depressing productivity is to provide arguments against the use of labor-
intensive techniques of production in industry, thereby keeping employment down.

By contrast, while officially advocating Africanization, trade unions have shown no interest since 1943 in
workers' education, and failed to cooperate with the government and, in many cases, with private employers when training facilities were set up.

Mediocrity of intermediate leadership, lack of involvement of top leaders in industrial problems and persistence of clan quarrels (within the "national union" and between unions), can be exemplified by quotations from labor reports. These show, better than quantitative data, the state of inefficiency that has been reached in Senegalese unionism. Appendix C shows judgements by industrial workers and shop delegates on trade-unionism since independence: Both deplore the deterioration of industrial policies.

Labor administration reports of 1963 show a conflict between two "tendencies" within the "national union." In the Thiès-Diourbel regions, "At all levels political issues between the two clans ... overshadowed ... industrial interests."[6] In Diourbel as well as in Thiès and in Louga, the classical model of two clans showed very clearly: Two competing clientships officially belonging to the same union fought with no time left for industrial problems to be considered: "The plethora of ... officials in quest of clientship ... actually provoked conflicts in enterprises where social peace prevailed so far ... ending up in the state of constant perturbation which now exists in most enterprises."[7] In Saint Louis, workers had reached a stage where involvement in clan quarrels was such that they worked "day for day ... in an atmosphere of mutual distrust";[8] there was no more room for tension between workers and employers (from whom the workers expected little), "workers being more concerned about the internal problems which divide them."[9] Lower union officials used the Labor Courts for purposes of their own, "raising the greatest possible number of individual disputes";[10] cases were brought to court in the name of illiterate employees often without their knowledge--compensation and damages being shared between the union official and the worker; membership dues were insufficient to pay officials so that courts contributed to financing the clan system in which lower officials are indispensable agents for recruiting clientship.

Respect for labor legislation is not the chief concern of union leaders; an alarming lack of discipline among shop delegates and workers was noted in 1963; industrial relations took an anti-expatriate turn due mainly to the fact that top leaders were absorbed by political problems of their own while the management of the unions was left to incompetent lower officials. Several cases of physical violence against employers were reported.

As the Labor Code gives shop delegates a very strong protection against dismissal, these constitute ideal

instruments for carrying out clan quarrels in the factories:
"This privileged class developed the feeling of personal
security to a dangerous extent."[11] Any steps taken by employers against delegates are likely to provoke strikes; in
many cases, shop delegates interfered more than usual with
the firms' hierarchy, opposing orders of the management in
matters such as working time, shifts, etc. Workers have
little choice and frequently accept the delegate's authority
by fear of losing his support (W 57); the Labor Administration of Dakar concludes that shop delegates "do not know
what their role is."[12]

A Congress of 500 delegates met in Dakar in May 1963.
It gave the rank and file an opportunity to express its
views; the chairman noted that "leaders ignore the working
class"[13] and suggested holding new elections; he added:
"The labor movements' crisis in Senegal is not due only to
the ideological struggle but also and above all to questions
of personal interest."[14] Elections were not held.

The efficiency of union leadership in industrial matters
has declined steadily since independence; the last increase in the legal minimum wage (ten percent in 1961) owes
little to union policy; the major causes of the unions'
mediocrity must be sought in enduring features of Senegalese
unionism and in the increasing uninvolvement of top leaders
in industrial matters. Under the official alibi of "ideology," divisions in the leadership contribute to creating an
immense gulf between union leaders and the workers whom they
are supposed to defend.

The unions have not significantly influenced the labor
market of Senegal in matters of wages and employment; they
have become largely political institutions helping to carry
out government labor policy, which will be examined in the
next four chapters.

*   *   *

How do government policies affect the labor market? The
first point to be analyzed is the labor doctrine of the UPS
party of President Senghor; this doctrine is part of a more
general ideology, which Senghor himself calls "African
socialism." It is shared by the government, the party and
the "national union" (which constitutes the bulk of Senegalese trade unions). How does the party view labor problems and what role does it impart to labor organizations in
independent Senegal?

We will then turn to the three principal means by which
the government influences Senegal's labor market: labor legislation, education and manpower training, and wage-determination.

Notes to Chapter 5

1. RIT 1950 to 1960; for 1956 figures, RIT Sénégal 1956
   (Dakar: Labor Inspectorate, roneoed, 1957), p. 67.

2. Notably expressed during the June 1956 session of the
   Grand Conseil d'AOF.

3. See Professor P. F. Gonidec's concept of mystique de
   l'égalite (notably in "L'Evolution du Syndicalisme en
   Afrique Noire" in Penant (1962), p. 167; also, see
   E. J. Berg, "French West Africa," in Labor and Eco-
   nomic Development, Walter Galenson, ed. (New York:
   John Wiley and Sons, Inc., 1959).

4. On clans, see W. J. Foltz, "Social Structure and Polit-
   ical Behaviour of Senegalese Elites" (New Haven, Conn.:
   Yale University Press, roneoed, 1964) on which some of
   this analysis relies; on castes, see David P. Gamble,
   The Wolof of Senegambia (London: International African
   Institute, 1957).

5. W. J. Foltz, op. cit.

6. Letter No. 230 (Regional Labor Inspectorate Thiès to
   Ministry of Labor, 1963).

7. Ibid.

8. Letter No. 167 (Regional Labor Inspectorate Saint Louis
   to Ministry of Labor, 1963).

9. Ibid.

10. Letter No. 595 (Regional Labor Inspectorate Kaolack to
    Ministry of Labor, 1963).

11. Letter CFB/GC (Regional Labor Inspectorate Dakar to
    Ministry of Labor, 1963); and Letter No. 241 DTSS "Note
    succinte sur l'évolution du mouvement syndical depuis
    l'indépendance et le climat actuel," 1963.

12. Letter No. 3 (Regional Labor Inspectorate Dakar to
    Ministry of Labor, 1963).

13.   Louis Coclès, Report for Italia Press Agency (Dakar:
      unpublished, May, 1963).

14.   Afrique Nouvelle (May 31, 1963).

6

"AFRICAN SOCIALISTS"
ON INDUSTRIAL LABOR
IN SENEGAL

President Senghor pays tribute "to the Negro-African labor movement,"[1] assuming--without evidence--that its "grievances ... were on purpose excessive" for political reasons and its refusal to work out any "constructive plan which would have given the workers satisfaction within the framework of political integration ... succeeded in discouraging the colonial power."[2] This interpretation of the union's history is not easy to reconcile with evidence showing the persistent use of the Equality Lever up to 1960. Senghor then criticizes post-independence trade-unionism in contrast with the politically "useful" role of previous labor movements. He criticizes the clan system and the lack of organization within the "national union"; he also exposes the main lines of his government's view of labor problems.

President Senghor makes it clear that "the role of trade unions is an advisory and not a managerial one"[3]; union leaders are offered opportunities to perform this advisory role by collaborating with the party and government; joint party-union committees meet to this effect. The governmental union participates in the Economic and Social Council where representatives of several sections of society discuss questions of national interest; it also participates in a purely advisory capacity in National Planning Commissions. Non-governmental unions are excluded from regular cooperation with the government.

In the eyes of the party, economic development should transcend ideological differences between unionists and favor unity of the labor movements.

The economic aspects of the "reconversion of labor movements" are underlined by the party. The main argument used for keeping down the trade unions' influence is based on "social justice": In Senegal "there are only 100,000 wage earners representing scarcely ten percent of the working

population. Without violating the most elementary rules of
democracy, (trade unions) ... could not speak for the entire
population which only the dominant party could legitimately
represent."[4] The scope of trade-unionism having been circum-
scribed in the perspective of the nation as a whole, the
party then limits the power of the unions within their own
sphere: "The annual income of an African civil servant is
about 360,000 cfa francs; that of a wage earner in the private sector is about 180,000 cfa francs; while that of a
peasant ... is about 10,000 cfa francs."[5] This analysis constitutes the basis of the government's wage policy which further consists of the statement that wages "can be raised only
in proportion to those of the underprivileged farmers."[6]
Trade unions are no longer justified in expressing economic
grievances; in the eyes of the party, the "wage freeze" is
morally and economically justified by the discrepancy in remuneration that exists between civil servants and workers on
one hand ("wage earners"), and farmers on the other hand.

    A second line of economic argument makes the point that
the Senegalese economy was built up in the sole interest of
metropolitan France: "In this system our country merely performed the roles of supplier of primary produces ... and of
forced consumer of manufactured goods" made in France;[7] this
type of policy could, according to the party, neither achieve
a rise in Senegal's standard of living, nor the implementation of an economic development policy. A necessary reconversion of policies therefore implies priority given to economic development so as to satisfy the needs of the population as a whole, the first objective being to satisfy the
needs of the "underprivileged peasants." Thus, the policy of
the government is to reduce, or at least stabilize, the gap
existing between incomes of the urban population and those of
peasants: "We cannot do less than to establish a fixed relationship between the standards of living of our 'quasi-
classes'."[8]

    A third reason for keeping the economic and political
influence of trade unions down is the employment policy of
the government and its concern for international competitiveness. According to the party, raising industrial wages by
unionist action would necessarily have three adverse consequences for Senegal: Maintaining--or increasing--unemploy-
ment, increasing the "general level of prices," and worsening
the terms of trade. The first causal relationship implies
that demand for labor responds negatively to increases in
wages; the second one rests on the assumption that a wage-
price spiral (cost-push inflation) is likely to develop in

Senegal; the third relationship implies that industrial exports represent an important share of Senegal's total exports
and that they compete on a "free market." If prices increase, "Senegalese exports will diminish as a result ...
factories will shut down, there will be a reluctance to invest and unemployment will increase"; "The unions must know
that the prosperity of Senegal depends on exports to such an
extent that they will never put forward any claims likely to
raise prices above world markets' ...".[9]

The government clearly aims at achieving political sub-
ordination of labor movements to the dominant party for political as well as economic reasons. It tries to keep wages
low because of "social justice" (peasants constitute the bulk
of the UPS' electorate) towards "underprivileged farmers," in
order to "increase employment" and keep prices competitive on
international markets.

Notes to Chapter 6

1. L. S. Senghor, On African Socialism (London: Pall Mall
    Press, 1963), p. 95.

2. Rapport sur l'Orientation Syndicale de l'UPS (Dakar:
    UPS 1963, roneoed). For a critical historical analysis
    of the political role of trade unions in French West
    Africa, see Guy Pfeffermann, "Trade Unions and Politics
    in French West Africa during the Fourth Republic,"
    African Affairs (July, 1967), pp. 213-230.

3. L. S. Senghor, op. cit., p. 95.

4. Ibid., p. 55

5. Ibid.

6. L. S. Senghor, op. cit., p. 97.

7. Rapport sur l'Orientation Syndicale de l'UPS, op. cit.

8. L. S. Senghor, op. cit., p. 56.

9. Rapport sur l'Orientation Syndicale de l'UPS, op. cit.

7

LABOR LEGISLATION AND ITS ECONOMIC IMPLICATIONS

The bulk of present-day legislation for industrial labor was introduced under the French Fourth Republic. Social concern almost always predominated over economic considerations with French MP's who were often ill-informed about colonial matters. The assumption of policy-makers was that France would always be present to help African territories finance the implementation of social legislation: After the Labor Code of 1952 had been partially enforced in Africa and production costs had risen as a result, a parliamentary commission of enquiry stated that "It is the role of France to consent the sacrifices necessary to restart ... the whole of Africa's economy."[1]

Rigid and complex administrative regulations were worked out for Africa at that time which favored concentration of powers with the public administration as a safeguard against private employers; these complex sets of legislation are not easy to modify--institutional change in matters of labor policy is difficult. These laws and regulations still constitute the backbone of Senegal's institutional framework in matters of labor: They have their roots in the "equality mystique" of the assimilationist post-war period and take little notice of the economic problems of independent Senegal.

The Labor Code of 1952 was one of the last monuments of assimilationist policy; it is enforceable in respect of Africans and expatriates alike, and reflects concern on the part of policy-makers for the welfare of the workers. We shall focus on the economic aspects of labor legislation.

The Code is the main source of labor legislation in Senegal as well as in the other former French colonies of tropical Africa; collective bargaining plays a subordinate part in the regulation of employment relationships; individual firms may conclude plant-level agreements with their staff on secondary matters only; individual employment

contracts are standardized and conform to the Code and to
collective agreements.

REGULATORY PROVISIONS

The more general regulatory provisions of the Code concern prohibition of forced labor and freedom of unionism.
While these provisions are of great significance to the
labor force as a whole, those regarding specific conditions
of employment are of more immediate relevance to individual
workers. The emphasis of the Code is on stability of employment, which is rather exceptional in developing countries; concern for stability of employment is one of the
striking results of assimilationist policy-making. How does
the Code attempt to achieve this aim?

Provisions concerning conclusion of employment contracts
are less indicative of the Code's spirit and have lesser
consequences on stability than those concerning the termination of contracts. The spirit of the Code is shown in provisions on suspension and breach of contract.

A contract is suspended (and cannot be unilaterally
broken by employers) in cases such as national service, industrial injuries, occupational diseases, pregnancy and recovery of female employees after birth of a child. Protection of female employees (who are entitled to fourteen
weeks' leave with pay in case of pregnancy) seriously reduced industrial employers' willingness to hire female employees and slowed down Africanization of secretarial jobs.
Moreover, a contract can be suspended, but not broken,
during strikes or lock-out respecting the legal procedure.

Employers have to keep jobs open during the period of
suspension and to take that period into account for calcu-
lating length of service premiums, etc. Employers who fail
to respect these provisions can be sued for damages. Collective agreements go even further than the Code in granting employees the right to leave work in cases of "grave
and unexpected events concerning their family" and in cases
of nonoccupational sickness and accidents, which--up to six
months--cannot involve a breach of contract; given "extended family" solidarities, these provisions embrace a very
wide field.

A contract is broken when one party fails to fulfill its
obligations; in fact, this concerns employers' more than
employees' obligations. The Code expressly enumerates ten

cases in which failure by employees to fulfill their con-
tractual obligations does not result in breach of contract
but in a mere suspension. Dismissals involve several financial transactions.

In case of dismissal a distinction is made between
"legitimate" and "illegitimate" dismissals. A worker can be
"legitimately" dismissed if he refuses to obey technical
orders, etc. The Code specifies that dismissals of employees should be accompanied by a written statement by the employer on his motives: "Dismissals without legitimate
grounds ... constitute an offence."[2] The burden of proof of
"legitimacy" rests on the side of the employers; this is
not even the case in France and may make it difficult for
employers to dismiss part of their personnel. Further, the
Code lists cases of "legitimate" dismissals (e.g., slowdown
of production).[3] Decisions to dismiss are only taken after
consultation between the management and shop delegates.

Employers are also bound to take the workers' qualifi-
cations, length of service and family situation into account when dismissing part of their personnel; ceteris
paribus, employers are legally obliged to dismiss the most
recently hired, the youngest and the least skilled workers
first; marriage raises "length of service" by one year and
so does each child. For twelve months dismissed employees
keep a priority of re-employment in case their firm recruits any labor during that period. Shop delegates enjoy
special protection against dismissal; the latter is subordinated to express consent of the Labor Administration.

The most important aspect of dismissal for the workers
is the economic compensation it entails; three kinds of
compensation are provided for by labor legislation. First,
notice of dismissal must be given in advance by the employer
(the length varies but is usually one week to one month);
obligations arising from the contract continue to bind the
parties after notice has been given; the employer must
grant workers who have been given notice leave of absence
of one day per week, for which normal wages must be paid, so
as to enable them to look for another job. In practice,
employers are not keen on keeping workers between the time
notice has been given and the actual date of termination of
the contract; usually, workers do not resume their work
once they have been given notice; in that case, the Code
obliges employers to give financial compensation (a) to
their employees; this amounts to the workers' wages between
the notice and the expiration of the period of notice.

Apart from this obligation, employers must pay compensation (b) for dismissal per se. Collective agreements include details on this point; the basis for compensation (b) is the workers' wage and length of service.

Moreover, if an employer is unable to prove that dismissal is based on "legitimate grounds," he may have to pay additional compensation (c) for "illegitimate dismissal" (licenciément abusif).

The combined effects of these three compensations are to reduce fluidity on the labor market.

Judgements by Senegalese Labor Courts indicate that the tendency of jurisprudence is to protect employees: For an employee to be regarded as having committed an offence requires almost criminal activities on his part (e.g., driving a truck without license, persistent drunkenness, theft).[4] A high percentage of cases brought to the Labor Courts consist in claims to compensate for dismissal: In 1956, 36 percent of all cases,[5] in 1959, 29 percent of all cases.[6]

In practice, the Code failed to ensure stability of employment: It is almost always possible for employers to invoke economic or technical reasons for dismissing workers "legitimately" (slowdown of production). But the Code did succeed in rendering dismissals expensive to employers and a source of income to dismissed workers (and for trade-union representatives defending their case in Court). The high percentage of dismissal cases brought to Labor Courts shows that the Code's provisions have not, as it had been hoped by policy-makers, helped stabilize the labor force; it acted as a disincentive to recruit seasonal labor and female African employees; it also rendered implementation of Africanization programs more difficult by (i) making it easier for employers to dismiss younger rather than older employees and (ii) making it very costly to dismiss highly paid expatriate employees.

Expatriate employers resent the fact that many Syro-Lebanese and African employers do not enforce labor legislation. This constitutes, in their eyes, a handicap in their competition with small-scale handicraft industries.

Control of enforcement is the responsibility of shop delegates, union officials and of the Labor Administration; only a very small proportion of firms interviewed stated that they had been regularly visited by Labor Inspectors since independence (E 73); union officials show only occasional interest in the social situation at plant level.

Hence, at present, responsibility for checking enforcement of
labor legislation at plant level mainly lies with shop delegates who often lack competence in these matters.

The second way in which the Code influences the labor
market is by its remedial provisions.

REMEDIAL PROVISIONS

The concern of policy-makers for the workers' welfare
was also reflected in the remedial provisions of the Code.
Two principal aspects of these provisions will be examined
because of their economic implications: The right to strike,
and the settlement of disputes.

Individual disputes arising between employers and employees are settled by Labor Inspectors acting as concilia-
tors and by specialized institutions called Labor Courts,
original creations by the 1952 Code. The main features of
Labor Courts are total absence of cost for either party for
their use, extreme rapidity of the procedure and the presence throughout the procedure of a professional magistrate.
Absence of fees and rapidity of the procedure have made the
Labor Courts very popular with industrial workers. The judicial procedure, legal assistance, acts and copies, payment
of experts and compensation for witnesses are all free for
the party introducing a claim; expenditure is met by the
Ministry of Justice.

The technical aspects of the procedure[7] show the policy-
makers' concern for efficiency. The Labor Courts in Senegal
handle well over 3,000 cases a year; they keep social tension at plant level down to a minimum. Senegalese workers
tend to accept judgements of the Courts even when these are
not in their favor: The fact that representatives of workers
and of employers cooperate with the magistrate in charge
brings justice closer to the parties and helps the latter to
accept the authority of the judgements.

Collective disputes are not handled by Labor Courts;
most collective disputes involve economic, political, and
social interests too important to be decided on by one magistrate. Compulsory conciliation and arbitration were in force
between 1937 and 1955. A very complex system that proved inefficient replaced the pre-war legislation in 1955.[8] A new
Labor Code of 1961 (that does not significantly depart from
its 1952 model) sought to adapt the machinery for settling
collective disputes to the political and economic situation
of the country as interpreted by the UPS party.

The right to strike is expressly recognized by the Senegalese Constitution "within the laws that rule it."9 On the
other hand, it is the policy of the government to contain
strikes. The procedure for settling collective disputes is
complex10 and subordinates the exercise of the right to
strike to a decision taken by the Minister of Labor; unless
authorization is given, strikes can break employment contracts of employees on strike.

The normal way to settle collective disputes is by conciliation and arbitration. Successful conciliation--by Labor
Inspectors--and arbitration have legal force for the parties
to the dispute and can be "extended" by decree to other employers and employees than those directly involved in the
dispute.

Arbitration is carried out either in law or in equity:
A collective dispute is a matter of law when it rests on
interpretation of labor legislation; in all other cases
disputes are judged in equity (i.e., without necessary reference to law); this is notably the case when a dispute
arises on wages or working conditions that are not foreseen
by law or collective agreement, as well as in the case of
disputes related to revision of collective agreements.

Combination of equity judgements by a council of arbitration composed exclusively of magistrates (professional
judges, often removed from economic realities) and of the
possibility of administrative "extension" turns the Senegalese machinery for settling collective disputes into a powerful economic instrument.

Two ways are open to workers wanting to improve their
material conditions by using the Senegalese remediary legislation: Either the council of arbitration or the Labor
Courts.

Before 1961, decisions of the arbitrators could be opposed by either party; an objection had the effect of setting a new judicial process in motion and prevented the attacked decision from being enforceable. Senegalese policy-
makers sought greater efficiency in modifying provisions
for collective disputes in 1961; they rendered the arbitrators' decisions immediately enforceable for the parties,
notwithstanding opposition or a recourse to the Supreme
Court. Further, decisions could be "extended" beyond the
parties by administrative acts: Either to one industry, or
to all private employers in Senegal. This had economic consequences: In practice, the dividing line between cases to

be judged in law and those to be judged in equity is not
sharp; the council of arbitration feels free to judge many
cases in equity. Therefore, the personality of the arbitrator has become a crucial factor for determining the spirit of
the machinery. At the lower level (first arbitrator) arbitrators are often chosen among academics; at the higher
level (council of arbitration) cases are in the hands of professional magistrates. Employers' associations often deny
the competence of academics and professional judges in matters of business administration.

From the point of view of labor unions, the mechanism
operates as follows: (a) An industrial employer--usually in
an expanding or a protected industry--grants an extra fringe
benefit to his employees after shop delegates have pressed
for obtaining it; (b) the union sends a notice to the Labor
Administration which opens a collective dispute; the union
claims that a dispute arose concerning the fringe benefit in
question in some factory--usually chosen in a marginal industry among firms in a difficult economic situation; (c)
the Labor Inspectorate attempts to conciliate the parties and
the attempt fails; at this point the Minister of Labor decides the case must be submitted to arbitration (thus rendering strike "illegitimate"); (d) the arbitrator judges either
in law or in equity and may recommend the fringe benefit in
question to be included into collective agreements; (e) employers' associations which are parties to the dispute appeal
and refer the case to the council of arbitration; (f) the
council (that does not include representatives of the unions
and employers' associations) may or may not subscribe to the
views of the first arbitrator; if it does, payment of the
fringe benefit becomes an obligation for employers in an
industry. Only the right to appeal to the Supreme Court on
grounds of legal error having been committed remains in the
employers' associations' power; the government may extend
the sphere of enforcement of the arbitration to the entire
private sector.

The scope of such a procedure ranges from one employer
to a whole industry. Three significant cases were dealt
with in recent years: The marriage premium, the "harmoniza-
tion of workers' and salaried staff's wage-grades," and the
transport allowance. The first issue was taken up unsuccessfully under the 1952 Code and again after 1961; it was
settled by conciliation, and employees of the groundnut-processing industry (the largest manufacturing industry) were
granted a premium for their first marriage equal to two weeks'
pay. The second case rests on the formal analogy between
wage-grade scales for workers and salaried staff, each consisting of eight levels; in 1958 unions demanded parity of

agreed wages between corresponding levels for workers and
salaried staff; the council of arbitration refused to judge
in favor of the unions.[11] The case was taken up again by the
trade union of printers to whom partial satisfaction was
given in 1961.[12]

In the case of the transport allowance, the mechanism
can be analyzed very clearly. In the minds of trade-union
leaders, transport allowances should cover the daily expenditure of those workers who do not live in the vicinity of
their place of work. The dispute opposed a national union to
the industrial employers' association. Prior to 1960, a decision on this issue would have been enforceable throughout
AOF. In 1958, the case was brought before an arbitrator who
gave partial satisfaction to the union. The union opposed
the arbitration because payment of the allowance had been
subordinated to conditions such as place of residence and
wage.[13] In 1959, the unions accepted the first arbitration,
but only at the factory level in the groundnut mills; in
1963, the case was taken up again in a wider context: A
motion by shop delegates[14] started the machinery of settlement of collective disputes. Conciliation failed;[15] the
arbitrator's judgement in favor of granting the transport
allowance[16] was attacked by the employers' associations. The
matter was referred to the council of arbitration and the
latter agreed, in equity, with the first arbitrator's judgement.[17] All that was left to do for the employers' associations was to appeal to the Supreme Court to verify the le-
gality of the procedure. But meanwhile the decision of the
council had become law to the parties. Transport allowances
amount to about 7,000 cfa francs per year per worker,
which represents little less than a month's wage for unskilled workers.

Legislation on collective disputes can thus transmit
benefits granted in one firm or industry to the industrial
sector as a whole or even to the whole private sector. Marginal firms such as shipyards, metalworks, etc., can be hard
hit by economic change generated in more prosperous industries by way of arbitrations in equity.

                    *   *   *

A second means for workers to increase their income is
the use of the Labor Courts. The most popular way of doing
so is to attack an employer in Court for having placed a
worker in a wage-grade that is inferior (by virtue of its requirements) to that which corresponds to the work actually

performed; in most cases workers are picked out and brought
to Court by lower union officials who take the initiative of
introducing the cases.

The concept of wage-grade based on the French system
was introduced by the first collective agreements. A Labor
Report of 1951 already criticizes them as being "a natural
source of difficulties and conflicts";[18] lack of precision
of certain job-description in collective agreements facili-
tates bringing these cases to Court.

The rigidity of wage legislation makes it very difficult
for employers to adjust individual wages to each worker's
performance. One of the ways in which employers can increase
a specific worker's wages without having to alter those of
other employees (which would conflict with the government's
"wage freeze" and might not achieve the desired result) is to
promote the worker to a higher wage-grade: Factors such as
length of service have become an important element in determining wage-grades. Young and efficient workers often find
that older, less-educated workers rank higher than themselves and perform less difficult tasks. Being promoted
from one wage-grade to the next represents an economic gain
of about 10 percent to 30 percent of the initial wage for the
worker. The introduction of factors other than the job-
description into wage-grade determination greatly contributed
to making the latter a major cause of industrial conflict and
of management difficulties.

*   *   *

Thus, machinery for settling industrial disputes can
perform two significant functions: It provides a channel for
efficient settlement of disputes arising at plant level,
thereby reducing social tension in the firms; it also provides a tool for trade unions and individual workers to increase the workers' income (and by way of corruption, that of
union officials) which restricts industrialists' freedom in
matters of wage-grades and fringe benefits. The initial aim
of policy-makers motivated by humanitarian rather than by
economic reasons--to protect workers from insecurity--does
not seem to have been attained. In a developing country, the
will of social policy-makers is not as powerful as economic
forces, especially if political change alters the background
as deeply as does transition from colonial dependence to political independence. Since the passing of the Labor Code,
despite the obstacles in the way of dismissals, employment
decreased. Labor Courts performed an economic role. So have
the institutions provided for settling collective disputes,

but their influence was exerted on income rather than on employment, and conflicted with the labor policy of "African socialism."

It was suggested in this chapter that assimilationist policy did not achieve all its objectives in the case of labor legislation; it will now be suggested that the same policy--assimilation--prevented the government's educational policies from meeting the requirements of industrial development.

Notes to Chapter 7

1. Assemblée de l'Union Française, Rapport d'Information sur les Conditions d'Application du Code du Travail Outre-Mer en AOF (Paris: February 2, 1954), No. 55, notably pp. 57-58, 64.

2. Labor Code of 1961, Article 51.

3. Ibid., article 47.

4. Travaux et Professions d'Outre-Mer is a periodical that is concerned with labor jurisprudence overseas; "legitimate" dismissal is one of the main recurring topics; see also, Martin Kirsch, Memento de Droit du Travail Outre-Mer (Paris: 1965); both publications are edited 57 avenue d'Iéna, Paris.

5. RIT Sénégal 1956 (Dakar: Labor Inspectorate, 1957), p. 34.

6. RIT Sénégal 1959 (Dakar: Labor Inspectorate, 1960), p. 98.

7. The maximum legal time allowed for cases to be dealt with is four weeks for Labor Courts and three months for appeals.

8. Decree of May 20, 1955 (AOF) which was violently attacked by trade unions until its abrogation by introduction of the Senegalese Labor Code of 1961.

9. Constitution of 1963, Article 20.

10. The procedure has three phases: (i) Conciliation by the
     Labor Inspectorate; (ii) arbitration in the first in-
     stance by one arbitrator chosen on a list of personali-
     ties by the Ministry of Labor (the list is drawn up
     jointly by that Ministry and the Ministry of Justice);
     (iii) arbitration in the second instance by a council
     of arbitration; this council is presided over by the
     President of the Cour d'Appel and other members are:
     One civil servant, magistrates and experts selected
     from the list mentioned previously. Altogether, cases
     must be dealt with within sixty-five days.

11. Judgement No. 20, December 1, 1958.

12. Judgement of November 27, 1961.

13. Opposition of December 17, 1958.

14. Dated 11 August, 1963.

15. October 3 and 10, 1963.

16. Judgement of October 10, 1963.

17. Judgement of January 30, 1964.

18. RIT Sénégal 1951 (Dakar: Labor Inspectorate, 1952).
     Statistics show the rise of conflicts on wage-grades:
     (Source: Labor reports)

     Conflicts on Wage-grades
     1946   4
     1947   5
     1948   24
     1949   53
     1950   61
     1951   284
     1959   1,962 (of which 436 to Court and the
                               rest to Labor Inspectorate)

     There is a correlation between the number of cases
     brought to Labor Courts and the index of industrial
     output; relative increases in industrial production
     (relative strengthening of workers' bargaining power)
     are matched year for year by relative increases in the
     number of cases submitted to courts: (Source: Sit. Ec.
     and Greffe of the Labor Court, Dakar)

18. (cont'd.)

Year	Ind.output	Absolute Variation	Rel.var.	Cases	Variation
1959	100			3,000	
1960	117	+ 17	+	3,400	+
1961	130	+ 13	-	2,600	-
1962	132.2	+ 2.2	-	2,550	-
1963	131.7	- 0.5	-	2,200	-
1964	138	+ 6.3	+	3,000	+

The smaller the risk of dismissal, the more numerous cases brought to Court.

CHAPTER **8** EDUCATION AND MANPOWER
TRAINING

What resources does Senegal allocate for education
and manpower training? What quantitative and qualitative
results does the government obtain? Is the educational
system adequate for the requirements of industrial development?

*   *   *

The educational system was one of the main instruments of the French for carrying out gradual assimilation
of its African dependencies to metropolitan standards. The
aim was "to ensure educational equality at each stage with
the corresponding institutions of metropolitan France.
Schools in the periphery were exact replicas of analogous
institutions at the centre."[1] The present educational system of Senegal differs only marginally from that of the
colonial time.

As in France, there are four main categories of educational facilities in Senegal, leaving out private schools:
(i) Primary schools that provide basic education within five
or six years; (ii) secondary schools (lycées and collèges)
that form a link between the primary schools and the universities; (iii) technical--or vocational--schools, running
parallel to secondary schools; (iv) higher education
facilities at the University of Dakar. Each of these chan-
nels is free of charge for Senegalese as well as for expatriate pupils and students--a system inherited from the
French.

Senegal spends over 4 billion cfa francs per annum as
current expenditure on education. This represents over 12
percent of the State budget for current expenditure.[2] Of
that, little less than one billion goes for vocational training. In addition, a large share of foreign aid accrues to
the educational system: Over 800 expatriate teachers work
in Senegal.[3] The University of Dakar is financed up to 80

percent by France (1966) and is not scheduled to come under
Senegal's sole financial responsibility before 1976. The
cost of French technical assistance in education exceeds 3
billion cfa francs per year. The total cost of the Senegalese educational system exceeds 7 billion cfa francs per
year, excluding private (mostly religious) establishments.
This represents over 5 percent of the Senegalese GDP.[4]

The rate of primary school attendance is higher in
Senegal than in many tropical countries in Africa; this is
due to early colonization and urbanization. The rate of
school attendance increases, but the law of diminishing returns works against such progress, mainly because marginal
increases now take place in rural areas.

TABLE 20

Government Primary Schools:
Attendance Excluding Expatriates

1958	68,393	
1959	77,400	+ 13%
1960	88,906	+ 15%
1961	107,788	+ 21%
1962	127,436	+ 18%
1963	150,573	+ 18%
1964	159,679	+ 6%
1965	178,350	+ 11%

Source: Services de la Statistique, Situation Economique du
Sénégal 1963 (Dakar, 1964), p.15; Services de la
Statistique, Situation Economique du Sénégal 1964
(Dakar, 1965), p. 13; Services de la Statistique,
Situation Economique du Sénégal 1965 (Dakar,
1966), p. 13.

About 36 percent of Senegalese children, including 47 percent
of all boys, go to school.

Primary school-leavers can either take a certificat
d'études primaires élémentaires (CEP)--awarded to successful
pupils after an examination, or attempt to enter secondary
school by ways of an entry examination, or enter a vocational
school.

Results for the CEP examination show a very low rate of success, thus a high rate of wastage:

TABLE 21

Final Examination for Primary Schools

	No. of Candidates*	Pass	% Fail
1961	13,254	6,309	52.5
1962	14,694	7,636	48.0
1963	17,095	7,156	58.0
1964	21,276	9,606	55.0
1965	25,373	12,339	51.4

* Includes expatriates and Syro-Lebanese.
Source: Services de la Statistique, Situation Economique du Sénégal 1963 (Dakar, 1964), p. 15; Services de la Statistique, Situation Economique du Sénégal 1964 (Dakar, 1965), p. 13; Services de la Statistique, Situation Economique du Sénégal 1965 (Dakar, 1966), p. 13.

Results for primary school-leavers attempting to enter secondary schools are even worse: Rate of failure, 64.5 percent in 1963.

Secondary schools cater for 18,374 Senegalese and 2,709 expatriate pupils (1965); statistics do not show the number of Syro-Lebanese pupils; these are included under "Senegalese" thus giving a magnified image of the number of Senegalese pupils attending secondary schools. Secondary schools lead to a brevêt d'études du premier cycle (BEPC) after about four years, and to the baccalauréat (that opens the doors of French universities) after a minimum of seven years. The rate of failure of Senegalese and Syro-Lebanese pupils in these examinations are: BEPC, 65.5 percent; baccalauréat, 23 percent (1963).[5]

*   *   *

Vocational schools do not enjoy high prestige value in France; the same is true in former French colonies of tropical Africa. Many of the pupils entering technical schools

unsuccessfully attempted to be admitted into a lycée before
applying for a vocational college.

Some 5,300 Senegalese and expatriate pupils attend technical schools. These lead to a certificat d'aptitude professionnelle (CAP) after four years, to a brevêt d'enseignement industriél (resp., commercial) (BEI) after a minimum of
six years, and to the baccalauréat technique after a minimum
of seven years. The CAP level of qualification corresponds
to that required for specialized, medium-skilled workers;
the BEI level corresponds to that of a highly skilled worker.

Statistics show that very few Senegalese pupils succeed
in obtaining any of these certificates.

TABLE 22

Certificates Delivered by Technical Schools

Certificate	Year	Candidates	Pass	Of which Senegalese or Syro-Lebanese
CAP	1962	242	128	91
(industrial)	1963	271	129	112
	1964	322	138	115
	1965	336	146	130
BEI	1962	79	60	25
	1963	48	31	n.a.
	1964	42	17	8
	1965	n.a.	n.a.	n.a.
baccalauréat	1962	6	6	1
technique	1963	25	23	8
	1964	33	26	11
	1965	35	24	13

Source: Services de la Statistique, Situation Economique du
Sénégal 1963 (Dakar, 1964), p. 15; Services de la
Statistique, Situation Economique du Sénégal 1964
(Dakar, 1965), p. 13; Services de la Statistique,
Situation Economique du Sénégal 1965 (Dakar,
1966), p. 13.

The average rate of failure of Senegalese pupils is of
about 65 percent for the baccalauréat technique, about 70

percent for the BEI and about 60 percent for the CAP. The
First National Plan foresaw an output of 100 Senegalese BEI
holders and 200 CAP holders for 1964; these previsions were
not reached.[6]

A synthetic table sums up quantitative information about
results, in terms of number of degrees obtained, of an educational system which functions at very high cost:

TABLE 23

Output of Certified Pupils (1965)

Primary schools:	206,431 pupils including expatriates 12,339 CEP obtained, including ex- patriates;
Secondary schools:	18,374 pupils, excluding expatri- ates 147 baccalauréats, excluding expatriates;
Vocational schools:	4,754 pupils, excluding expatri- ates 130 CAP (industrial) excluding expatriates 25 BEI (1962) excluding ex- patriates 13 baccalauréats techniques, excluding expatriates

Source: Services de la Statistique, Situation Economique du
Sénégal 1963 (Dakar, 1964), p. 15; Services de la
Statistique, Situation Economique du Sénégal 1964
(Dakar, 1965), p. 13; Services de la Statistique,
Situation Economique du Sénégal 1965 (Dakar,
1966), p. 13.

*   *   *

What are the main causes of the high rate of failure and
wastage?

The main reason for the very poor economic performance
of the educational system is the fact that the latter is--
despite political independence--geared to France rather than
to Senegal; the particular aims of French educational policy

"very elevated perhaps but certainly wholly irrelevant for
the future success and prosperity of Africa, were successfully achieved."7 The proportion of French teachers among
teachers working in Senegal reveals the main causes for lack
of adaptation of secondary and vocational schools, as well as
of higher education, to the country's needs:

TABLE 24

Proportion of French Teachers (1964)

Primary schools:	3.6%
Secondary and Vocational schools:	93.3%
University (full professors):	100.0%

Source: Services de la Statistique, Situation
Economique du Sénégal 1964 (Dakar, 1965).

French families living in Senegal and the Senegalese
"upper class" exert pressure on the government for maintaining French standards of examination and tuition; about 20
percent of secondary school-attenders were French in 1963.
Diplomas such as the CAP, the BEI, the BEPC and the baccalauréat are valid in France as well as in Senegal.

Technical assistants teaching in Senegal usually work in
that country for a relatively short period (two to four
years) after which they resume their normal careers in
France; thus, teachers are mostly unwilling to depart radically from their normal methods and standards for such short
periods of their careers. Teachers of the older generation
who "stayed behind" after independence tend to dispense a
type of tuition which they grew accustomed to during the
colonial period. These factors make it very difficult indeed
to implement new educational policies.

Attempts by the colonial administration to set up specialized schools for vocational training of Africans alone
failed; a center for training medium-skilled workers was set
up in Dakar in 1951 for supplying adequate labor for implementing the FIDES programs; this center had to be closed
down in 1958 after demand for skilled labor had declined in
public works; it trained only a handful of people.

The syllabuses of vocational schools reflect the "neo-
colonial" position of Senegal. They are composed of two

parts: In addition to the purely technical part, Senegalese vocational schools teach literature, history, geography,
languages, etc., all patterned on French syllabuses. The
inclusion of classical education into the syllabuses of the
vocational schools makes it possible for industrial trainees
to contemplate entering university, or administrative employment. While this shows concern on the part of French policy-
makers for "equality of opportunities," it constitutes a
major source of waste in Africa. A Zweckentfremdung--diver-
sion from the original purpose--occurs. Both traditional
caste divisions and the present price, wage and social preference system, resulting from colonial rule, weigh against
pupils concentrating on the purely industrial part of tuition. There is a strong preference for nonmanual jobs in
Senegal, justified to a great extent by wage-differentials
between manual and nonmanual jobs; thus, many pupils attending vocational schools intend to "switch over" to
secondary schools that open the doors to scholarships in
France; if they fail "switching over," they do not readily
accept the idea of having to perform manual work for the rest
of their lives. The vocational part of tuition--by far the
most expensive--is largely wasted.

      In fact, many vocational school-leavers enter public ad-
ministration; most of these become primary school teachers.
Those who do enter industry are often reluctant to undergo
the slow process of adaptation and promotion inherent in factory work. They (rightly) consider themselves part of a
small privileged élite, which makes their integration with
less-educated workers a problem rarely satisfactorily overcome. Only a minority of vocational school-leavers are
found in an industry or trade for which they were trained,
two to five years after they have left school.

      A follow-up survey[8] was carried out to determine the
rate of wastage in vocational schools; this survey covers
school-leavers of 1960 to 1962. It indicates their occupational status in 1963 and 1964 and covers 176 school-leavers.

TABLE 25

Occupational Status of School-Leavers with
Industrial Training (Senegalese only)

		(a)	(b)	(c)	(d)	(e)	(f)
After 3 years	CAP	82	42	49%	3	19	18
(1960 leavers)	BEI	14	4	71%	-	4	6
	No Cert.	17	2	87%	5	3	7
After 2 years	CAP	33	7	79%	2	18	6
(1961-62 leavers)	BEI	9	4	55%	-	5	-
	No Cert.	21	4	81%	6	3	8
Total		176	63	64%	16	52	45
Percentage		100	35.8		9.1	29.5	25.6

(a) Senegalese pupils leaving vocational school with indus-
    trial training;
(b) Of which, employed in industry or trade corresponding to
    training;
(c) Percentage not employed in industry or trade correspond-
    ing to training;
(d) Of which, unemployed;
(e) Studying;
(f) Employed outside industry.

Note: Four Senegalese pupils obtained a baccalauréat tech-
       nique and must be added to the list.

Source: Enquêtes Relatives à la Situation des Anciens Elèves
         des Etablissements d'Enseignement Technique (Dakar:
         Centre National d'Orientation Professionnelle, 1963
         and 1964).

This survey shows that 18 percent of pupils training to become medium-skilled workers are employed outside industry
after two years; 22 percent after three years. This trend
seems to be even more marked after five to six years.[9]

Only 35.8 percent of all vocational school-leavers
covered are employed in the field for which they were trained; the higher the level of the certificate held, the higher the proportion of school-leavers not employed in industry:

Certificate	Percentage not employed in industry
CAP (industrial)	57.5
BEI	65.0
baccalauréat technique	100.0

The larger the amount of general education dispensed for higher certificates may account for this progression.

Among former pupils of industrial schools who were not employed in industry, most became public employees: Of forty-five former pupils employed out of industry, thirty-five were public employees (many of them primary school teachers), five were employed in commerce and five elsewhere.

Sixty of the school-leavers who obtained a CAP stated the number of jobs which they had had since leaving school. Turnover is high: 23 percent of these former pupils had two jobs in three years, 16 percent three. Justification for changing jobs were "dismissal" (65 percent) or "dissatisfaction with too hard work" or "too little pay."

The ILO set up a new type of vocational school for industry in 1962. This experimental establishment attempts to avoid some of the handicaps of State-run schools; it provides tuition for Africans only, thus being in a better position to adapt to Senegalese needs. It operates in closer cooperation with private industry than State-run schools and operates on a principle which is new for Senegal. Pupils share their time between periods of school tuition and periods of factory work of four months each. It is hoped that the percentage of wastage among school-leavers will be reduced in this way, and adaptation to actual factory work eased. The first school-leavers came out in June 1965; it is too early to assess the efficacy of the new system.

*   *   *

Senegal and France spend considerable sums on education, notably on vocational training. The rate of school attendance in primary schools is high by African standards, but the rate of failure among Senegalese pupils is also high. The main reason for this is the persistence, in secondary and vocational schools, of policies geared to France rather than to Senegal's needs. Vocational schools are not specialized enough and do not remedy scarcity of supply of skilled and

supervisory Senegalese labor. Few industrial trainees become and remain industrial workers in the field for which
they were trained.

There has been almost no effort so far at coordinating
the government's vocational training policy with plans of
private firms. From the point of view of industrial development, Thomas Balogh was quite justified, in the case of Senegal, in stating that the system "unnecessarily constituted a
hindrance rather than a help":[10] The present output of industrial labor could be obtained at much smaller cost, and
sums saved used for more productive purposes, if educational
policies were modified.

Notes to Chapter 8

1. Thomas Balogh, "The Problem of Education in Africa", The
    Centennial Review of the Michigan University, Vol. VI,
    (No. 4, 1962), pp. 534-535.

2. Budget Général 1963-1964 (Rufisque: Government of Sene-
    gal, 1964).

3. Notes sur la Coopération Française au Sénégal (Dakar:
    Mission d'Aide et de Cooperation, 1964). There were
    1,410 French technical assistants--not counting French-
    men directly employed by the Senegalese government--in
    Senegal in 1964.

4. Comptes Economiques du Sénégal 1959-1962 (Dakar: Ser-
    vices de la Statistique, 1964).

5. Corresponding rates for expatriate pupils are about
    39.5 percent and 7.5 percent.

6. Plan Quadriennal de Développement 1961-1964 (Dakar:
    Ministry of Planning, 1961), p. 137.

7. Thomas Balogh, op. cit.

8. Enquêtes Relatives à la Situation des Anciens Elèves des
    Etablissements d'Enseignement Technique (Dakar: Centre
    National d'Orientation Professionnelle, 1963 and 1964).

9. Based on interview with the head of the ILO mission in
    charge of manpower training in Dakar, 1964.

10. Thomas Balogh, op. cit.

CHAPTER **9** THE GOVERNMENT'S
INFLUENCE ON WAGE-
DETERMINATION

Finally, the government affects the labor market by means of its policy of wage-determination. How significant is the State's influence on wage-determination? How does it affect effective wages?

There are three main reasons for which the State has great influence on industrial wages in former French colonies. Firstly, most private employers used to pursue "cheap labor" policies in colonial times; unless the administration determined wage rates at a higher level, employers tended to pay wages that did not cover the basic expenditure of workers. Private firms became used to rely on wage-determination by the government. Secondly, a high percentage of the wage-earning labor force is employed by the State. This sets minimum standards that private firms tend to adjust to. Thirdly, in African economies a great number of employees are unskilled workers; they do not earn much more than the legal minimum wage rate. This is a result of the structure of the economy in which industrial firms use much larger quantities of unskilled labor than is the case in industrialized countries. These three factors contribute to giving the government a wage-leadership and an effective role in determining wages.

Industrial wages can be broken down into (i) basic, and (ii) social wages. Basic wages consist of the hourly or monthly wage and of fringe benefits paid out by employers; social wages are paid out by a government agency and vary according to the workers' family situation.

THE GOVERNMENT'S INFLUENCE ON BASIC WAGES

Wage-determination policies of the colonial administration were patterned on the French, without adopting all the provisions in force in metropolitan France; basically, the metropolitan and the colonial systems were identical. The Senegalese government took over the wage-determination machinery from the French.

The national (or territorial) minimum wage rate was introduced into Africa in 1925.[1] Previously, wages were determined by custom. The administration sets a rate called
<u>salaire minimum interprofessionnel garanti</u> (smig). On the
basis of this rate, trade unions and employers' associations
may conclude collective agreements that include agreed rates
for different degrees of qualification. No agreed rate can
--by law--be inferior to the national rate, but employers are
free to pay wages in excess of that rate and do usually pay
premiums and gratuities in addition to the basic wage.

The administration determines the national minimum rate
on the basis of a standard budget representing the theoretical expenditure of an unmarried unskilled worker; it exceeds the <u>minimum minimorum</u> below which human beings cannot
survive but ignores expenditure relating to wives and children. The main differences between the metropolitan and the
colonial systems is that in France, the evolution of the smig
is automatically geared to changes in a cost-of-living index,
whereas in the colonies, it was fixed from time to time by
the administration that remained free to choose when to raise
the rate.

Although a commission including representatives of trade
unions and employers' associations was set up by the Code of
1952 for following the evolution of the theoretical standard
budget, the administration alone determines the minimum wage;
the commission plays a purely consultative role. The commission is called in by the administration.

Although there are two minimum wages in Senegal--one for
urban areas and one for rural ones--most industrial workers
fall into the first category: For the purpose of this study
the national minimum rate is that of the majority of industrial workers, which is slightly higher than that for the
rural areas; the two rates vary parallel to each other.

The structure of the standard budget was slightly modified since its first introduction; its progress cannot be
interpreted strictly in the same way as that of a cost of
living index; however, the relative weight of food and nonfood expenditure remained the same over time. A great number of industrial workers are paid no more than the minimum
rate.

In March 1964, the structure of the standard budget was
as follows:

TABLE 26

Standard Budget for Unmarried Unskilled Worker*

Expenditure	Percent
Food	42.30
Rent	19.20
Clothing	8.99
Coal and Fuel	5.47
Hygiene	3.40
Bedding	3.27
Furniture	1.51
Laundry	1.30
Light	0.96
Maintenance	1.20
Miscellaneous	8.20
Tax	4.20
Total	100.00 = 100,179 cfa francs

*The adequacy of this budget is questioned in Appendix E.
Source: Statistical Services, Dakar.

Legal working time under the Labor Code is forty hours
per week; the determination of the theoretical minimum
hourly wage is achieved by dividing yearly expenditure by
2,080 hours (in the sample shown above, the hourly wage would
be 48.16 cfa francs).

*   *   *

Collective agreements include agreed rates that apply to
all employees; almost all workers are covered by collective
agreements that have been made compulsory by administrative
decision, in the same way as arbitrations.

The essential point in wage-determination is that very
little liberty is left to employers to adapt each worker's
pay to his actual performance or to the particular policy of
the firm. Jobs are defined by industry; employees are divided into broad categories: (i) Workers, (ii) salaried
staff, (iii) supervisors, and (iv) management. For each
group--in practice only for workers and salaried staff--
agreements include job-definitions (that may or may not be

tied to qualifying tests or vocational certificates). Agreements tie each job-definition to a certain wage-grade. The latter is the essential criterion that determines the actual wage. Agreed rates are linked to a hierarchy of wage-grades; it is the wage-grade, rather than the job actually done, which determines wages paid out to industrial workers.

The metropolitan scale was adopted in a simplified form in Senegalese collective agreements:

Wage-grade for Industrial Workers

I	Unskilled workers
II	Unskilled workers participating in "the productive process"
III	Assistant-workers trained for part of a job
IV	Workers specialized in operating a machine
V	Skilled workers
VI	Skilled workers having practical and theoretical training
VII	Very skilled workers (by Senegalese standards)
M1, M2, etc.	Foremen

In practice, it is extremely difficult to draw a line between groups of wage-grades. Industrial managers are not agreed on a common policy. The four lower grades grosso modo include unskilled workers, the next three grades skilled workers; workers of the seventh grade have supervisory responsibilities in certain firms.

Wage-differentials are also determined by collective agreements. The range of the scale depends on the industry; it reflects the situation of the labor market at the time agreements were concluded (most of them before independence). The structure of the wage scale does not vary considerably from industry to industry; it is only in the case of very skilled workers and foremen--both scarce--that there is a noteworthy difference between industries.

TABLE 27

Wage Scales in Manufacturing Industries and Construction
(1965)

Wage-grades:	1	2	3	4	5	6	7
Hourly wage in cfa							
Manufacturing*	44	51	55.75	70.60	90.50	105	134.25
Construction	44	51	55.75	68.00	86.00	104	191.00
Index							
Manufacturing	100	118	126	160	205	237	310
Construction	100	118	126	154	194	236	435

*Manufacturing includes: Food industries, fats and oils,
miscellaneous industries, mechanical engineering, auxiliary
transport industries; it excludes energy, mining, textiles
and printing.
Source: Charles F. Brun and Georges Vermot-Gauchy, Salaires
          1961-1962 (Dakar: Clairafrique, 1962).

   Both the national minimum rate and agreed rates bind employers; in many cases employees are paid above the rate.
Payments above the rate reflect the effective state of the
labor market; they enable expatriate labor to exert its own
bargaining power. Payments above the rate enable employers
to escape the egalitarian provisions of the Labor Code; expatriate labor hired in Europe can be paid higher wages than
African labor and expatriate labor hired locally.

*   *   *

   The relationship between the three wage factors (smig,
agreed rates and payment above the rate) varied in the course
of time; the practical problem that arises is to know what
effect a rise in the smig has on agreed rates. Legislative
evolution brought about a stiffening of the links between
these two elements: Before the Labor Code of 1961, there was
no legal obligation for employers to tie actual wages to the
national rate, provided no actual wage was inferior to the
latter. Employers were free to pass on or not to pass on
changes in the national wage rate to wages of skilled workers. The agreed hourly wage rate of unskilled workers

(wage-grade I) is equal to the smig. This kept the structure
of wage scales flexible in each industry; it was the task of
bilateral commissions to adapt agreed wage rates to the evolution of the labor market and of the cost of living, industry by industry.

Trade unions pressed for a modification of this system--
feeling that all workers did not derive equal benefits from
increases in the national minimum rate; as a result, the
Labor Code of 1961 provides that agreed wages linked to the
wage-grades should be related to the national minimum by
fixed coefficients.[2] The concern of the legislator was to
avoid long discussions whenever the national rate was modified.

This policy of crystallizing existing wage scales in
each industry raises a number of problems. In the short run,
it prevents trade unions and employers' associations from
increasing rates of one particular wage-grade without raising
all wages in an industry. This makes it difficult for employers to adapt to changes in the relative scarcity of, and
demand for, certain types of labor.

In the long run, more serious problems will arise; the
process of economic development implies raising the general
level of qualification of the labor force and training a
larger number of foremen and technicians in Senegal. It may
imply a change of techniques of production which would increase demand for certain types of labor--notably supervisory
and skilled labor--once manpower training has become more
adequate. A comparison between agreed rates in force in
France and in Senegal shows that the present scarcity of
skilled labor is reflected in a wider opening of the scale in
Senegal than in France:

TABLE 28

Agreed Wage Scale in Manufacturing

Wage-grades:	1	2	3	4	5	6	7
Index							
Senegal	100	118	126	160	205	237	310
France*	100	102	103	112	124	136	154.7
Ratio	1.	1.15	1.22	1.43	1.65	1.74	2.

*Agreed rates for metal workers in Lyon, February 1961.

Source: Charles F. Brun and Georges Vermot-Gauchy, Salaires
          1961-1962 (Dakar: Clairafrique, 1962); Brun and
          Vermot-Gauchy, "La Question des Salaires au Séné-
          gal", Afrique Documents (1965, Supplement No. 2).

While basic wages of unskilled workers were 2.25 times higher
in France than in Senegal, in the case of skilled workers
there was little difference in the wage of a Senegalese worker in Dakar and a French worker in Lyon (this is due mainly
to the fact that French workers did work as skilled workers
in Senegal as well as in Lyon at the time collective agreements were signed).

    It must be borne in mind that this approach to inter-
national wage-comparisons is misleading; it tends to minimize the gap between wages in France and in Senegal. Whereas the majority of workers in Senegal are unskilled--their
wage being only slightly, if at all, higher than the legal
minimum rate--this is not the case in France, where average
wages exceed minimum rates by a substantial margin. Furthermore, social security is more developed in France than in
Senegal; hence, the cost of labor is much higher there for a
given basic wage, than in Senegal. These two points need to
be illustrated.

    Average hourly earnings of industrial workers (excluding
foremen) in mechanical industries were about 68.1 cfa francs
in Senegal and 205.5 cfa francs in France.[3] Retail prices
for food and prime necessity goods (including water and electricity) are about 31 percent higher in Dakar than in
France.[4] On this basis, the real wage-differential between

workers in France and Senegal is 3.95:1. The cost-differential
is even higher because of social security contributions; indirect wages amount to 56.5 percent of basic wages in France
and do not exceed 20 percent in Senegal. The average real cost
of labor is therefore about 5.15 times higher in France (1964)
than in Senegal.

Freezing agreed wage scales by instituting a fixed relationship between them and the national minimum rate introduced a further element of rigidity into wage-determination
in Senegal. It may influence the willingness of industrial
managers in the future to move from one point on the production function to another: At present relative costs, African
supervisors and skilled workers may well become too expensive
in the future, when a greater number of Senegalese will have
been trained; this will (i) delay the introduction of more
labor-intensive methods of production thereby keeping employment figures down and (ii) further discourage Africanization.

*   *   *

Freezing the relationship between national and agreed
wages also crystallizes the relationship between wages in
different industries; while differentials between unskilled
workers of different industries are not considerable, this
is not the case with the higher skills. Here also, the
cost-differentials express the state of the labor market before independence:

TABLE 29

Indexes of Agreed Wages Related to Wages in Manufacturing

Wage-grades:	1	2	3	4	5	6	7
Manufacturing	100	100	100	100	100	100	100
Mining	100	100	100	99	99	99.5	108.5
Construction	100	100	100	96	95	99	143
Salaried Staff	100	101.5	105.5	104	116	116	128

Source: Charles F. Brun and Georges Vermot-Gauchy, Salaires
1961-1962 (Dakar: Clairafrique, 1962).

The low degree of occupational specialization in lower
skills--common to developing economies--accounts for the fact

that workers of the three lowest wage-grades are paid the
same agreed rates in each of the three occupational scales;
it is only for the higher grades that differences appear.
Differentials between industrial and commercial wages (salaried staff) are, in general, weighted in favor of the latter;
the crystallization introduced by Senegalese legislation in
1961 may well prove harmful to the distribution of labor between sectors in the future, if a policy of industrial development is to be pursued.

As for payments above the rate, a legal dispute is in
progress at present to determine whether these should also
follow increases in the minimum wage rate; this matter affects expatriates rather than African employees and is therefore left out of this study.

The wage policy of the Senegalese government is to link
actual wages very tightly to the national minimum wage rate
which is determined by the administration alone. Neither
trade unions nor employers' associations have any direct
means of influencing decisions of the administration in this
matter.

The second channel through which the government influences wage-determination is by social wages.

THE GOVERNMENT'S INFLUENCE THROUGH SOCIAL WAGES

The standard budget used by the administration as a
basis for minimum wages does not include expenditure related
to the workers' families. Attempting to remedy this situation, the French introduced a system of social security into
their overseas possessions. The system discussed below concerns employees of the private sector only: Public employees have a system of their own that is more favorable to employees than that in the private sector.

Introduction of social security into Africa in the
1950's rested on certain sociological assumptions shared
by many French deputies and by part of the colonial administration; the main assumption was that industrialization and
urbanization had disrupted the traditional family structure,
depriving urbanized workers of the security attached to the
traditional system; the new social security system covers
risks such as occupational injuries and sickness, old age,
and the financial burden of raising children (family allowances). To what extent traditional societies did in fact
cover these risks is a debatable matter; it is also doubtful

whether traditional solidarities were, in fact, entirely disrupted by urbanization. We will focus on family allowances
(that constitute the bulk of social wages) as a complement to
basic wages and question the adequacy of the system of social
wages in an African context: How does the system work? What
influence does it have on income and costs?

In few territories of tropical Africa has the implementation of social security been as comprehensive as in Senegal. The Senegalese system works in favor of all private employees, Africans and expatriates alike, regardless of their
income, as in France.

All risks, except old age, are placed under the responsibility of a national fund (caisse de compensation) created
under the 1952 Code's provisions. It is governed under the
supervision of a tri-partite board including representatives
of the government, trade unions and employers' associations.
Contribution to the fund is compulsory for employers; employees do not contribute.

At present, and since 1958, each child entitles his
family to an allowance of 650 cfa francs per month. The
government contributes 250 cfa francs per child (included in
the 650), and thereby, as well as through its voice in the
fund's board, influences the rate of social wages.

Fifty-one thousand employees applied for family allowances in 1963. This represents almost all Senegalese private
employees with children (slightly under 80 percent of all
private employees). The same year, 136,000 children were
covered in 39,000 families (excluding children of less than
one year of age). The structure of families having children
of one year of age or more is interesting, because it leads
to (i) analyzing the impact of polygamy on social security
costs (and the impact of social security on polygamy) and
(ii) showing the significance of family allowances for industrial workers.

TABLE 30

Structure of the Families (1963)
(Excluding children of less than 1 year)

Families having one child	25.6%
two children	22.7%
three children	17.7%
four children	13.0%
five children	8.7%
six children	5.0%
seven children	2.9%
eight children	1.8%
over eight children	2.6%

Source: Rapport d'Activité de la Caisse de Compensation
1962-1963 (Dakar: Caisse de Compensation, 1964).

Interviews (W 13 and W 14) show that slightly less than
29 percent of married workers are polygamous; the distribution of monogamous and polygamous families according to the
number of children shows the following pattern:

TABLE 31

Number of Children and Polygamy

Number of Children	Percent of Polygamous Families
0	5.2
1	13.0
2	9.0
3	17.5
4	25.0
5	43.0
6	55.5
7	60.0
over 7	62.0

Source: Interviews: W 13, W 14.

The average number of children per wage-earner is 3.08 for monogamous and 5.93 for polygamous families. In as far as these data are representative, it is tentatively possible to evaluate the fraction of social wages that is paid out to polygamous families (using social security fund data for sums distributed to families of various sizes). The fraction of social wages distributed to polygamous families is by no means insignificant:

Sums distributed to monogamous families (1963):
                                    620.45 million cfa francs

Sums distributed to polygamous families (1963):
                                    302.55 million cfa francs

Moreover, there is evidence that the proportion of large families increases over the years, while the proportion of smaller ones decreases:

TABLE 32

Families Receiving Family Allowances in Senegal

Percentage of families having:	1-3 children	Over 3 children*
1960	72.0	28.0
1961	70.1	29.9
1962	68.2	31.8
1963	66.0	34.0

*Children over 1 year only.
Source: Rapport d'Activité de la Caisse de Compensation 1962-1963 (Dakar: Caisse de Compensation, 1964).

There is not only an increase in the share of social wages accruing to one of these groups (over 3 children) but to each group having respectively 4, 5, 6, 7, 8 and "over eight" children; there is a decrease for each group of families having 1, 2 or 3 children.

The average size of families covered by the scheme increased from 2.8 children of over one year of age (1960) to 3.1 (1963). This represents an increase of about 11 percent in the average size of families. It is not possible to

conclude that family allowances favor polygamy and encourage
natality; however, a trend towards larger families must be
noted among beneficiaries of family allowances.

The adequacy of introducing social security measures
initially meant as a means to encourage population growth in
France after 1945 into African countries where polygamy is
accepted, is questionable: The cost of family allowances for
polygamous families is considerable and the effects on population growth are not necessarily in accordance with the
government's desire to raise GNP per head. If allowances
were distributed only to monogamous employees (or, in the
case of polygamous ones, only for children of the first wife)
the sums distributed would be reduced by slightly over 20
percent.

What do family allowances mean to industrial workers in
terms of their basic wages?

Official statistics place industrial employees in one
of three income-groups. Two of these groups include most
African employees; the third group mainly includes expatriates. Average yearly income[5] of employees of Group I is
156,000 cfa francs per year; that of employees of Group II
is 255,000 cfa francs (both basic wage and fringe benefits,
excluding social wages).

The impact of family allowances on income can be shown
in a table:

TABLE 33

Impact of Family Allowances on Workers' Income (per year)

No. Children over 1 year	Social Wage (in cfa)	% of Families	Social Wage in % of Nonsocial Wage	
			Group I	Group II
0	nil		nil	nil
1	7,800	25.6	5.	3.05
2	15,600	22.7	10.	6.10
3	23,400	17.7	15.	9.15
4	31,200	13.0	20.	12.20
5	39,000	8.7	25.	15.25
6	46,800	5.0	30.	18.30
7	54,600	2.9	35.	21.35
8	62,400	1.8	40.	24.40
20	156,000		100.	61.00

Source: Rapport d'Activité de la Caisse de Compensation 1962-1963 (Dakar: Caisse de Compensation, 1964).

Social wages represent a considerable percentage of non-social wages, notably in the case of unskilled workers; most workers in Senegal belong to the first income-group; the incentive to increase the size of the family is stronger for poorer workers (the relative marginal social wage being higher than for workers in the higher income-group). Since the actual income of a great number of unskilled workers is as low as 105,000 cfa francs per year, the effect of social wages on income can be very marked; social wages of unskilled workers who are fathers of four children usually amount to little less than 30 percent of their basic wage (i.e., 23 percent of their total income). Since the cost of raising children is subject to economies of scale (clothing, etc.), there may be an incentive for poorer workers to enlarge their families up to the point where a switch from monogamy to polygamy has to occur; at the very least, it can be said that the present system does not create a disincentive for workers to adopt this attitude.

*   *   *

Viewed as a cost, social wages are shared between the government and private employers. Leaving out old age insurance, the cost of the system is well over one billion cfa francs per year:

Cost of Social Security

| 1961 | 1,240 billion cfa francs |
| 1962-1963 (12 months) | 1,394 billion cfa francs |

The breakdown of contributions shows that employers carry most of the financial burden:

Distribution of Costs (1962-63)

Employers	62.5%
Government	31.7%
Other Resources	2.5%
Deficit	3.3%
Total	100.0%

The breakdown of wage-bills of two semi-public institutions[6] shows that the cost of all compulsory social security contributions amounts to about 15 percent of the wage-bill; in some industries it may amount to 20 percent.

*   *   *

Finally, fringe benefits must be mentioned: They include overtime payments, three weeks' paid holiday per year, length of service premiums, etc. They can amount to about 20 percent of the basic wage. Most fringe benefits are ruled by collective agreement; some are ruled by plant-level agreements.

The question that remains to be answered is how private employers react to government influence on wage-determination.

REACTIONS OF INDUSTRIAL EMPLOYERS

The institutional framework aims at unifying wage policies in industrial firms; enterprises interviewed fell under collective agreements or similar regulations (E 42). Most employers did not feel the need to adapt the collective agreements' provisions on wages to their particular situation; others signed plant-level agreements complementing and adapting these provisions to the particular situation of their firms (E 43).

FIGURE 5

Dakar: Employment, Population, Minimum Wage

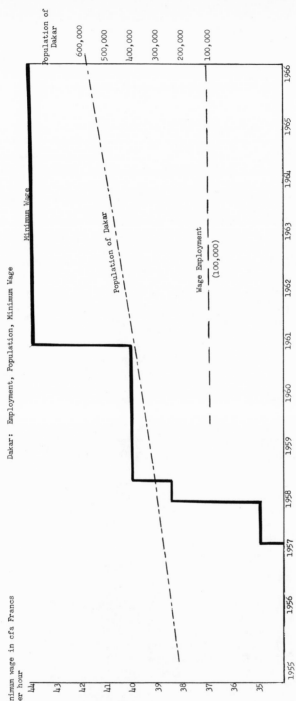

Source: Services de la Statistique, Dakar.

131

Most employment contracts are verbal (E 44); administrative declarations that include the workers' wage-grades serve as a basis for wage-determination.

The similarity between collective agreements ruling different industries constitutes the essential element of coordination of wage policies between the firms interviewed (E 45); for 68 percent of employees in the firms interviewed the level of wages paid out is that of collective agreements; 21.5 percent of establishments (covering 12 percent of employees) paid higher wages than those determined by collective agreements. The rest of private employers worked out a wage-grade system of their own by plant-level agreements.

It seems that the nominal wages of the majority of industrial workers in fact correspond to the agreed rates linked to the national rate; the latter has not been raised since August 1961, while family allowances remained at the same level since 1958. Most employers do not adjust their lowest wages to changes in any cost-of-living index; they leave the wage-leadership to the government and wait until the administration raises the national minimum wage rate before changing their own workers' wages.

The workers' nominal wages progressed by "jumps"; there is no relationship between the evolution of nominal industrial wages by ratchets and the supply of labor: Migration into Dakar continued after wages were frozen in 1951 at the same rate as before--about 24,000 people per year (see Figure 5).

Overtime payments are also coordinated. They are governed by the Labor Code; since most firms operate for over 40 hours a week, most workers earn more than basic agreed wage rates. Most entrepreneurs interviewed said that their workers were employed for 42 or 48 hours a week (E 51). Overtime rates of collective agreements provide the following increases:

Overtime Payments (Basic rate = 100)

40 hours	100
41st and 42nd hours	109
43rd and 44th hours	111
45th and 46th hours	114
47th and 48th hours	122

*   *   *

In conclusion, the government's influence on wage-determination is very great indeed; it tends to crystallize existing wage rates and relative wages, leaving only little freedom to industrial employers. These usually conform to government legislation and collective agreements in matters of wages and only a minority of them pays higher wages than is legally necessary to their staff.

*   *   *

Having examined the labor policies of employers, trade unions and the government, it is now time to sum up: Given the influence of imperfections on the labor market, what do we expect to find in reality?

Under "competitive conditions," wages are likely to be very low--not much higher than agricultural earnings--and employment relatively low, too. How do market imperfections affect wages and employment in industry?

The multiracial structure of employment and the grave psychological difficulties in manpower training and African-ization in private industry have been shown; so far the government has exerted little pressure on industrial firms as regards encouraging them to step up the pace of African-ization. In the long run, the slower Africanization is, the less attractive labor-intensive methods of production and the higher total labor costs. It appears that the slowness of Africanization found in Senegalese industry tends to keep in-dustrial employment down. Trade unions do not exert a sig-nificant role on the labor market any more; they contribute to crystallizing present relative wages (as between qualifi-cations and as between industries) and to spreading marginal wage increases throughout the industrial sector through ar-bitration. However, trade unions are not now in a position to force the government to raise the crucial national mini-mum wage rate. Their policies focus on very short-term ob-jectives--the only ones that appeal to the rank and file--which are sometimes self-defeating (pressure for employers' credit to workers, overtime policy meant to increase employ-ment, etc.). In general, trade-union leaders are incapable of, or unwilling to, pursue long-term policies likely to maximize employment and real wages; their lack of interest in matters as essential as manpower training, noted ever since 1943, is symptomatic in this respect. All in all, it appears that trade unions have a marginal influence: It is hardly possible at present to find "imperfections due to trade unions" on the labor market.

In contrast, government influence on the labor market is
extremely strong. Although the government failed to achieve
greater security of employment for industrial workers through
labor legislation, it influences wages and employment, in the
short and in the long run through manpower training and wage
policies. Neither of these two policies is particularly con-
ducive to faster Africanization in the private sector: Manpower training does not provide adequate supply of skilled
and supervisory labor to industry; crystallization of present
relative wages is likely to slow down Africanization in the
long run.

Both trade unions and government share an ideology of
"African socialism" as presented by President Senghor. This
conveys the image of relatively well-off wage-earners (by
Senegalese standards) who, despite the wage freeze, enjoy a
much higher standard of living than "underprivileged peasants." Thus, it is to be expected that the government will
maintain the national minimum wage rate below equilibrium.

Despite the fact that Africanization is not encouraged
by labor policies, the cost of labor is still much lower in
Senegal than in France. Therefore it may be expected that
techniques of production in Senegal should differ from those
in use in France, and be less capital-intensive. Imperfections on the labor market seem likely to keep the level of
industrial wages close to equilibrium or below it; they
show no signs of encouraging a substantial increase in employment in the immediate future.

*   *   *

Thus, we expect to find relatively well-off industrial
workers--despite the wage freeze--and techniques of production
reflecting the low cost of African labor. Whether or not
these expectations are justified and how the features of the
labor market of Senegal affect growth, are the next problems
to be considered.

Notes to Chapter 9

1. Decree of October 22, 1925 (AOF) in force in Senegal as
    from March, 1929.

2. Labor Code of 1961, article 85.

3. Charles F. Brun and Georges Vermot-Gauchy, <u>Salaires</u>
    <u>1961-1962</u> (Dakar: Clairafrique, 1962).

4. <u>Annuaire Economique de la France 1965</u> (Paris: Govern-
    ment Publication, 1966); <u>Bulletin Statistique et</u>
    <u>Economique Mensuel</u> (Dakar: Services de la Statistique,
    periodical).

5. Data for 1963.

6. <u>Rapport d'Activité de la Caisse de Compensation 1962-</u>
    <u>1963</u> (Dakar: Caisse de Compensation, 1964).

PART **III** INDUSTRIAL LABOR AND
ECONOMIC DEVELOPMENT IN
SENEGAL: EFFECTS OF
POLICIES AND ALTERNATE
POLICIES

We will now try to find an answer to the following questions: What effects do actual features of the labor market
have on industrial workers' real wages and standard of
living? How do they influence the choice of techniques in
industry? What effect might be achieved on industrial development if imperfections on the labor market were removed?

This analysis focuses on two very important problems:
(i) The real income of industrial workers, which is significant both politically and in view of "balanced growth" programs; and (ii) the choice of techniques that influences the
long-term evolution of industrial employment.

CHAPTER **10** SENEGALESE WORKERS'
INCOME

What effects do labor policies have on the incomes of
African workers? First, we shall try to see how real wages
for African workers have changed since 1957; secondly, we
shall try to determine what share of the industrial wage-bill
accrues to African workers; thirdly, we will evaluate the
actual disposable income of African workers.

TREND OF REAL WAGES

The evolution of wages is only known with precision as
far as the national minimum wage rate and agreed rates are
concerned; it has been seen that actual earnings are closely
geared to agreed rates, themselves tied since 1961 to the
national minimum wage rate.

Three periods can be distinguished since World War II:
(a) From 1945 to 1952 the minimum wage rate rose considerably--
adjustments were made on eight occasions in order to match the
evolution of prices; (b) from 1953 to 1958 the rise was less
pronounced; however, the introduction of the 40-hour week in
1953 increased the actual income of employees by 20 percent;
(c) from 1958 onwards the minimum rate showed great
stability:

TABLE 34

Minimum Wage Rate (Dakar) per Hour,
in Current cfa Francs

From	Rate	From	Rate
1945	4.0	1953 (July)	27.15
1946	5.5	1953 (December)	28.10
1947	7.75	1956	31.0
1948 (February)	10.0	1957	35.0
1948 (July)	13.15	1958 (August)	38.50
1949	17.0	1958 (December)	40.0
1950	18.5	1961 (August)	44.0
1951 (February)	20.6		
1951 (November)	23.4		

Source: Ministère du Travail, Salaires 1963-1964 et Evolution
des Salaires depuis 1937 (Dakar: roneoed, 1964).

The yearly rate of increase diminished with time:

Index 1945 = 100   1951 (November) = 585

average increase: 70 points per year

Index 1953 = 100   1965   = 162

average increase: 4.8 points per year

Agreed rates varied in the same way as the national
minimum rate:

TABLE 35

Agreed Rates (Dakar) and Minimum Rate

Year	Minimum rate	Rate (a)	Rate (b)	Rate (c)
1946 (Base Year)				
1952	+ 425%	+ 322%	+ 290%	+ 307%
1958	+ 56.5%	+ 70.8%	+ 60.3%	+ 58.0%
1965-66	+ 20.3%	+ 11.8%	+ 25.2%	+ 17.9%

(a) = construction, Vth wage-grade.
(b) = manufacturing industries, Vth wage-grade.
(c) = clerk, IVth wage-grade.

Source: Same as Table 34.

Between 1946 and 1952 the national minimum wage rose faster
than agreed rates for skilled workers; since 1952, however,
there was no great difference between the rates of growth of
the national and agreed rates. Before 1961, changes in the
minimum rate were usually reflected in changes in the agreed
rates; since 1961 they are (by law) necessarily reflected.

Agreed wage rates in force in Senegal since August 1961
are shown below, before introducing the price factor into the
analysis.

TABLE 36

Agreed Rates (Senegal since 1961)
in cfa Francs per Month
(assuming working week of 45 hours)

Wage-grade	Manufacturing Industries	Commerce
First	8,675.35	7,627
Second	10,055.50	9,075
Third	10,992.05	10,725
Fourth	13,767.0	13,200
Fifth	17,843.60	18,150
Sixth	20,702.50	21,120
Seventh	26,469.50	29,975

Source: Charles F. Brun and Georges Vermot-Gauchy, Salaires
          1961-1962 (Dakar: Clairafrique, 1962).

The main obstacle to an evaluation of real incomes is the
absence of reliable cost-of-living indexes. Qualitative
changes may make long-term comparisons meaningless.[1]

Three different methods will be used here to appraise the
evolution of real incomes: (1) The first is based on government estimates of the minimum standard budget of unskilled unmarried workers and on a survey of family budgets carried out
in 1960-61; (2) the second one is based on government price
indices for expatriate consumption in Dakar based on 1945 ex-
penditure-pattern (revised in 1960); although a parallel
appears to exist between price indices series for European and
African consumption-patterns, it is not known up to what point
this parallel exists; information for 1961-64 suggests that
the directions of the trends are the same, but it is not known

whether the rates are also parallel; (3) the third method is
also based on the government's estimate of unskilled workers'
standard budget; it consists in relating the evolution of the
theoretical wage rate (that which enables workers earning
minimum wages to buy the standard budget's "bundle") to that
of the actual minimum wage rates. The first and third methods
seem to provide the most reliable indices; they may understate
the cost of living since they are government estimates. The
survey used with the first method covers the African population of Dakar; it exceeds the field of industrial labor.

The first method shows that industrial workers' real income rose between 1957 and 1959--both in terms of the total
cost of living and in terms of cost of food alone.[2] Between
1959 and 1960, there was a decline in purchasing power; after
1960, a period of stability. However, in terms of food only,
which is the most relevant aspect for poorer workers, the decline of 1959-60 was not followed by recovery: Decrease has
been continuous.

TABLE 37

Real Wages = First Approach

Year	Minimum Wage Rate/Cost of food (index)	Variation
1957	100	
1958	126	+ 26
1959	not available	
1960	119	- 7 (since 1958)
1961	117	- 2
1962	116	- 1
1963	112	- 4
1964	98	- 14
1965		

Year	Minimum Wage Rate/Cost of living (index)	Variation
1957	100	
1958	110	+ 10
1959	120	+ 10
1960	109	- 11
1961	110	+ 1
1962	112	+ 2
1963	111	- 1
1964	104	- 7
1965		

Source: Government Estimate of Cost of Living (unpublished).

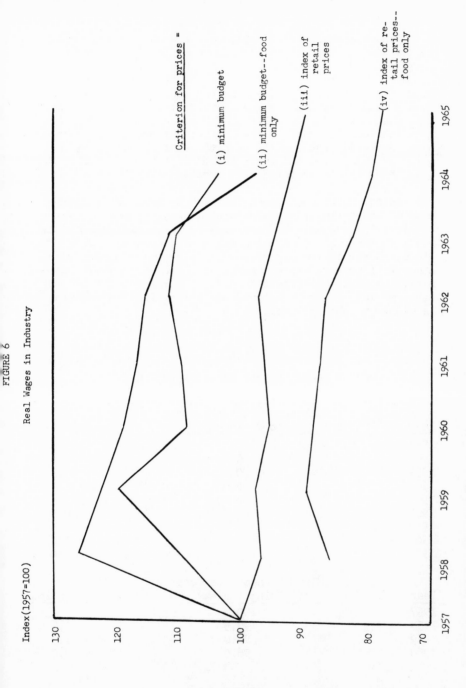

FIGURE 6

Index(1957=100)

Real Wages in Industry

Criterion for prices =

(i) minimum budget

(ii) minimum budget--food only

(iii) index of retail prices

(iv) index of retail prices-- food only

130   120   110   100   90   80   70

1957   1958   1959   1960   1961   1962   1963   1964   1965

Source: Services de la Statistique, Dakar.

143

Senegalese workers seem to have reached a maximum real
income towards the end of the period of "semi-autonomy"
(1959); since independence there has been an erosion of real
income back to the 1957 level. Recent measures of price-
control do not seem to have affected real income. The position of the poorest workers has probably worsened slightly
less than that of others since 1959, because prices of rice,
groundnut oil and sugar, as well as of tinned milk and bread
have increased less quickly than those of fresh vegetables,
dairy produce, fish and meat; consumers of meat and fish have
seen their income decrease more substantially in real terms.

Using the second method is risky because of the remote-
ness of the series' starting point (1945, revised in 1960);
however, the evolution of the cost-of-living index for Europeans in Dakar is not meaningless in the case of food expenditure, as far as the higher- and medium- income groups among
industrial workers are concerned (skilled workers and foremen); these rely on imported goods to a larger extent than
other workers--therefore their pattern of food expenditure
is closer to that of expatriates.

TABLE 38

Real Wages = Second Approach

Year	Minimum Wage Rate/Cost of Food (index)	Variation
1957	100	
1958	86.5	- 13.5
1959	90.0	+ 3.5
1960	89.0	- 1
1961	88.0	- 1
1962	87.5	- 0.5
1963	83.0	- 4.5
1964	80.0	- 3.0
1965	78.6	- 1.4

Year	Minimum Wage Rate/Cost of Living (index)	Variation
1957	100	
1958	96.5	- 3.5
1959	98.0	+ 1.5
1960	96.0	- 2.0

(cont'd)

TABLE 38 (Cont'd)

Real Wages = Second Approach

Year	Minimum Wage Rate/Cost of Living (index)	Variation
1961	97.0	+ 1.0
1962	98.0	+ 1.0
1963	95.0	- 3.0
1964	93.0	- 2.0
1965	91.2	- 1.8

Source: Services de la Statistique, Bulletin Statistique et
Economique Mensuel (Dakar).

There the variations of real income do not coincide with
the previous approach for the period 1957-59, although a rise
in real income between 1958 and 1959 is confirmed; however,
afterwards the evolution coincides with the previous one: (a)
Steady decline of real income in terms of food since 1959; (b)
acceleration of the downward movement since 1963; (c) rather
even evolution of purchasing power in general between 1959-60
and 1962; (d) decline of purchasing power in general since
1963.

A graphic representation of these two approaches (see
Figure 6) shows that there appears to have been a downward
trend in real income in terms of food since 1959 that was relatively slow until 1962 and much faster from then onwards.
There may have been a slight increase in purchasing power for
goods other than food between 1960 and 1962 (although it is
likely that much of this increase is due to inaccurate observation of nonfood prices).

The third approach to real income is particularly reveal-
ing of the government's policy of freezing nominal wages.
Comparing the theoretical hourly minimum wage rate to the actual one shows how the government reacted to changes in the
cost of living; the theoretical rate is computed by dividing
the yearly standard budget of unskilled unmarried workers--as
worked out by the government--by 2,080 hours; this corresponds
to a 40-hour week. Since the standard budget is defined as
being the minimum socially acceptable one, the very fact that
the legal minimum wage is inferior to it can only be interpreted as a deliberate policy of keeping nominal wages stable
(in accordance with the idea of "African socialism" on urban
versus rural fractions of the population). Figure 7 clearly

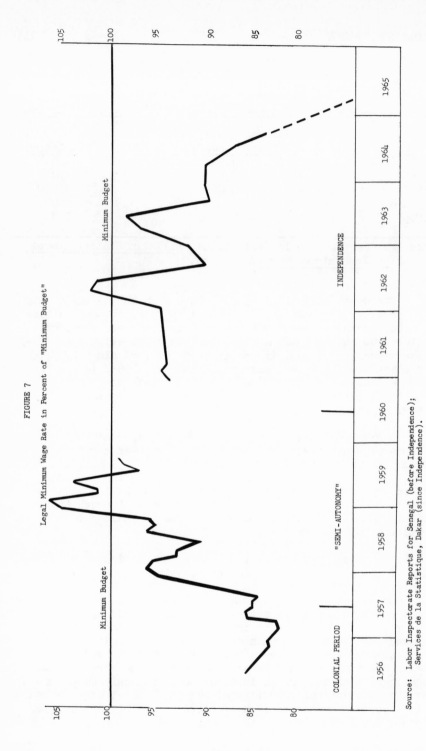

FIGURE 7

Legal Minimum Wage Rate in Percent of "Minimum Budget"

Source: Labor Inspectorate Reports for Senegal (before Independence);
Services de la Statistique, Dakar (since Independence).

shows how real incomes declined after independence, notably
after 1962. The extrapolation in dotted line on the right is
based on the evolution of retail prices since September 1964.

In conclusion, since 1962 all indicators of real income
have declined. Whether the 1957 level of real income has been
reached in 1964 depends on the perspective chosen; it seems to
have been reached in terms of workers' expenditure on food--
the main element in the unskilled workers' standard of living.

Three general remarks can be made: (a) Unskilled workers' real income in Senegal in 1965 is not higher than it was
in 1956; (b) prices for food--especially fresh food--have
varied in such a way that variations of real income in terms
of food have been greater (both upwards and downwards) than
those of real wages in general terms, i.e., than items other
than food; (c) whether there has been an increase in real
income between 1957 and 1959 mainly depends on the sources
used; it seems that real wages declined from 1962 onwards,
whichever criterion is used.

The policy of freezing nominal wages is not specific to
the Senegalese government; most West-African governments
yielded to the combined influences of expatriate pressure
groups (to keep wages low) and of ideas of "distributive
justice" particular to "African socialism." A comparison
between two six-year series of minimum wage rates reveals that
Senegal's policy is characteristic of the former French
colonies of West Africa and Togo.

The periods chosen are 1954-59 and 1960-65; except
for Guinea--which became independent in 1958--this makes it
possible to compare the evolution of minimum wage rates during
the six years preceding independence and that during the six
first years of independence. All the countries chosen inherited the bulk of 1952 labor legislation; actual wages
closely follow the evolution of minimum wage rates.

TABLE 39

Yearly Averages of National Minimum Wage Rate (1st area) Indexes

	1954	1955	1956	1957	1958	1959	Increase	No. of increases
Ivory Coast	100	100 X	119 X	158 X	176	176	76	3
Dahomey	100	100	100 X	125 X	158	158	58	2
Upper Volta	100 X	124	124 X	188	188	188	88	2
Mauritania	100	100	100	100 X	120 X	145	45	2
Niger	100 X	138	138 X	186	186 X	213	113	3
Senegal	100	100	100 X	124 X	142	142	42	2
Sudan	100 X	109	109 X	124 X	156 X	185	85	4
Togo	100 X	107 X	118 X	125 X	142 X	157	57	5
Guinea	100	100	100	n.d. X	148 X	172	72	2

Average increase per year: 11.76   Total: 25

TABLE 39 (cont'd)

	1960	1961	1962	1963	1964	1965	(1966)	Increase	No. of increases
Ivory Coast	100 X	108	108	108 X	114	114	114	14	2
Dahomey	100	100	100	100 X	114	114	114	14	1
Upper Volta	100	100	100	100	100	100	100	0	0
Mauritania	100 X	121	121	121	121	121	121	21	1
Niger	100	100 X	112	112	112	112	112	12	1
Senegal	100 X	110	110	110	110	110	110	10	1
Mali	100	100	100	100	100	100		0	0
Togo	100	100	100	100 X	109	109	109	9	1
Guinea	100	100	100	100	100	100		0	0
							Total:		7

Average increase per year: 1.46

X = Upward shift of rate.

Source: BCEAO, Rapports Annuels (Paris: BCEAO, 1959-65).

The average increase declined from 11.76 to 1.46 points per
country between 1954-59 and 1960-65; average interval
between upward shifts rose from 1.55 to 4.22 years; there has
been no increase in minimum wages since three to eight years,
according to the countries.

Prices have risen since independence. Official statistics
underestimate the rise, which is superior to that of minimum
wage rates; even official price indexes show the trend:

TABLE 40

Cost of Living for Africans in West African Capitals

	1960	1961	1962	1963	1964	1965
Ivory Coast (Abidjan):	100	111	105.5	110.9	114.2	116.6
Food only:	100	n.d.	n.d.	115.2	121.3	121.3
Upper Volta (Ouagadougou):	100	116	117	122	124.5	122.6
Niger (Niamey):			100	99.9	100.1	105.3

Source: BCEAO, Rapports Annuels (Paris: BCEAO, 1959-65).

African employees' purchasing power declined after independence
in the former French colonies of West Africa; in this respect
the situation of Senegal is representative of that of other
former member-territories of AOF and Togo.

The government wage freeze effectively reduced real wages
in industry since 1961-62, in the case of Senegal. We must
now turn our attention to Senegal's present wage structure and
find out what share of the industrial wage-bill accrues to
African employees.

AFRICAN AND EXPATRIATE WAGES IN INDUSTRY

The material used in this section consists of printouts
from the Social Security Fund's IBM accountability system; it
concerns the months of December 1962 ("D 62") and 1963 ("D 63").
These statistics have no absolute value because they do not
cover all Senegalese firms, and because the coverage of the two

series used differs slightly. However, they show the structure
of wage income and the distribution of wages among different
social groups, notably between European and African employees.

Firms are classified according to industry; "industry" and
"public works and construction" were selected. Comparisons between results for these two industries and those for the entire
private sector--including commerce and transportation--show
that the private sector's wage structure does not differ much
from that of "industry."

Firms are further classified according to their size (in
terms of manpower): (i) Under twenty employees, (ii) twenty
employees or more.

Wage-earners are classified according to their income
(basic wage including overtime payment and premiums). The
first group ("Group I") includes employees paid on an hourly
basis (mainly workers); the second group ("Group II") includes
employees paid on a monthly basis and whose wages do not
exceed 45,000 cfa francs per month; the third group ("Group
III") includes those employees whose wages -- worked out on a
monthly basis--exceed 45,000 cfa francs.

Effective average wages will be evaluated for each of
these groups: Then, the distribution of actual wages will be
shown.

Evaluation of average wages (all wages in cfa francs)

(a)   i.   Industry, Group I

Date	No. of employees	Wage income	Average wage
D 62	no data	192,933,440	about 13,000
D 63	no data	214,391,967	(assuming 45 hrs.* per week worked)

Number of hours wage paid out in Dec. 1962:
   2,687,180

Number of hours wage paid out in Dec. 1963:
   2,392,807

ii. Industry, Group II

Date	No. of employees	Wage income	Average wage
D 62	5,300 (all firms)	144,337,150	19,800 *
D 63	5,755 (all firms)	169,032,207	23,000 *

iii. Industry, Group III

Date	No. of employees	Wage income	Average wage
D 62	2,894	313,683,303	108,000
D 63	2,976	387,674,163	130,000

(b) i. Public works and construction, Group I

Date	No. of employees	Wage income	Average wage
D 62	no data	100,545,542	about 14,000
D 63	no data	94,871,509	(assuming 48 hrs. ** per week worked)

Number of hours wage paid out in Dec. 1962:
1,026,613.

Number of hours wage paid out in Dec. 1963:
1,300,059.

ii. Public works and construction, Group II

Date	No. of employees	Wage income	Average wage
D 62	805	20,603,436	23,800
D 63	679	18,495,545	21,000

iii. Public works and construction, Group III

Date	No. of employees	Wage income	Average wage
D 62	526 (firms of 20 em- ployees and	54,669,384	104,000
D 63	493 more)	63,876,682	129,000

---

*   Forty-five hours is the average working-time in in-
      dustry if nonpermanent unskilled workers are taken
      into account (Source: Ministry of Labor).
**   Average working-time in public works and construc-
      tion (same source).

The structure of income-groups can now be shown:

| | Wage-earners | | |
Income-groups:	I	II	III
Industry D 62:	14,900	5,300	2,894
D 63:	13,400	5,755	2,976
P.W. & C. D 62:	5,900	805	567
D 63:	6,800	679	543

These statistics make it possible to present the structure of the wage-bill:

Distribution of wages among occupational groups (all
wages cfa francs)

(a) i. Industry, December 1962

Group	%-age of employees	%-age of wage income	Average wage
I	64.5	30.0	about 13,000
II	23.0	22.0	about 20,000
III	12.5	48.0	108,000

coverage: 23,094 employees earning 650.8 million
           cfa francs.

ii. Industry, December 1963

Group	%-age of employees	%-age of wage income	Average wage
I	60.6	27.7	no data
II	26.0	22.0	about 23,000
III	13.4	50.3	130,000

coverage: 22,131 employees earning 771.1 million
           cfa francs.

(b) i. Public works and construction, December 1962

Group	%-age of employees	%-age of wage income	Average wage
I	81.1	57.6	no data
II	11.1	11.4	about 23,800
III	7.8	31.0	104,000

coverage: 7,272 employees earning 175.2 million
           cfa francs.

ii. Public works and construction, December 1963

Group	%-age of employees	%-age of wage income	Average wage
I	84.75	53.6	no data
II	8.45	10.4	about 21,000
III	6.8	36.0	129,000

coverage: 8,022 employees earning 177.3 million
           cfa francs.

There is no continuity between the three income-groups;
they correspond to different types of labor. According to the
number of employees included in each of the groups, it appears
that they represent the following types of labor: Group I
includes all manual workers; Group II includes salaried staff
and some supervisory labor; Group III includes management and
higher technical staff.

This interpretation is cross-checked by the fact that
only the first occupational group is paid on an hourly basis;

it also corresponds to information on monthly wages of workers, salaried staff and managers; furthermore, the proportion of employees included in Group III corresponds grosso modo to the percentage of expatriate employees in Senegal:

TABLE 41

Distribution of Wages

		Industry	P.W. & C.
(a)	Expatriate labor force in percent of total labor force:	10.3	6.0
(b)	Group III in percent of all groups:		
	December 1962	12.5	7.8
	December 1963	13.4	6.5

Source: Ministère du Travail, Statistiques de la Sécurité
         Sociale (Dakar: roneoed, 1964).

Only a few Africans fall into the highest income-group (Group III) while all the expatriate labor force does.

*   *   *

These statistics reveal that (a) the lowest income-group (Group I) includes over 60 percent of the labor force in industry, over 80 percent in public works and construction; the average monthly wage in this income-group is less than 15,000 cfa francs per worker; this corresponds to agreed wages for workers of the IIIrd and IVth wage-grades. Although they form by far the most numerous group, African workers only draw a relatively small share of wage income: About 30 percent in industry and 55 percent in public works and construction; the ratio: Share of wage income/share of employment, is equal to 0.5 : 1 in industry and 0.55 : 1 in public works and construction. (b) The medium income-group (Group II) forms about 25 percent of the labor force in industry and about 10 percent in public works and construction. The average monthly wage of employees in this income-group is slightly over 20,000 cfa francs per employee; this income-group draws a share of total wage income corresponding roughly to its numerical importance: 22 percent in industry and about 11 percent public works and

construction; the ratio: Share of wage income/share of
employment is 0.88 : 1 in industry and 1.1 : 1 in public
works and construction.

(c) The remarkable point is that the higher income-
group (Group III) stands out in all respects: The average
monthly wage of employees included in this group is five
times higher than that of employees of the medium income-
group while the number of employees included in Group III is
small; the average wage of employees belonging to this income-
group is 104,000 to 130,000 cfa francs per month; this excludes gratuities and payments in kind such as free housing,
energy, car, paid holidays in Europe for employees and their
families, etc. The absolute level of wages in the higher
income-group is very high by international standards. Although they form the least numerous group, managers, technicians and expatriate supervisors draw a tremendous share of
wage income: Nearly 50 percent in industry, about one-third
in public works and construction. The ratio: Share of
income/share of employment is equal to 3.85 : 1 in industry
and 4.7 : 1 in public works and construction.

Economic accounts for 1959[3] show the distribution of
wages among different groups of wage-earners by industry; although Africanization has progressed in many industries since
1959, data on this subject-matter is scarce: Any fairly
recent data is of interest. The over-all proportion of expatriate and African wages was of (respectively) 47 percent and
53 percent in 1959, while in 1963 it was about 42 percent and
58 percent. Changes that have occurred between 1959 and 1963
are twofold: (i) The number of expatriates decreased by about
10 percent; (ii) the wage-differential between Africans and
expatriates widened. It seems--although there are little data
other than employers' interviews on this question--that the
decrease in the expatriate wage-bill due to reduction in
expatriate employment has been greater than the increase due
to rises in wages.

FIGURE 8

Distribution of Industrial Wages
(December 1963)

Percent of Industrial Wage-bill

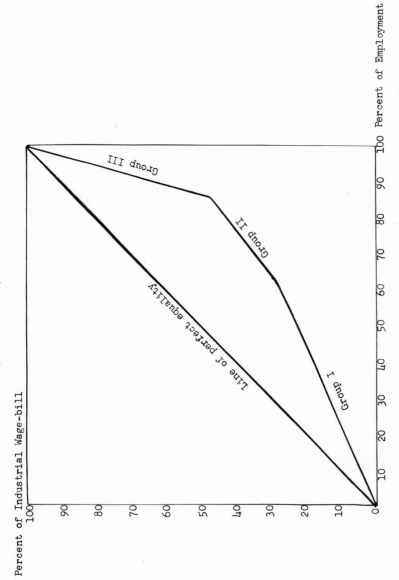

Percent of Employment

Source: Social Security Fund, Dakar.

157

TABLE 42

Structure of Industrial Wage-bill and Employment (1959)

Industry	% of Expa-triates on Total Staff	Expatriates' Wages (in bil. cfa fr.)	Africans' Wages (in bil. cfa fr.)
Food Industries	7.0	0.76 (32%)	1.65 (68%)
Fats & Oils		0.45	0.97
Grain & Flour		0.16	0.33
Sugar & Drinks		0.10	0.20
Meat & Canned Food		0.07	0.15
Energy & Mining	13.7	0.40 (49%)	0.42 (51%)
Energy		0.24	0.20
Mining		0.16	0.22
Textile & Leather	5.0	0.23 (39%)	0.36 (61%)
Public Works & Construction	10.2	2.15 (47%)	2.42 (53%)
Transport	5.9	1.56 (47.5%)	1.71 (52.5%)
Other Industries	16.0	0.98 (53%)	0.86 (47%)
Chemicals		0.05	0.05
Construction Materials		0.25	0.25
Metal Engineering		0.30	0.25
Woodware & Furniture		0.16	0.13
Tobacco & Matches		0.06	0.05
Miscellaneous		0.16	0.13

Source: La Planification en Afrique Noire (Paris: Ministère de la Coopération, 1964), Vol. V, Table 27.

It seems that Africanization has progressed since 1959 in public works and construction, in textile industries and in transport. The reduction in the expatriate labor force in public works and construction from 10.2 percent (of total labor force) to 6 percent increased the share of the wage-bill accruing to African workers from 53 percent to about 66 percent (average 1962-63), i.e., an increase in African purchasing power in nominal terms of about 24.5 percent (assuming total employment remained the same).

In 1959, in seven out of fifteen industries, the expatriate wage-bill equalled or exceeded that of African employees.

*   *   *

This highly unequal wage distribution is characteristic of post-colonial economies; a comparison between France and Senegal brings this point out:

TABLE 43

Structure of Wage Income in France and Senegal
(1962)

Ratio: Share of wage income/share of employment in France* and Senegal.		
Management:	France	1.9 : 1
	Senegal	3.85 to 4.7 : 1
Salaried Staff:	France	0.83 : 1
	Senegal	0.88 to 1.1 : 1
Workers:	France	0.85 : 1
	Senegal	0.5 to 0.55 : 1

*   Commerce and industry.

Source: Social Security Fund IBM Printout; Le Monde (October 21, 1964).

Managers and higher technicians draw about twice the share of total wage income per head in Senegal than in France; contrariwise, workers draw 1.6 times more of the wage income per head in France than in Senegal.

By now it clearly appears that (i) the workers' income in real terms declined since political independence, and (ii) expatriate employees absorb a tremendously large share of industrial wages. In order to evaluate the workers' actual disposable income, we shall now switch from a macro-economic to a micro-economic perspective.

INDUSTRIAL WORKERS' INCOME

On the basis of interviews carried out in Senegal in 1964-65, what is the disposable income of Senegalese workers? What is the "extended family" influence on the workers' standard of living?

This study only concerns permanent industrial workers-- casual and seasonal labor is excluded; evidence is based on 188 interviews (W 61 to W 81). The sample is slightly weight- ed in favor of better-off workers; however, the analysis of the "extended family" influence on income is not much affected by this bias. Workers of the lower wage-grades (notably casual and seasonal labor) earn less than indicated in this study; the average income of workers in the study corresponds to that of workers of wage-grade V.

The Disposable Income of Industrial Workers

"Disposable income" is defined as:

  (i)   Basic wage plus
 (ii)   Social wage plus
(iii)   Nonwage income minus
 (iv)   Tax minus
  (v)   Repayment of Debt (+ Granting of Credit) minus
 (vi)   Sums sent to relatives who remained in home
         villages.

The disposable income is that share of income which is avail- able for current expenditure to workers and the people they support.

The basic wage constitutes the bulk of the workers' income; it varies according to wage-grade, length of service and overtime. Basic wages in the sample ranged from 6,400 to 105,250 cfa francs per month.

TABLE 44

Distribution of Workers According
to Their Basic Wages

Basic Wage (cfa)	Percent of Workers (cumulative)
Below 10,000	12.0
Below 15,000	38.0
Below 20,000	58.0
Below 25,000	74.0
Below 30,000	83.0

Interviews: W 61.

One-half of the workers interviewed earn less than 17,000
cfa francs per month; one-quarter of them less than 12,500 cfa
francs. Most frequent values in the series were: 8-9,000;
12-13,000; 15-16,000; 21-22,000; and 25-26,000. For each of
these levels (and only for these levels) there are over 5
percent of the workers. The average monthly basic wage of
workers was found to be 21,000 cfa francs. Total wage income
of the workers amounts to 3,948,100 cfa francs per month.

Basically, wages depend on wage-grades; the following
table shows a comparison between agreed wage rates in manufacturing industries calculated on the basis of 48 hours per
week, and rates observed in the sample. Several factors account for differences between the two series. For the two
lowest wage-grades, observed wages are lower than agreed rates
because the sample includes many young workers who work less
than 48 hours a week (notably in the food industries). The
agreed rates for wage-grades I and II roughly correspond to a
44-hour week; also, young workers do not receive seniority
premiums. Discrepancies at the other end of scale can be
explained by scarcity of highly skilled workers in Senegal and
by seniority premiums for elder skilled workers.

TABLE 45

Agreed Wage Rates (Manufacturing Industries) and
Observed Rates (Including Overtime and Premiums)

Wage-Grade	Agreed	Index	Observed	Index
I	9,305	100	8,400	90.2
II	10,652	100	9,200	86.4
III	11,789	100	11,800	100.1
IV	14,685	100	14,000	95.3
V	19,138	100	19,300	100.8
VI	22,204	100	22,500	101.3
VII	28,389	100	32,500	114.5
M	26,610 to 53,780		45,000	

Source: Charles F. Brun and Georges Vermot-Gauchy, Salaires
1961-1962 (Dakar: Clairafrique, 1962); Interviews:
W 61.

Of the workers interviewed 70.6 percent receive family
allowances that are proportional to the number of children
registered with the Social Security Fund. Taking basic and
social wages into account, the distribution of workers among
wage levels shows the following pattern:

TABLE 46

Distribution of Workers According
to their Total Wages

Total Wage (cfa)	Percent of Workers (cumulative)	Difference from Basic Wages
Below 10,000	8	- 50%
Below 15,000	35	- 8%
Below 20,000	54	- 7%
Below 25,000	69	- 6.75%
Below 30,000	82	- 1.2 %

Source: Interviews: W 61, W 62.

Average income has shifted upwards; half the workers earn less than 18-19,000 francs; one-quarter earn less than 13,500. The most frequent values in the series were: 12-13,000; 13-14,000; 14-15,000. For each of these levels (and only for these levels) there are over 5 percent of the workers.

The addition of social wages reduces the number of peaks in the curve; instead of five most frequent wage levels, there are only three, and these are adjacent to each other so as to form a single bloc (12,000 to 15,000). The shift towards higher incomes is particularly marked for the lower income-group.

Social wages reduce inequality in income-distribution to some extent, thus fulfilling one of the objectives of French policy-makers. Social wages represent between 1 and 43 percent of the workers' basic wages. The monthly rate of family allowances is 650 cfa francs per declared child:

TABLE 47

Social Wages in Percent of Basic Wage

Social Wages in Percent of Basic Wages	Percent of Workers
1 to 5	21
6 to 10	22
11 to 15	27
16 to 20	12
21 to 25	7
26 to 30	negligible
31 and more	7

Source: Interviews: W 61, W 62.

For 57 percent of workers interviewed, social wages amounted to over one-tenth of basic wages; for 30 percent of them, they amounted to over 15 percent of basic wages.

Nonwage income: For some 80 percent of workers, wages constitute the only regular source of income; 17 percent of workers occasionally earn some extra income in performing small services (e.g., electrical and mechanical repairs, etc.) outside their normal working hours. Only 2.2 percent of those interviewed said that their wives had a regular income. A

number of Senegalese workers own some cattle in their home
villages and some chickens and goats in town, but it is difficult to appraise the influence of such ownership on the standard of living. It does not seem that nonwage income is of
great consequence in the workers' budget; except for 8.5 percent who live at their own parents' home, their wage represents
the main source of income for the urbanized part of the "extended family."

Tax: Not all the workers interviewed were taxpayers;
this is due to imperfections in the tax-collecting administration rather than to the low level of industrial wages.

For those who pay taxes, those are determined by (a) the
level of income, (b) the place of residence, and (c) the
number of dependents (wives and children). The latter feature
is a legacy of French policy encouraging large families; income tax is assessed on the following basis: Husband and
wives count for one share each; children count for half a
share each; income (husband's + wives') is divided by the
number of shares and assessed on the resulting sum.

Moreover, when that sum is inferior to 100,000 cfa francs
per year there is no income tax at all.

An example shows how large families are favored by such a
system:

Basic wage: 40,000 cfa francs per month = 480,000 cfa
                  francs per year

Family Situation	Income Tax
single:	15 percent
married:	
1 wife, no child	10 percent
1 wife, 1 child	2 percent
1 wife, 6 children	nil
2 wives, 3 children	nil

The system discriminates against European-type families and is
of questionable benefit in a polygamous developing country
that does not suffer from underpopulation.

In the sample, 21.4 percent of the workers did not pay
any tax; 57.2 percent of them paid less than 500 cfa francs per
month; 18.5 percent paid between 501 and 1,000 cfa francs per
month; only 2.9 percent of the workers paid more than 1,000 cfa
francs per month.

Debts: Although only 41.4 percent of workers interviewed admitted they had any debts, it seems that the actual
proportion of indebted workers is higher.[4] Only 7.7 percent
of the workers interviewed said they had lent money to
friends: Sums lent were relatively small and prospects of
recovery uncertain.

TABLE 48

Debts Expressed in Monthly Terms[*]

less than 5,000 francs	75% of indebted workers
5,001 to 10,000 francs	18%
over 10,000 francs	7%

*   The sums indicated correspond to the total
     amount of debts divided by the number of months
     for repayment.
Source: Interviews: W 66.

Expressed as a percentage of basic wages, repayment of debts
represents a large fraction of income:

TABLE 49

Workers' Indebtedness

Monthly Repayment of Debts in Percent of Basic Wages	Percentage of Indebted Workers
1 to 5%	4.0%
6 to 10%	24.0%
11 to 15%	28.0%
16 to 20%	17.4%
21 to 25%	12.6%
26 to 30%	4.0%
31 to 35%	5.0%
36% and more	5.0%

Source: Interviews: W 61, W 66.

The total sum of monthly repayments of debts is roughly
equivalent to the total sum of social wages: (for 188 workers)

Repayment of Debts: 309,700 cfa francs
Social Wages: 316,300 cfa francs

Money sent home: One of the features of urbanization in
a society where traditional family solidarities are strongly
developed is the transfer of goods and money from the wage-
earning fraction of the population to those who remain in the
traditional sector of the economy. Although only about 34
percent of workers interviewed said that they regularly send a
part of their income to relatives in the country, additional
information indicates that this figure understates reality;
many workers send home considerable fractions of their income
but do not do so at regular intervals, or else they send goods
(e.g., rice, groundnut oil, sugar, etc.) rather than cash.
Figures indicated here exclusively concern regular transfers
of money.

TABLE 50

Income Sent Home

Sums Sent Home (of workers sending regularly)	Percent of Workers
500 francs per month and less	14%
501 to 1,000 francs	28%
1,001 to 2,000 francs	35%
over 2,000 francs	23%

Source: Interviews: W 61, W 64.

These sums represent the following fractions of basic wages:

Sums Sent Home (as percentage of basic wage)	Percent of Workers
1 to 5%	28%
6 to 10%	34%
11 to 15%	11%
16 to 20%	11%
21 to 25%	11%
over 25%	5%

The total sum of transfers home amounted to 112,340 cfa
francs for the sample as a whole (average per worker sending
money home is about 1,800 cfa francs per month) which is about
3 percent of the basic wage.

Disposable Income: The elements of disposable income can now be related to each other.

TABLE 51

Disposable Income

Item		Monthly sum for whole sample (cfa francs)	Index
	(i) Basic wage	3,946,100	100
+	(ii) Social wage	316,300	108
+	(iii) Extra income	negligible	108 +
-	(iv) Tax	about 30,000	108
-	(v) Repayment of debts (+ granting of credit)	309,700	100
-	(vi) Money sent home	112,340 +	97 -
	Disposable income	3,810,000	97 -

Source: Interviews: W 61, W 62, W 63, W 64, W 66, W 69, W 70.

This represents a disposable income of about 20,000 cfa francs per worker--a relatively high figure when compared to that of casual and seasonal unskilled workers.

The workers' expenditure is indicated in Appendix F.

The "Extended Family" Impact on the Workers' Standard of Living

Income figures per worker convey a highly misleading image of standards of living. They merely constitute a first step in an attempt to find out how the standard of living of urban industrial workers compares with that of peasants or other fractions of the population. In a society in which the "extended family" system prevails, the number of dependents who are fed (and often clothed) at the wage-earners' sole expense, thereby curtailing his income, must be taken into account.

The "extended family" is defined as an urbanized group of persons who partly or entirely depend on the income of one wage-earner for subsistence. The extended family can be broken down into the "nuclear family," comprising the wage-

earners' wives and children, and the nonnuclear family"
comprising other relatives.

An analysis of the size of the extended family alters the
image of per head incomes of individual workers considerably:
Both nuclear and nonnuclear families are remarkably large--
the first as a result of absence of birth control and of polygamy, the second because of traditional family solidarities.

The number of wives is the first element that affects the
size of the extended family. Only 13.8 percent of workers
interviewed were unmarried:

Number of Wives	Percent of Workers
0	13.8%
1	61.2%
2	21.3%
over 2	3.7%

Senegalese families are large: The average number of
children for monogamous workers is 3.08; that for polygamous
ones nearly twice as many: 5.93.

Over three-quarters of workers interviewed had children;
the curve representing the distribution of workers according
to the number of their children does not decline steadily--
probably as an effect of polygamy:

TABLE 52

Workers' Children

Number of children	Number of workers
none	40
1	25
2	24
3	18
4	20
5	21
6	9
7	10
8	8
9	4
10	2
11	2
12	3
13	1
14	1
over 14	none

Source: Interviews: W 14.

The number of persons maintained at the workers' expense is much larger than statistics concerning wives and children suggest. Unemployed relatives enjoy the hospitality of wage-earners and often move into their houses. Usually the non-nuclear family consists of elderly relatives from the provinces (mother-in-law, grandparents, etc.) and of children (nephews and nieces). Except in the case of young unmarried workers living at their own parents' home, it is rare to find more than one wage-earner per household. As soon as Senegalese job-seekers find stable employment, they set up their own households.

Figures indicated here may seem remarkably high by European standards; however, they do not include the numerous temporary guests--who come to stay in town for periods ranging from a few days (usually after wages have been paid out) to several weeks. Therefore, in order to have a fair idea of the extended family's impact on the workers' standard of living, figures indicated must--in spite of their magnitude--be taken as minima:

TABLE 53

Size of Extended Family

Size of Extended Family Fed (and Sometimes Clothed) at the Workers' Home-- Excluding the Workers Themselves	Percent of Workers
2 to 4	14.0%
5 to 7	25.5%
8 to 10	27.5%
11 to 13	17.0%
14 to 16	7.0%
over 16	9.0%

Source: Interviews: W 15.

One hundred eighty-eight workers in the sample maintain at least 1,614 persons, excluding themselves, permanently at their homes; the average size of the extended family is remarkably great by Western--although not necessarily by African--standards: 9.63 persons (including wage-earners themselves). Cases of extended families of over twenty people are not uncommon; the largest extended family encountered in the sample was of thirty people.

On a macro-economic level, this roughly corresponds to the ratio of wage-earners (about 100,000) to total urban population (about 800,000) in Senegal.

The impact of the extended family on the wage-earners' standard of living is extremely heavy; this fact is hardly ever mentioned in literature on economic development, although it is quite a common phenomenon in rapidly expanding cities where employment lags behind urbanization.

The deflating effect of family redistribution on income is tremendous; not to take this social factor into account when comparing incomes completely distorts the image of reality; nonetheless, extremely few income comparisons in developing economies do take social redistribution among members of extended families into account.

The impact of the extended family on workers' income can best be shown in an example: While average disposable income of workers in this sample is about 20,000 cfa francs per month, the per capita income--taking into account the family, but not transfers of money home and payments to nonpermanent visitors --is about 2,075 cfa francs (US $8.38).

One of the few analyses that does take this factor into account[5] concludes that unskilled workers in Senegal often earn as little as 900 or 1,000 cfa francs per month per head.

Present labor policies of private employers, trade union and government have led to (i) a declining trend in real wages for industrial workers, (ii) the absorption of a large share of the wage-bill by expatriate foremen, managers and clerical staff, (iii) low standards of living for industrial workers; the latter fact is due mainly to the impact of extended family responsibilities on industrial workers. The low standard of living of industrial workers conflicts with the doctrine of "African socialism" that emphasizes the "over-privileged" condition of industrial workers; by European standards, Senegalese workers are not in the slightest "over-privileged." The question of the relationship between urban and rural incomes will be dealt with in Chapter 12, when we will try to find what would happen if present imperfections of the labor market were removed.

Having seen the effect of policies on the workers' incomes, we must now turn to the long-term problem of employment and analyze the crucial question of choice of techniques. What are the determinants of capital-intensity in Senegalese

industry? How do labor policies--with their present and past
imperfections--influence the choice of factor-proportions in
industry?[6]

Notes to Chapter 10

1. E. J. Berg computed a series of indices of import-purchasing
    power for Dakar workers in "Real Income Trends in West
    Africa 1939-1960" in Economic Transition in Africa, M. J.
    Herskovits and M. Harwitz, eds. (New York: Routledge and
    Kegan Paul, 1964), p. 224:

1946	106
1947	105
1948	86
1949	100
1950	108
1951	112
1952	113
1953	142
1954	173
1955	175

2. See Appendix E.

3. La Planification en Afrique Noire, Vol. V (Paris:
    Ministère de la Coopération, 1964), Tables 27 and 28.

4. Based on conversations with industrial managers.

5. Charles F. Brun and Georges Vermot-Gauchy "La Question des
    Salaires au Sénégal," Afrique Documents (1965, Supplement
    No. 2). Average income figures of that study were de-
    flated by extended family data found in the interviews for
    this study.

6. Recent legal development confirms the existence of a link
    between the size of the extended family and widespread
    indebtedness: A law adopted in Feb. 1967 (Law No. 10)
    puts a ceiling to the value of presents that families are
    allowed to exchange on the occasion of family celebrations
    and prohibits sacrificing more than one animal per cele-
    bration. The object of this law is to attack the major
    cause of indebtedness in Senegal. This law is the first
    part of a new Code of the Family.

CHAPTER	11	THE CHOICE OF TECHNIQUES IN FORMER FRENCH TROPICAL TERRITORIES

This chapter does not intend to discuss the question of optimum factor-proportion, but merely aims at throwing some light on two aspects of the question of choice of techniques that are relevant in this book: (i) How much of recent economic theory is relevant to actual problems of choice of technique[1] in the area considered? (ii) what are the actual determinants of factor-proportions in Senegalese industry?

THE RELEVANCE OF SIMPLIFIED MODELS TO FORMER FRENCH TROPICAL TERRITORIES

The general issue at stake can be expressed in a simplified form: "How far does unemployment or the availability of cheap labor in the underdeveloped economies provide a case for relatively less capital-intensive techniques?"[2] On the basis of neo-classical economic theory according to Meade and Solow, the existence of high interest rates and low wages in underdeveloped economies should lead to the prima facie expectation to find relatively labor-intensive methods of production to be favored there. A. K. Sen writes that ceteris paribus there is a case for less capital-intensive methods of production in countries with cheap labor, whether the objective considered by policy-makers be maximizing social marginal productivity or re-investible surplus.[3]

However, the very abundant recent literature on the question suggests that the problem is highly complex. A first point to be clarified is the question of objectives: What aim do policy-makers and theoreticians have in mind when choosing a certain factor-proportion? The choice of an objective implies that of a maximization function and also taking a certain set of constraints into account. Second, there is, parallel to the choice of objective, that of a criterion; criteria are usually conceptually more refined than policy objectives and serve as instruments of measurement of success or failure in attaining the chosen objective. Thirdly, there is the question of knowledge (which may be viewed as merely

one of the constraints in the maximization function); each
criterion brings with it the need for knowledge of relevant
data for present and future; only availability of a critical minimum amount of data makes it possible to outline an
optimum path of development from the point of view of factor-
proportions. Finally, there is the problem of implementation, that centers on the question of the type of decision-
making structure existing in the economy considered; it
usually focuses on the degree of centralization of the
planning mechanism. Bearing these four aspects in mind, we
can turn to recent economic literature and to the characters
of the economies under study, to try to answer the first
question posed at the outset of this chapter.

     Early post-war literature dealt with the problem of factor-
proportions with the question of reconstruction of Europe
in mind. The problem was mainly how to use scarce capital
resources in the most effective way in the short term so as
to restore minimal standards of living and economic viability
in Europe. The maximization function which responded to this
concern usually focused on output in the short term. Polak
and Buchanan[4] had this objective in mind when they wrote
their contributions to the question of factor-proportions in
the early post-war period. Constraints taken into account in
this context have little relevance to present developing
economies: In the immediate post-war period objectives had a
fair chance to be attained through availability of a highly
skilled "reserve" of labor, consumption patterns that had
been "accidentally" depressed and would, given availability
of goods and services in sufficient quantity, resume their
pre-war "ratchet," and through availability of Marshall aid
on soft terms.

     Later, literature focused increasingly on poor coun-
tries and objectives shifted accordingly. Literature emphasized the need to absorb the labor surplus available and
favored strategies of development that relied to a large extent on small-scale industries; India's experience illustrates the fact that constraints such as social cost, quality
and competitiveness of output had not always been given sufficient attention by policy-makers before launching a program emphasizing labor-intensive methods of production. It
also became clearer that the question of time-horizon was
critical. The common objective of most economists is to
maximize employment and standards of living, but divergences
appear as to priorities in time. Some economists consider
an economy as a whole, in a welfare-economics perspective;
others stress the need for policies maximizing the rate of
growth. Both among economists with a welfare-economics

approach and those wishing to maximize growth rates, there
are differences in opinion as to the point in time when objectives should be realized. It should be mentioned, pour
memoire, that within the realm of private enterprise, policy-
making considerations such as the rate of profitability remain in the center of focus.[5]

Early post-war literature focused on maximizing the
ratio of output to capital; the criterion used to achieve a
fast recovery of Europe's economies is sometimes referred to
as the "rate of turnover." It is not very relevant for economies with no surplus of skilled labor, where consumption
patterns have to be shifted upwards from a very low level as
part of a development strategy, and that cannot count on
massive inflows of aid on soft terms. Economists who adopted
a welfare-economics approach focused on the "social marginal
productivity" (or SMP) as defined by A. E. Kahn,[6] taking the
economy as a whole and not just one sector or one industry
into account. Likewise, certain Marxist economists, like
Charles Bettelheim,[7] and also Maurice Dobb,[8] adopted an over-
all perspective. Others, like Galenson and Leibenstein[9]
adopted the rate of re-investible surplus as the critical
criterion on the assumption that maximizing that rate would
maximize investment, thus employment in the longer run.[10]
The critical influence of the choice of a criterion (and of
a time-horizon) on the choice of techniques is evidenced
very clearly by literature.[11]

Each criterion brings with it the need for relevant
knowledge. To analyze the question of factor-proportions in
an "operational" frame of mind it is perhaps not necessary
to have precise and detailed knowledge for the present and
for future points in time of all the relevant data. Usually
studies on factor-proportion carried out by governments concern a limited range of alternatives for a small number of
commodities. However, analyses such as Sen's, or Fei and
Ranis'[12] rely on availability of critical data such as marginal productivity of labor (in certain types of societies,
average productivity of labor) in agriculture, cost of labor
to the advanced sector of the economy (or to the economy as
a whole). Even on the conceptual level there are differences
in opinion as to the way to evaluate labor costs, "one of the
most important determinants of the degree of mechanization":[13] Dobb, Galenson and Leibenstein value labor at the
wage cost, while Kahn considers labor to be free. In fact,
much depends on the perspective adopted. In a welfare-
economics approach, for example, extra consumption that will be
induced in the process of development in the advanced sector
of the economy by extra employment is usually deducted as a
cost to the economy as a whole.

Implicitly or explicitly, recent literature on factor-proportions assumes the existence of a centralized structure of decision-making in which the central organization has powers to decide and implement factor allocation, if not in the economy as a whole, at least as far as additions to the capital stock are concerned. Sen explicitly supposes public ownership of means of production in the "new sector" (additions to the capital stock);[14] other economists who do not spell out this basic assumption share it implicitly, for their reasoning would not be effective if it were otherwise.

In former French colonies in Africa, government objectives as to factor-proportions are usually rather vague.[15] The Senegalese government, as most other Franc area governments, expressed the desire to maximize employment in the short and medium term, thus encouraging investment that creates maximum employment in the short and medium run (e.g., most "Investment Codes" discriminate in favor of investment that adds substantially to industrial employment). At the same time, however, development plans explicitly aim at maximizing growth of GDP per head. The possible conflict between these two objectives is never dealt with explicitly. It is thus not entirely clear which objective lies in the forefront of government preoccupations.

Looking at the question of criteria and constraints, one faces a rather fundamental difference between much of economic theory and African conditions. Most of theoretical literature is primarily concerned with countries suffering from widespread unemployment. Indeed, economists started to work on the problem of factor-proportions to try to help countries that are burdened with large surpluses of labor, like India, China, etc. A. K. Sen assumes a very elastic supply of fully committed labor from agriculture to the advanced sector of the economy and is "concerned primarily with ... 'over-populated' economies."[16] It is very doubtful whether there is such a surplus in most parts of Africa. In Senegal, labor had to be brought in at the time of most intense agricultural activity from neighboring countries during the colonial period (the administration bearing the cost of transport) every year, to help with the groundnut crop. Case studies have shown supply inelasticity of fully committed labor to the advanced sector in other African countries,[17] stressing seasonal constraints. The social cost of withdrawing labor from agriculture may, as monographs suggest, be high relative to income in African conditions, thus placing severe limitations on the applicability of theoretical models devised for over-populated areas.

The criterion of maximum surplus is also of questionable relevance in the present institutional framework of the Franc area. Transfer of capital is entirely free between member-countries of the Franc zone; outflows of factor income payments from Africa to France are at a high level at present. Maximizing the rate of re-investible surplus is not synonymous with maximizing investment. In all likelihood, if no restrictions are put in the way of capital flows between Franc zone countries, a policy achieving maximization of surplus in foreign-owned industry would thereby keep factor income payments abroad at a very high level rather than employment.

The question of time-horizon affects to some extent the relevance of criteria. The Senegalese government formulated its economic objectives within the framework of four-year plans. The plan currently implemented is for the years 1965-1969 and there is no "prospective" plan at present for investment beyond 1969. Thus, since some criteria normally assume a longer period for objectives to be attained than others, a short time-horizon such as that of the Senegalese government makes criteria such as SMP or "rate of surplus" less relevant than, say, maximization of the ratio: employment/output in the short run, which seems to be that of the government.

The question of knowledge is one of the causes of concern in most African countries. Statistical services devote most of their time trying to collect, and to keep up to date such very basic information as population, employment, output, value added, etc. Wide differences exist in most African countries (including Senegal, which has one of the best statistical services in tropical Africa) between various estimates of employment, and even as to the number of firms in industry (because of small-scale enterprises). Although general decisions as to factor-proportions can be made even in the absence of refined statistical data, the poor state of knowledge does constitute a hindrance to working out socially desirable factor-proportions.

However, even assuming availability of reasonably accurate data on marginal productivity of labor, wage rates, employment, capital costs, etc., the question of the decision-making structure still remains. Governments in the tropical member-states of the Franc zone have become accustomed to view private industry as a realm of expatriate dominance; over and above laying down certain constraints through taxation, labor legislation, etc., governments usually are in no position to determine factor allocation in industry. Investment decisions are usually taken abroad, at the center of decision-making of international firms, with the optimization function pertaining to those international firms as a whole in mind. The interests of African states and that of local plants are taken into consideration insofar as they affect the over-all advantage of the firm, within the broad framework of often world-wide objectives. Insofar as centralized decision-making by government is essential in the applicability of the theoretical treatment of the question of factor-proportion, the latter loses much of its relevance in the case of Franc-area countries of tropical Africa.

Finally, it seems that even when governments are in a position to formulate and implement industrial policies, it is doubtful whether the problem of factor-proportions would be in the center of preoccupations. Normally, governments outline general objectives such as maximizing GDP per head, encouraging industrial development along the lines of available natural resources and markets, making the best use of foreign exchange, containing inflationary pressures and keeping the foreign debt service ratio within reasonable limits. The question of factor-proportion usually arises when employment objectives are examined, a question often subordinated to the constraints outlined before. Also, governments desiring to increase employment in industry find it easier to influence the choice of industries rather than the choice of techniques within industry. Governments might through investment licenses and/or taxation and subsidies, encourage labor-intensive industries such as textiles, light manufacturing, etc., to come into the country, and discourage foreign investment in relatively capital-intensive industries, rather than attempting to influence investment and recruiting policies within industries. There is need for empirical studies as to the capital-intensity of various industries in developing countries. Insofar as colonial administration encouraged textile, food, and light manufacturing industries to settle in Senegal, one can say that (explicitly or implicitly) it pursued a policy concerning factor-proportions, favoring relatively labor-intensive industries. Since independence no such trend can be discerned (investment since independence includes such capital-intensive industries as fertilizer and oil refining, as well as some more labor-intensive light manufacturing plants).

ACTUAL DETERMINANTS OF CAPITAL-INTENSITY IN SENEGAL

Bearing the reservations to the applicability of simplified models in mind, we can now pose the second question

and try to analyze actual determinants of factor-proportions
in Senegal.

All tropical member-states of the Franc zone are poor:
Gross national product exceeds $200 per year per head in only
two cases (Gabon and Ivory Coast), and this includes expatriates. GNP per head of the African population is much lower
(by as much as 30 percent or more in many countries). In
these countries, capital is scarce and there is, in the short
run, abundance of unskilled labor available to the advanced
sector. Yet, despite government objectives expressed in national plans to maximize employment, and despite factor en-
dowment, the industrial centers of Dakar, Abidjan, Cotonou,
Douala, Libreville, Pointe Noire, those of Madagascar and the
mining companies in the interior have adopted relatively
capital-intensive methods of production that do not markedly
differ from those that can be found in France.

In the following discussion of determinants of capital-
intensity we shall emphasize the fact that many over-simplified
arguments on the question allow for two homogeneous inputs--
"labor" and "capital," when in fact none of these factors are
homogeneous. "Capital" and "labor" can be broken down into a
great number of heterogeneous components, each pointing to a
different optimum factor-proportion.

*   *   *

One reason for which little use is made of labor-intensive
methods of production is the low productivity of unskilled
African labor that may offset the effects of lower wages (than
in developed countries). In turn, productivity of indigenous
labor depends a great deal on the degree of mechanization in
the firms: Most industrial employers interviewed in Senegal
believe that productivity-differentials between expatriate and
African labor mainly depend on that factor (E 37). Large investments in technically advanced capital goods are viewed by
expatriate employers as a prerequisite to an economic use of
cheap labor.

Bauer and Yamey pointed out the fact that complemen-
tarity between labor and capital may be more important than
their substitution:[18] "It has sometimes been found that
cheap unskilled labour can be used economically only if
methods are highly mechanised." Often, a "preliminary" investment is a necessary condition for using any amount of
unskilled labor (e.g., mining, railroad building, etc.). In
these cases, there are in fact several processes that necessarily follow each other in a certain order. The first

process may be fairly capital-intensive (fixed technical
coefficient of production, or at least limited choice of
techniques); the other processes--that cannot take place
before the first capital-intensive process has itself taken
place--may show a greater degree of substitution of labor for
capital. There is no single production function in these
cases, but a production function for each process.

But Bauer and Yamey's argument appears to rest on two
other reasons which are closely related to each other: (a)
Qualitative factors on the factor and the product market depend on the degree of mechanization; (b) managerial difficulties decrease as capital-intensity increases.

(a) The more machine-paced operations determine the
rhythm of production in a plant, the less scope there is for
poor performance for an untrained labor force; machine-paced
operations usually involve some conveyor-belt process; conveyor-belt processes are used only for large-scale production. Although theoretically labor-intensive machine-paced
operations might be conceived, it is usually the case that
operator-paced processes are less capital-intensive than machine-paced operations. Hirschman implies (on the basis of
empirical knowledge) that in general machine-paced operations
require a higher capital-intensity than operator-paced
ones.[19] The use of capital-intensive methods of production
reduces the scope for imperfections and irregularities in
output. Therefore, entrepreneurs often use highly mechanized
assembly-lines and conveyor-belts in order to force workers
to adapt their rhythm to that of the machine. Despite a high
degree of capital-intensity, the main textile firm in Senegal
loses about 30 percent of its output because of qualitative
defects due to human causes;[20] attempts to use less capital-
intensive methods of production led to even greater losses.
Capital-intensive methods of production and machine-paced
operations increase the homogeneity of labor and therefore
minimize losses due to poor output.

(b) Some of the main features of a low-productivity
labor force are extreme scarcity of efficient foremen and the
very great difficulties involved in organizing the work of
large numbers of workers. Capital-intensive methods of production reduce the need for supervisory labor by setting minimum standards of coordination for unskilled workers.

In both cases, a "lump" of investment is a prerequisite
rather than a substitute for using ill-trained indigenous
labor.

In the former French colonies of tropical Africa, the
wage rate for unskilled workers is kept above the equilibrium
level by government intervention; indigenous employers, who
are not controlled as sharply as expatriate ones by Labor
Inspectorate, usually pay their employees below the national
minimum or agreed rate. Considerable concern arose in Senegal when it became clear to the government that most small-
scale business hired labor without declaring it to the administration, thus escaping the obligation to contribute to
social security. A law passed in 1962[21] prohibits "unde-
clared employment and labor without employment contract."
Lack of efficient administration and the Labor Courts' awareness that many indigenous firms are not able to stand higher
wages prevented steps from being taken to enforce the law;
large expatriate firms feel discriminated against in the enforcement of labor legislation.

Industrial employers also found labor far from inexpen-
sive at the prevailing minimum rate, considering the low
level of productivity. Maurice Dobb made this point very
clearly: The choice of techniques is affected by the fact
that "the productivity of labour in the underdeveloped areas
is low given the capital-intensity."[22] The cost of unskilled
labor in Senegal is about 420 cfa francs per day, including
social contributions (US $1.72). Interviews with industrial
employers clearly indicate that the larger the number of
workers employed, the more difficult it becomes to supervise
them so as to keep marginal productivity above marginal cost.
Supervisors are notoriously bad in former French colonies of
tropical Africa: Each firm may have a very small number of
supervisors capable of organizing the work of unskilled employees placed under their authority; but beyond the point
where the few relatively efficient supervisors are fully oc-
cupied, marginal productivity of labor drops sharply. The
law of diminishing returns plays as a variable factor (unskilled labor) is combined with a fixed factor (supervision).
According to expatriate employers, a point is soon reached
where the marginal productivity of African workers under
African supervision drops below US $1.72 per day. There,
too, more capital-intensive methods of production are a substitute for more supervision of unskilled labor.

The supply-elasticity of Senegalese supervisory labor is
presently very low; the quality of supervisors turned out by
vocational training schools is usually too poor to satisfy
industrialists' requirements, for reasons which were shown
earlier.

The cost of expatriate supervision is very high indeed:
It was found by the French planners who made detailed studies
of the Senegalese economy that served as a basis for setting
up the First National Plan, that "if the expatriate labour
force represents 20 percent of the African labour force, ...
total costs of labour is the same as in France."[23]

It is therefore uneconomic to increase the productivity
of African labor by reinforcing expatriate supervision; the
sole comparative advantage of Senegal to France--cheaper
labor--might be offset.

A comparison between average wages and labor costs
throws some light on the seemingly exorbitant cost-
differential between African and expatriate labor costs:

TABLE 54

Cost-differential Between African and Expatriate Labor

Monthly Values (in cfa francs)

(i) Average wage of a <u>cadre moyen</u>* in France
(1964):   78,000

(ii) Average wage of a <u>contremaître</u>[+] in France
(1964):   66,750

(iii) Average cost of supervisory labor, including
indirect labor costs of 56.5% of wage in
France (= (i) + (ii) / 2):   113,375

(iv) Average wage of expatriates in Senegal (1963):   130,000

(v) Average cost of expatriate labor in Senegal
(1963):   over 230,000

Hourly Values (in cfa francs)

(vi) Average cost of Senegalese workers (permanent
workers only) (1963):   81.7

(vii) Average cost of workers in France (1964):   321.5

---

*cadre moyen: lower executive or technician.
[+]contremaître: foreman.

Source: <u>Annuaire Statistique de la France 1965</u> (Paris: Government Publication, 1965); <u>Le Monde</u> (December 12-
13, 1965); Social Security Fund IBM Printout
(Dakar); Ministère du Travail, <u>Statistiques de la
Sécurité Sociale</u> (Dakar: roneoed, 1964); Interviews
with industrial managers.

It appears that wages for expatriates are about 1.8 times
higher in Senegal than wages in France--this is due to ex-
patriation and to a higher general level of prices in Senegal than in France (the index of cost of living used by
United Nations personnel implies that the cost of living was
16 percent higher in Dakar than in New York City in 1964).

The cost of expatriate labor in Senegal is over twice
as high as the cost of the same type of labor in France.
Conversely, the average cost of Senegalese labor (workers)
is much lower than that of workers in France (ratio 1:3.95).

Thus it appears that the a priori surprisingly high
cost-differential between African and expatriate labor in
Senegal is due both to the relative cheapness of African labor and to the high cost of expatriate labor (all comparisons
with similar types of labor in France).

At present the expatriate labor force represents about
11 percent of the African labor force in Senegal; total
labor costs are thus lower than in France--but a significant
increase in expatriate supervision is quite likely to push
total labor costs up to the French level.

It appears, in the case of Senegal, that "Wage rates
above the equilibrium level /and shortage of efficient domestic supervisory labor7 ... encourage the use of more cap-
italistic methods" of production.[24] High capital-intensity
goes with low supervision per worker.

*   *   *

Overtime payments are paid out to hourly paid African
labor only--expatriates are paid by the month. This makes it
in the African workers' interest to maximize the number of
hours worked; there is a tendency for African labor--under
the influence of trade unions--to reduce their effort during
the first forty working hours of each week in order to increase the amount of work to be performed under overtime conditions. This depresses average productivity of labor and
further encourages employers to use machine-paced, rather
than operator-paced, methods of production. Expatriate employers are strictly bound by provisions on overtime payment
included in collective agreements.

The trade unions' policy is self-defeating in this
respect (as in others which have been mentioned before):
Capital-intensive methods of production keeping down

employment opportunities in the long run are favored by the union's policy of "creating more work" in the short term.

*　　*　　*

Standardization of capital goods is a further reason for industrial managers not to depart significantly from "European-type" factor-proportion. The range of capital goods supplied by advanced economies corresponds to the needs of buyers in industrialized countries, rather than to those of the minority of industrialists operating in backward economies. The only alternative solution for the latter is to purchase second-hand equipment at a lower cost; this is rarely done because of the high spare and maintenance ratio required and because of risks of qualitative imperfection of the products.

The expatriate labor market also imposes certain constraints on the choice of techniques. Young expatriate technicians have a high mobility. International firms encourage mobility and often use their scarce expatriate labor force in several plants all over Africa. A fair degree of standardization between sister-plants in different territories reduces expatriate labor costs: Similar factor-proportions are chosen by foreign firms for their plants operating in the former French countries of North and tropical Africa.

*　　*　　*

Objective differences in productivity between tropical and temperate developed countries undoubtedly exist. Diseconomies of small scale, inadequacy of external economies available to firms, lack of industrial tradition with the labor force play a considerable role. In Senegal's cement factory (producing about 200,000 tons per year) productivity of labor measured in terms of tons of output per working hour is low: Although equipment used is the same in the two cases, it is 2.3 times higher in cement plants in France than in Senegal. The "environmental" factors depressing productivity reinforce the employers' belief that capital-intensive methods of production are the best way to use indigenous labor; in many cases there is no clear awareness on the part of expatriate employers of the distinction between "environmental" and individual factors affecting productivity of labor.

The case of Senegal's match factory reveals what the potential choice of techniques might be in that country

were the present capital stock to be replaced. The factory
was accidentally destroyed in 1960. Labor-intensive methods
of production--making great use of female manpower--were replaced by fairly capital-intensive ones when the factory was
reconstructed:

<u>Match Factory, Dakar</u>

Period	Employment (African)	Expatriate Staff
Before destruction	900-1,000	15
After reconstruction	130	5

Total capacity of production remained unchanged.

*   *   *

Monopoly position and tariff protection increase the industrial firms' ability to depart from the (social) optimum
allocation of factors. This means that the absence of need
for international competitiveness helps industrial enterprises to refrain from departing from their "traditional"
capital-intensive policies often dating back to colonial
times when the supply of skilled African workers was very
much smaller than it is today.

The planning experts who examined the Senegalese economy
before setting up the First National Plan already observed
that "The privileged position of certain firms which enjoy a
monopoly in the local market reinforced by tariff and geographical protection, enables them ... to depart from the
/social7 optimum allocation of real factors in the country
and seemingly to escape economic logic of perfect competition. The very fast rate of amortization and high profit
rates which this position confers explain part of the paradox."25

*   *   *

However, an upward limit to capital-intensity is reached
when absence of external economies, hardships of the tropical
climate and maintenance difficulties endanger capital equipment; "The absence of a kind of sympathy which, in the end,
establishes itself between Man and Machine, makes that the
latter does not operate well /in Senegal7 and wears out
quickly."26 Very advanced equipment has a short lifespan in
Africa; beyond a certain degree of technical complexity of

the capital equipment it becomes necessary to add to the expatriate labor force of technicians. According to industrial entrepreneurs in Senegal, the upward limit to capital-intensity is reached when they feel that adding to the stock of capital would require hiring an expatriate technician at a cost that would offset the gains from using more efficient machines. There is a marked preference in Senegal, as in other parts of Africa, for intermediate technology and sturdiness is valued more than technical sophistication.

*   *   *

Most industrialists interviewed stated that there was "no choice" for them, in practice, between different factor-proportions (E 23); they said that the degree of capital-intensity is pre-determined.

Eckhaus pointed out this question on the theoretical level which seems to be fairly common in dualistic economies: "Suppose that, whatever the actual characteristics of the production function and degree of technical substitutability of factors, businessmen believe that they face a production function with constant coefficients ... the expansion path ... would be independent of the factor-price ratios, and therefore, of the supply curve of labour."[27] However, there are factors that help understand the point of view of industrialists operating in Senegal.

The main reason for which there is "no choice" is the rigidity of commercial structures for capital goods: There is a limited choice of capital equipment available on the market (notably on the French market where most Senegalese firms buy their capital equipment). Firms which order equipment have to "take it or leave it"; they are not in a position to bring manufacturers of capital goods to modify their product in order to match the special needs of tropical firms.

More sophisticated entrepreneurs do realize that there is a choice between alternative factor-proportions; but they deny the usefulness of thinking in terms of an aggregate production function: They realize that for each process within a factory (there are over 25 processes in Senegal's agricultural equipment factory) there is a different choice of techniques, and different degrees of substitutability of labor for capital. In the minds of these entrepreneurs, there may be two or three alternatives for each production function (for each process). However, for technical reasons, once a certain factor-proportion is chosen for one of the processes,

the choice of techniques is restricted by technical constraints for other processes. Thus there may be over 25 production functions for each factory; aggregate production
functions have little practical significance. In the minds
of the more sophisticated entrepreneurs, the "no choice"
proposition means that there may be a choice of factor-proportion for one of the processes of production, but that
once a decision is taken concerning that process, technical
constraints sharply reduce freedom of choice for the rest of
the factory.

                    *   *   *

However, there is still room for shifts in the production function despite the managers' belief. Firms can be
broken down into (a) central operations which are usually
machine-paced and tied to some mechanical or chemical process; (b) ancillary operations such as transportation,
maintenance, handling of goods, cleaning, etc. The factor-
proportion can be different in the two sections of each factory; in Senegal, the first tends to be capital-intensive,
but this does not often extend to ancillary operations.

The simultaneous existence of two sections with different capital-intensities need not affect productivity adversely as long as "plant operations as a whole are process-
centred ... since the central process still would indirectly
set the pace /but not the capital-intensity7 of all operations in the plant."[28] Arguments in favor of using capital-
intensive methods are more convincing in the case of central
than in that of ancillary operations; in the case of the
latter there is a real choice between different degrees of
capital-intensity, while for central operations there may be
no such choice. There is no "take it or leave it" proposition in the case of operations other than central ones;
there remains a very wide range of possible shifts on the
production function in most industrial firms in Senegal.

Economic history shows that changes in the choice of
technique occurred in ancillary rather than in central operations. The organization of harbors and roadbuilding in Senegal before and after 1952 shows the existence of a margin of
maneuver in the case of ancillary operations.

As a result of the introduction of the 40-hour week in
French West Africa in 1953--an effect of enforcing the new
Labor Code--cost of labor increased by about 20 percent.
While the factor-proportion remained largely unaltered in
central operations of industrial firms, more labor-saving

methods of production were introduced in ancillary operations; Labor Reports for South Senegal point out that there
was a marked shift in favor of mechanization in handling
operations, transportation, ship loading, unshelling of
groundnuts, roadbuilding and construction: "The general
spread of mechanization in handling goods created important
unemployment among the unskilled labor force";[29] this fact
was interpreted by the labor administration: "The ordinary
African labor force (unskilled and unspecialized) /has been7
used uneconomically so far, because its cost was very
low."[30] Part of the decline in employment in the late colonial period can be attributed to this trend. There is still
room for further adaptation in the techniques of production
in the ancillary operations of the firms visited in Senegal.

                        *   *   *

    The reasons for choosing fairly capital-intensive meth-
ods of production were summed up by the manager of the Senegalese match factory justifying increased mechanization of
operations in his establishment: (a) The quality of the product had improved greatly--making it capable of facing international competition--as a result of mechanization; (b)
problems of personnel management and supervision had been
greatly alleviated and labor relations in the firm had improved; (c) the rate of absenteeism fell; (d) piece-work
could be replaced by hourly wages representing a better remuneration for most workers; (e) the need for expatriate
supervision was reduced; reducing the number of expatriates
enabled the firm to raise the quality of the expatriate labor
force, thereby making it less likely to be attacked by the
government on political grounds for Africanization; (f) the
new plant--as reconstructed--is very similar to a recently
built sister-plant in the Ivory Coast; this reduces over-all
costs for the international firm to which both factories
belong.

    A simplified diagram sums up factors determining the
choice of techniques in industrial firms in the former French
colonies of tropical Africa:

FIGURE 9

Choice of Techniques

K_1 K_2 = Area of Choice of Capital Investment

L_1 L_2 = Area of Choice of Employment

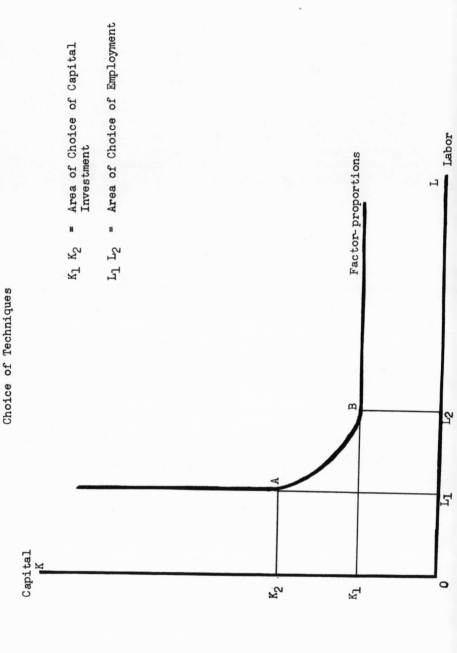

188

Figure 9: Point A represents the upward limit to the use of
capital-intensive methods of production; it is determined mainly
by (a) the short life-span of technically very advanced equipment in developing tropical countries; (b) the point where marginal returns of additional equipment are offset by a need for
and by the cost of additional expatriate manpower. Point B represents the downward limit to the use of capital-intensive methods of production; it is determined mainly by the point where
the legal minimum (or agreed) wage rate equals marginal productivity of African labor under minimum expatriate supervision
(i.e., in the case of Senegal, when marginal productivity of unskilled labor falls under US $1.72 per day).

Factors exerting an influence in favor of labor-intensive
methods of production are: (a) Scarcity of capital and high
rate of interest common to most developing countries; (b) a-
bundant supplies of unskilled labor in the short run (which
can--given proper training--be transformed eventually into a-
bundant supplies of skilled and supervisory labor); (c) low
level of industrial wages in comparison with France; low cost
of labor in comparison with France; (d) small scale of the
domestic market which restricts the economical use of highly
capital-intensive methods of production whenever these are subject to discontinuities;[31] (e) monopoly position and protection
which enable firms to delay mechanization even when there are
reasons to produce on a more capital-intensive basis.

Factors exerting an influence in favor of capital-intensive
methods of production are: (a) The difference between the very
low productivity of labor in the absence of mechanization (and
proper supervision) and the much higher productivity of labor in
machine-paced operations; (b) constraints due to "environmental"
influences on productivity; (c) qualitative requirements on the
product market--a factor of increasing importance in the event
of a geographical diversification and expansion of foreign trade
advocated by most African governments; (d) the very high cost
of expatriate supervision; the fact that in view of a possible
departure from its present "liberal" attitude towards expatriate
manpower, the government may make it desirable for industrial
firms to reduce the number and increase the quality of their expatriate manpower in order to increase its "political accept-
ability"; (e) standardization in the factor market (capital
and expatriate labor); (f) problems of personnel management
and industrial relations at the plant level; (g) compulsory
overtime payment system for African labor force; (h) monopoly
position and protection from foreign competition which
also enables firms to operate on a more capital-intensive

basis than the equilibrium level because very high profits
and fast amortization are made possible by market imperfection.

*   *   *

However, all these factors do not provide a complete explanation of the paradox of capital-intensive methods of production in Senegal; indigenous firms--that command a negligible share of the market--are far more capital-and-energy-
saving than expatriate ones. Payment of wages below the
legal minimum rate may be one of the factors explaining the
discrepancy between methods of production of indigenous and
expatriate firms. However, this reason does not appear sufficient.

The answer must also be sought in the fundamentally
dualistic character of the economy which has been perpetuated
since the colonial period: There are, in fact, not one capital market and one labor market, but a much larger number of
markets. They come under four groups: (i) Labor markets
that are available to indigenous enterprises; (ii) labor markets that are available to expatriate firms; (iii) capital
markets that are available to indigenous firms; (iv) capital
markets that are available to expatriate firms; (there may be
a certain degree of overlapping between these four groups).

Some of these groups of markets can, in turn, be broken
down into more specific factor markets: Unskilled labor,
skilled labor, supervisory labor, managerial labor; short-
term capital, medium-term capital and long-term capital, etc.

The "liberal" system of the Franc zone involves entire
freedom to transfer men and capital from France to Africa and
vice-versa--but for health requirements and minor restrictions to emigration of African labor; this facilitated the
rise of European enterprise in Africa but constituted a handicap to the growth of African enterprise, notably in industry; the "liberal" system of the Franc zone embracing one
developed and a large number of nonindustrial countries
worked in favor of expatriate and against indigenous industries in tropical Africa.

Expatriate firms have access to European financial markets; they base their investment decisions on long-term
rates of interest in Europe and can issue shares in Paris,
Frankfurt, Zurich, etc. Indigenous firms have no access to
these financial markets and find it extremely hard if not

impossible to finance long-term investments. The rate of
interest in Africa--if adequate savings are available, which
is not necessarily the case--is considerably higher than in
Europe; credit is scarce, risks on the lender's side are
quite considerable in view of the past unfavorable record of
African industrial entrepreneurship in Senegal. One important factor that should never be omitted from an analysis of
African enterprise in Senegal is the pressure of the extended family: The extended family system makes any attempt at
a capital-forming use of funds an almost superhuman feat.
Most often, available surplus is dissipated in private consumption by the entrepreneur and his extended family.

    Some of the necessary short- and long-term credit is
provided to expatriate firms by local branches of interna-
tional--formerly exclusively French--banks in Senegal; but
treasury requirements and medium-term credit are usually provided by a mere transfer of funds from European headquarters
to local branches of industrial firms. The economic and financial solidity of these firms justify low rates of interest. There, too, indigenous firms find it more difficult to
obtain credit, and when they obtain it, the rate of interest
is much higher than is the case for expatriate firms.

    Dualism on the market for managerial labor further in-
creases dualism on the capital market. Expatriate firms
which operate on a fairly large scale--by African standards--
and have their "roots" in France, have access to the French
market for managerial and higher technical labor; they can
recruit students graduating from the grandes écoles (e.g.,
Hautes Etudes Commerciales, Polytechnique, etc.). There are
frequent advertisements in French newspapers for graduates
of these institutions--the élite of French students--to work
overseas for expatriate firms. Moreover, the scale of expatriate firms enables them to afford a fair degree of specialization at the managerial and technical level: Each
department is staffed and/or headed by specialists. Indigenous firms are in no such position. They cannot hire expatriate labor either in France or in Senegal; they are unable to offer competitive wages, and lack the French "roots"
necessary for recruiting in a sellers' market; they cannot
either offer guarantees of stability of employment. Moreover, it is doubtful whether many Frenchmen would contemplate
working for small indigenous firms--there are, in fact, very
few private industrial firms of over 20 employees managed by
Africans. Finally, the small scale of African firms and of
their respective markets does not make specialization at the
managerial and technical level economical: Even if it is assumed that an African firm succeeded in recruiting an

expatriate manager of high professional quality, the diver-
sity of tasks to be dealt with by him would put him into an
inferior position, when compared with competing large-scale
firms with specialized departments. Dualism on the market
for managerial and technical labor thus increases the difficulties African firms face when trying to obtain medium- or
long-term credit on favorable terms, because it cuts them off
from the main sources of competent management, thereby further reducing their creditworthiness.

*   *   *

The price of entry is very high in terms of cost of
competent managers, organizers, finance and marketing, etc.
All factors of production--except unskilled labor--are harder
to find and to organize for indigenous than for expatriate
firms.

*   *   *

But is unskilled labor at the minimum wage "cheap"? At
the lower end of the scale, the situation is biased in favor
of small indigenous firms: These are able to hire unskilled
(sometimes even skilled) workers below legal rates, often
"holding" their employees by granting them credit in excess
of their ability to repay, so that these are "bound" to the
firm. This seems to be the case in many African and Syro-
Lebanese enterprises. African firms have a very fair chance
of escaping provisions of labor legislation on minimum wages:
They often fail to register their employees with the Labor
Administration, thus saving social security contributions
(about 15 to 20 percent of basic wages); they have often
been found to pay their employees at rates equal to one-
fourth of agreed rates, thereby reducing the cost of unskilled labor to about US $0.45 per day. Labor Inspectors
and Courts have no means (and often no desire) to exert effective control since this would inevitably result in increasing unemployment by wrecking small African firms. Expatriate firms are bound by labor legislation because of
their political position, their scale, and the presence of
shop delegates in firms of over ten employees; their books
must remain available to Labor Inspectors at any time. To
expatriate firms, the cost of unskilled labor is about US
$1.72 per day (since August 1961).

Thus we are faced with the irony of a government trying,
in the context of a doctrine of "African socialism" to keep
labor costs low, and which, in fact, maintains the level of
wages well above equilibrium.

The result of these discriminatory markets is that investment planning and the choice of an economical factor-
proportion are basically different for expatriate and indigenous firms: Competent management and cheap capital are
available only to expatriate firms; conversely, unskilled
(and possibly little-skilled) labor is available to indigenous and Syro-Lebanese firms at a cheaper cost than it is to
expatriate firms.

The various factor markets are summed up in the following table. It shows the lack of validity of concepts such
as "homogeneous" labor and capital determining the choice of
techniques in a dualistic country:

TABLE 55

Factor Markets and Choice of Techniques

Factors	Indigenous Firms	Expatriate Firms
DOMESTIC FACTORS		
Labor		
Unskilled labor below legal rate:	A+	NA*
Unskilled labor at legal rate:	A+	A+
Skilled labor:	A-	A-
Supervisory labor:	A-	A-
Capital		
Short-, medium- and long-term credit:	A-	A-
FOREIGN FACTORS		
Labor		
Skilled labor:	NA	A-**
Supervisory labor:	NA	A-**
Managerial and technical labor:	NA	A-**
Capital		
Short-, medium- and long-term credit:	NA	A+
OPTIMUM FACTOR-PROPORTION	Capital Saving	Capital-intensive, Expatriate Labor-saving

  * For institutional reasons shown above.
 ** Assuming scarcity of labor in France as is the case since 1958.

Legend: A = available
        NA = not available
         + = abundant
         - = scarce

*   *   *

The discrepancy between expatriate and indigenous firms --as far as methods of production are concerned--can best be explained by dualism in the various factor markets. In the absence of such dualism, there are strong arguments in favor of the general use by African and expatriate firms alike of intermediate techniques of production (possibly, in a closed economy, of "African-type" factor-proportions). The "liberalism" of the Franc zone system--as that of any "liberal" system including developed as well as developing countries-- emphasized the discriminatory factors at work in the policies of private firms and of the government (notably in education and manpower training).

Historically, large capital-intensive expatriate firms established themselves in Africa; with independence and political "balkanization" of the federal entities came the erection of nationalistic tariffs. The factories set up by the French were large enough to meet the requirements of the countries in which they operate and to export when this is possible; there is little or no room left for African industry. The latter can develop only "in the shadow"[32] of existing firms. The educational policies and the wage policies of the French and the Senegalese governments left the former French colonies of tropical Africa without an indigenous élite of industrial workers, accountants, managers, technicians, etc., able and willing to start enterprises. African enterprise is confined to labor-intensive activities such as housebuilding, repair workshops, confection, etc. In production of consumption goods it can compete only in manufacturing goods of inferior quality, taking advantage of external economies provided indirectly by expatriate firms (e.g., marketing, including publicity), such as imitation BATA tennis shoes, etc.

The monopoly position and greater long-term growth potential of expatriate industrial firms came as a result of a partly liberal system; they are most unlikely to be challenged by African enterprise.

At least three ways are open to the Senegalese government in the future: (i) National development banks giving credit at a relatively low rate of interest could be enlarged in scope; however, in the absence of competent African industrial managers and given the pressure of extended families on African managers, it is probable that the scope will be limited very soon by the smallness of the capacity of African enterprises to absorb capital profitably; (ii) the government could augment its financial participation in expatriate firms; this is of limited value, however, since the funds

available for such participation are scarce and greatly
needed for other uses, and because there is little chance of
the government acquiring sufficient financial power to influence the expatriate firms' policies (e.g., accelerating
Africanization at the managerial level, lowering retail
prices, reducing outflows of capital, etc.); (iii) ultimately it seems that basic changes in educational and wage policies alone might favor the development of African enterprise.

The Franc zone framework--which provides excellent institutions to expatriate firms--discourages significant departure from present factor-proportions, making it unlikely
that employment objectives of the government for industry
will be attained in the present state of the market.

Neither labor nor capital can be analyzed in terms of
homogeneous factors of production. Six main factors determine the preference for rather capital-intensive methods of
production: (i) Lack of local supervisory and technical
skills; (ii) the fact that the government keeps minimum
wages well above equilibrium rates; (iii) high cost of expatriate labor keeping total labor costs high; (iv) standardization encouraging mechanization; (v) monopoly positions and tariff protection; (vi) the structure of the capital market.

There is still room for changing techniques of production one way or the other.

The government can act on most of the factors listed
above, particularly on factors (i), (ii) and (v) through its
educational policy and its wage policy and by acting on
tariffs. Insofar as it can act, the government is responsible for keeping employment in industry down to its present
level. An action by the government on point (vi) is conceivable; but such action raises wider political problems,
which will be discussed in the last chapter.

*   *   *

Contrary to what was expected on the basis of the
analysis of market imperfections, we found that the standard
of living of African workers is low (because of declining
real wages, high expatriate wages and the impact of the family system), despite the fact that--paradoxically--government
policy maintains minimum wage rates well above equilibrium
level. The question of the relative income of peasants and
industrial workers remains to be examined.

Furthermore, instead of finding preference for labor-intensive methods of production, we found that expatriate firms have very strong reasons to operate on a fairly capital-intensive basis, thus keeping short-term employment prospects bleak.

What alternative labor policies might satisfy the objectives of the Senegalese government?

In the next chapter, analysis will be confined to domestic factors. We will first examine whether there is a case for setting up a "balanced growth" program in Senegal; and then, a "second-best solution" will be analyzed: What effects might higher wages for industrial workers have on the factor and on the product market? Next, the problem of wages and employment will be replaced in its natural context, and we will try to find how the family system influences policies for industrial labor.

Senegal's position in the context of the international post-colonial political and economic framework will be shown in the last chapter; the questions to be answered--which in fact are the key questions for development--are: (i) How does Senegal's post-colonial political situation influence labor problems and growth? (ii) Could changes in Senegal's political position help the government of that country achieve its economic objectives?

Notes to Chapter 11

1. By factor-proportions, we mean the ratio of capital to labor as measured for practical purposes by the ratio of cost of fixed and working capital to cost of labor (wage-bill including indirect labor costs such as social security, etc.). This definition is most often used in economic theory. Entrepreneurs and planners may, before creating an additional unit of production, have a fair idea of the respective costs of capital and labor. Other ratios depending on gross output or on value added may be useful ex post, but are less easily predictable ex ante than capital and labor costs.

2. A. K. Sen, Choice of Techniques (Oxford: Blackwell, 1960), pp. 64-65.

3. A. K. Sen, op. cit., p. 65.

4. N. S. Buchanan, International Investment and Domestic
    Welfare (New York: H. Holt and Company, 1945); J. J.
    Polak, "Balance of Payments Problems of Countries Recon-
    structing with the Help of Foreign Loans," Readings in the
    Theory of International Trade, H. S. Ellis, L. A. Metzler,
    ed., (Philadelphia: Blackistan, 1949).

5. On actual conditions of policy-making in the private
    sector and their effect on choice of techniques, see R. L.
    Meek, "Ideal and Reality in the Choice between Alterna-
    tive Techniques," OEP (November, 1964).

6. See A. E. Kahn, "Investment Criteria in Development Pro-
    grams," QJE (February, 1951), p. 39. Social marginal
    productivity takes into account "the total net contribu-
    tion of the marginal unit to national product, and not
    merely that portion of the contribution (or of its costs)
    which may accrue to the private investor."

7. Charles Bettelheim, Studies in the Theory of Planning
    (London: Asia Publishing House, 1959); Charles Bettel-
    heim, Some Basic Planning Problems (London: Asia Publish-
    ing House, 1961).

8. Maurice Dobb, "A Note on the Discussion of the Problem
    of Choice between Alternative Investment Projects,"
    Soviet Studies, Vol. II, No. 3 (January, 1951); Maurice
    Dobb, "A Note on the So-called Degree of Capital-Intensity
    of Investment in Underdeveloped Countries," Economie
    Appliquée, No. 3 (July, 1954); Maurice Dobb, "Second
    Thoughts on Capital Intensity," Review of Economic
    Studies, Vol. XXIV.

9. W. Galenson and H. Leibenstein, "Investment Criteria,
    Productivity and Economic Development," QJE (August,
    1955).

10. An empirical study by G. Ranis in Pakistan "Production
    Functions, Market Imperfections and Economic Development,"
    Economic Journal (June, 1962), shows some of the diffi-
    culties met when trying to conciliate theory and real
    conditions with factor-proportion problems.

11. See, notably, A. K. Bagchi, "The Choice of Optimum Tech-
    nique," Economic Journal (September, 1962).

12. J. C. H. Fei and G. Ranis, "Unlimited Supply of Labour and the Concept of Balanced Growth," Pakistan Development Review, Vol. I, No. 3.

13. A. K. Sen, op. cit., p. 61.

14. Ibid., p. 17.

15. None of the national development plans implemented at present in former French colonies in tropical Africa spell out this problem in an analytical way.

16. A. K. Sen, op. cit., p. 13.

17. See in particular C. Clark and M. Haswell, The Economics of Subsistence Agriculture (London: Macmillan, 1964); and R. F. Lord, Economic Aspects of Mechanized Farming at Nachingwea in Tanganyika (London: HMS Office, 1963).

18. P. T. Bauer and B. S. Yamey, The Economics of Underdeveloped Countries (Cambridge: Cambridge University Press, 1959), p. 124.

19. A. O. Hirschman, The Strategy of Economic Development (New Haven, Conn.: Yale University Press, 1958), p. 146. The fact that machine-paced operations are generally more capital-intensive than operator-paced ones is not based on any principle; it is merely a result of empirical observation. Hirschman accepts this view implicitly: "Since machine-paced operations are typically more capital-intensive than operator-paced ones ...". A. O. Hirschman, loc. cit.

20. Based on interview.

21. Law No. 62-47, February 2, 1962. A commentator of this law wrote: "Workers who work without employment contract ... are ill-paid and often less than the smig," Charles F. Brun, Droit du Travail, Vol. I (Dakar: Clairafrique, 1962).

22. Maurice Dobb, "Second Thoughts ...," op. cit.

23. CINAM, "Rapport sur les Perspectives de Développement au Sénégal," Rapport Général sur l'Industrialisation (Paris: CINAM, 1960), Chapter 11-7-12. A numerical example may illustrate implications in terms of labor costs:

23. (cont'd.)

	Per Month
Average cost of labor in France (all workers)	58,800 cfa
Average cost of African labor in Senegal	24,000 cfa
Average cost of expatriate labor in Senegal	230,000 cfa
Then, 120 workers in France cost	7,056,000 cfa
100 African workers in Senegal cost	2,400,000 cfa
20 expatriates in Senegal cost	4,600,000 cfa

Total labor costs for 120 men:
France   7,056,000 cfa
Senegal   7,000,000 cfa

(Source: Annuaire Statistique, op. cit.)

24. P. T. Bauer and B. S. Yamey, op. cit., p. 125. See also:
     P. T. Bauer, "Regulated Wages in Under-developed Coun-
     tries," The Public Stake in Union Power, Philip D. Bradley,
     ed. (Charlottesville: University of Virginia Press, 1959).

25. CINAM, op. cit.

26. Ibid.

27. R. S. Eckhaus, "The Factor-Proportions Problem in Under-
     developed Areas," American Economic Review (September,
     1965). Eckhaus acknowledges his indebtedness to F. M.
     Bator for this point.

28. A. O. Hirschman, op. cit., p. 152. For comments on the
     concepts of process-centered versus product-centered ac-
     tivities, see: A. O. Hirschman, ibid., p. 151.

29. RIT Sud Sénégal 1957 (Kaolack: Labor Inspectorate, 1958),
     p. 153.

30. RIT Sud Sénégal 1956 (Kaolack: Labor Inspectorate, 1957),
     p. 9.

31. Assuming that expatriate firms do not depart from present
     policies, it is to be expected that international agree-
     ments enlarging the product-market beyond Senegal's borders
     (e.g., a West African Common Market) would increase capital-
     intensity by making it possible to enlarge the scale of
     production.

32. By that expression we mean that African firms can use
     marketing activities and innovations, etc., of larger

32. (cont'd.)

 expatriate firms, which constitute, in their perspective,
external economies. A somewhat similar situation was
found in Pakistan where "small firms may wish to remain
small, since they stand to do better outside the reach of
factory legislation and under the umbrella of an oligopo-
listic price structure." G. Ranis, "Production Functions,
Market Imperfections and Economic Development," <u>Economic
Journal</u> (June, 1962), p. 345.

12

LABOR POLICIES AND
INDUSTRIAL
DEVELOPMENT

BALANCED GROWTH IN SENEGAL

From its statements and from the National Plan, it appears that the government of Senegal intends to allocate investment in such a way as to achieve balanced growth of the sectors of the economy. Is there a good case for initiating a process of balanced growth in Senegal?

Early literature on balanced growth is closely linked to the idea of a "big push" of investment expenditure and to lowering costs through external economies. Rosenstein-Rodan bases his early article[1] on Allyn Young's analysis of external economies,[2] inaugurating an important stream of controversy around demand-orientated strategies of economic development.

The basic idea of balanced growth in a closed economy, given a determined time-horizon, is simple: "Each industry must advance along an expansion path determined by the income elasticity of consumer demand for its product".[3] The fundamental consideration is that the very narrowness of the market in backward countries, a symptom of underdevelopment, is also a cause of underdevelopment, and that acting on this factor may stimulate economic growth. There is little doubt that the narrowness of Senegal's market constitutes one of the main causes of its low level of development. Thus, there is reason to examine the relevance of balanced growth theories to that country.

Nurkse and Myint distinguish at least three types of balanced growth programs (leaving out those that include more than one country): (i) The first and most comprehensive program embraces the economy as a whole and requires coordination on all fronts, including agriculture; (ii) a narrower version (following Allyn Young's pattern) leaves agriculture out; it includes directly productive investment and overhead (social and economic); (iii) a third version of balanced growth, as put forward by Professor Nurkse focuses on the expansion of the industrial sector, especially that part of industry manufacturing light consumer goods.

The first type of balanced growth program does not seem to have much chance of raising standards of living in Senegal in the light of the past performance of the government, especially in the agricultural realm. As Hla Myint puts it: "Given the logic of the balanced growth path, the rate of development of the whole economy will be determined by the rate of expansion in its slowest moving component part."[4] Undoubtedly agriculture qualifies for the latter role in Senegal, because of its overwhelming economic importance to the economy, and because of lack of technical progress in that sector. Unless a radical improvement in policy-making and implementing occurs it is questionable whether development of Senegal in the short run and the medium run should be tied to that of agriculture if this can be avoided. In the long run, however, it is clear that agricultural development will be a conditio sine qua non for economic growth, since over three-quarters of the population derive their main source of income from that sector.

The second version of balanced growth may appear more attractive for Senegal. However, the very narrowness of the market in the initial period of the exercise may provide a source of difficulties in the short run and medium run. The success of such a program including overhead investment requires large public funds for transport, energy, communication, education, public health, etc. Many of these investments are subject to indivisibilities and discontinuities in the production function limit the degree of flexibility during the development process. It is often not possible to balance "lumpy" investments in a reasonable way (i.e., at a socially acceptable cost) in a small economy; productive investment might lag behind nondirectly productive investment. It is doubtful whether, even if sufficient public funds were available, such a program would be the best possible strategy for raising income and growth rates in a country of slightly over three million inhabitants with less than $200 GNP per head per year.

The narrowest version of balanced growth may well be the most adequate for Senegal since it could develop from the already diversified manufacturing sector. Labor is not lacking and high returns to capital might make investment possible.

However, it is doubtful in view of the short-term time-
horizon in industry whether investment would in fact be
forthcoming. Nurkse is fully aware of the fact that his
analysis is limited to the demand side of the development
process and does not imply that the supply side is any less
relevant: "We have been considering one particular facet of
our subject. The more fundamental difficulties that lie on
the supply side have so far been kept off-stage for the sake
of orderly discussion."[5] In present conditions of political
uncertainty and pessimism on the part of industrial entrepreneurs, adequate supplies of private capital cannot be taken
for granted.

Moreover the point was made by E. S. Mason[6] that not only
is capital not available in perfectly elastic supply, but
"Implicit in the balanced growth argument is the assumption
that entrepreneurship, both in the sense of managerial capacity and of ability to recognize investment opportunities, is
available in unlimited supply. If entrepreneurship, however,
is a--if not the--scarce factor ... It may ... be impossible
to exploit simultaneously the large number of complementary
incentives of a stronger sort than are implied in the equal-
returns-at-the-margin goal of balanced growth" to stimulate
entrepreneurship if the latter is sluggish and in short supply. In Senegal, only expatriate entrepreneurship could, at
very high cost, fill the gap between requirements and indigenous supply. Given the present pessimism of foreign investors,
it is doubtful whether availability of entrepreneurship can be
assumed in the next few years in quantities such as to make a
balanced growth program feasible.

Availability of data and structure of decision-making are
also important, as in the case of choice of techniques. Authors differ in their judgements as to the degree of centralization required for successfully carrying through a balanced
growth program.   V. V. Bhatt suggests that "Planning or pro-
gramming ... is an integral part of ... balanced ... growth."[7]
This view is shared by W. Arthur Lewis, Paul Streeten and
S. K. Nath. Nurske suggests first that coordination might be
effected within the private sector,[8] but later draws a distinction between "balanced growth as a method and balanced
growth as an outcome or objective"[9] and accepts the need for
"alternative possibilities" such as central planning. It is
evident that the structure of decision-making in Senegal does
not conform to a need for government influence on investment
coordination in industry. Given the competitive character of
international private firms operating in Senegal (competition
on an international scale) and reluctance to invest caused by

a feeling of political uncertainty, the possibility of private
firms co-ordinating their investment programs on their own
over a period of several years can safely be ruled out.

We will not come back to the question of data; suffice it
to remind that V. V. Bhatt, in his discussion of balanced
growth, suggested that "Balanced growth discussion implies
more or less perfect knowledge of the constraints of condition-
ing factors such as technical and demand relations, propensity
to save, possibilities relating to foreign trade and assistance and the growth of the labor force."[10] Even though for
policy-making purposes availability of refined data needed for
thorough academic discussion may not be indispensable, it must
be borne in mind that aggregate variables and parameters often
lack sense in a dualistic society; they must be broken down
into indigenous and expatriate realms, and this further complicates the problem of data.

Assuming, however, that the necessary prerequisites concerning decision-making structure and data were realized, the
question remains whether small African countries lend themselves to be the starting point of balanced growth processes.

In Senegal, as in many other African economies, the
structure of industry is strongly marked by the colonial past.

Industrialization did not, in fact, deeply modify the
colonial pattern of economic flows. There are two groups of
industries in Senegal: (i) Those which process domestic
products (groundnuts, phosphate, tuna fish, etc.) for export
and (ii) those which process imported raw materials and semi-
finished goods for sale on the domestic market; the two groups
of industries parallel each other and merely constitute inter-
ruptions in the traditional colonial import-export flows:
Capital, energy, semi-finished goods, some raw material,
skilled labor and management are imported; output mainly consists in light consumer goods. There is no "heavy industry"
in Senegal.

A table of industrial intermediary consumption established in 1959 shows how little interdependence there is between industries in Senegal. Sub-sectors often buy intermediary goods within themselves (i.e., some firms buy their
inputs from other firms in the same sub-sector).

TABLE 56

Domestic Intermediary Consumption in Industry (1959) Senegal

(in million cfa francs)

Products:	Industries:										Domestic Intermediary Consumption			
	(1)	(2)	(3)	(4)	(5)	(6)	(7)	(8)	(9)	(10)	(11)	(12)	(13)	(14)
(1) Fats-Oils	190													
(2) Wheat-Flour		1200												
(3) Candy-Soft Drinks				10										
(4) Meat Cans														
(5) Chemical Ind.					50						.	180		
(6) Construct. Mat.						120					.	1280		
(7) Metal Eng.	30		20	150		30	160	40	40		. 10	430	30	
(8) Woodwork							190	10	80		.	120		
(9) Textile & Leather		110	40								.			
(10) Matches, Tobacco											.			
(11) Misc. Ind.		10	10	10		40	10	20	20	10		20		
(12) Public Wks. & Constr.		30	10	20	10	10	20	10	20		10	2010	10	120
(13) Energy		50	60	20	10	20	20	20	90			60	230	10
(14) Mining		10			40									

Total Domestic Intermediary Consumption: Manufacturing Industries
(excluding agriculture & services)   (within dotted frame) :   2,630,000,000 cfa.
       Public works, construction,
       energy and mining: 5,290,000,000 cfa.

Total Imported Intermediary Consumption: Manufacturing Industries: 4,230,000,000 cfa.
(excluding agriculture & services)
       Public works, construction,
       energy and mining: 3,110,000,000 cfa.

Source: La Planification en Afrique Noire (Paris: Ministère de la Coopération, 1964), Vol. V, Tables 27 and 28.

For industry as a whole, domestic industrial inputs represent 52 percent of total industrial inputs. Domestic intermediary consumption within the manufacturing industry represents 38.3 percent.

The following table shows what percentage of inputs is constituted by domestic inputs for exchanges within manufacturing industries. Nil means 0 percent domestic input:

TABLE 57

Percentage of Domestic Inputs

	(1)	(2)	(3)	(4)	(5)	(6)	(7)	(8)	(9)	(10)	(11)
(1) Fats-Oils	25			100							
(2) Wheat-Flour		88	nil								
(3) Candy-Soft Drinks		nil	nil								
(4) Meat Cans											
(5) Chemical Ind.	nil	nil	nil		25	nil		nil	nil	nil	nil
(6) Construction Mat.						100					
(7) Metal Eng.	100	100	100	100		100	21	80	100		100
(8) Woodwork								70		nil	
(9) Textile & Leather	52	50						100	9		
(10) Matches, Tobacco											
(11) Misc. Ind.	100	33	50	100		66	100		50	50	nil

Source: La Planification en Afrique Noire (Paris: Ministère de la Coopération, 1964), Vol. V, Tables 27 and 28.

On a total of forty inter-industrial exchanges (manufacturing) thirteen do not include any imported inputs; thirteen do not include any domestic input.

Interviews with industrial managers confirm the lack of inter-dependence of Senegalese industry (E-8). Groundnut-oil manufacturers declared that they depended almost 100 percent on domestic inputs (excluding capital and expatriate labor); all other industrial firms interviewed depend almost entirely on imported inputs (except for unskilled and medium-skilled labor).

The different segments of the industrial sector are ill-
integrated among themselves as industry as a whole is ill-
integrated into the Senegalese economy. Backward linkages
connect Senegalese industry with foreign firms; industrial
growth in Senegal increases industrial activity abroad. The
growth of any one segment of the industrial sector has few,
if any, repercussions on other local industries, just as
growth of the industrial sector as a whole has little influence on the growth of the traditional sector.

Multiplier effects are exerted abroad rather than in
Senegal; in no way do industries constitute a "leading sector"
likely to constitute a sound basis for national economic
development.

Thus, it is possible in the case of Senegal and of most
other small African economies to subscribe to H. W. Singer's
judgement: "The doctrine of balanced economic growth has
severe limitations in its applicability to underdeveloped
countries. While it rightly insists on marketing difficulties
as a cause of low-level equilibrium and rightly shows that the
marketing difficulty can be overcome by a broadly based balanced investment program, it fails to come to grips with an
even more fundamental problem of underdeveloped countries,
i.e., the shortage of resources"; furthermore, "while supply
of goods may create its own demand, unfortunately in underdeveloped countries demand for factors does not create its own
supply."[11] The lack of prospect for massive capital inflow
into Senegal and the leakages through foreign linkages bring
us to examine alternative demand-orientated policies for
industrial development.

EFFECTS ON FACTOR AND PRODUCT MARKETS
OF CHANGES IN WAGE POLICY

Demand for industrial goods can be increased (a) at constant real wages, by enlarging employment or (b) employment
remaining constant, by increasing real wages and purchasing
power of industrial workers. There are several reasons for
focusing on the problem of influencing demand by acting on
wages.

Firstly, the present wage-pattern does not provide a
satisfactory standard of living to industrial workers; the
national wage rate--although it is above equilibrium--is inferior by more than 15 percent to the "minimum budget" of
unmarried unskilled workers, as worked out by government
services, while most workers have to support a large family as
well as themselves.

A second reason is that the government has few means of influencing economic policies in private industry. Political factors and inefficiency of administration restrict the government's possibilities of action in this respect. However, the administrative cost of using the wage-determination machinery is low, and the implementation of possible measures can be efficiently controlled without involving complex practical aspects--as would be the case of company taxation, price control or reploughing of profits. The government would remain entirely free, while implementing a wage policy, to intensify its efforts to develop the traditional sector of the economy.

The question of alternative wage policies will be posed in the following terms: What would happen if industrial wages for African workers rose by, say, 20 to 25 percent?

There would be effects on the factor market and on the product market.

Effects on the Factor Market

On the demand side, costs of production would be affected by a rise in wages; employment might decrease as a result. The wage policy of the government should therefore be expressly tied to increasing pressures for Africanization in private industry.

Gradually replacing expatriate by African employees might reduce labor costs considerably. Presently, about 8.1 percent of the industrial labor force is composed of expatriates; these absorb 42 to 48 percent of the industrial wage-bill (the lower figure will be used in this chapter). 91.9 percent of the industrial labor force is composed of Africans; these absorb little more than half the wage-bill. The cost-differential between African and expatriate labor--for the same type of employee--often exceeds 1 : 3. It appears that Africanization can offset the cost of higher wages for Africans.

The following hypothetical model shows this point; it is assumed that (a) productivity-differentials between Africans and expatriates have been ironed out--which is possible over ten years--by adequate training; (b) that the cost-differential between African and expatriate labor remains constant.

It may be recalled that a decline in the number of expatriate employees in public works and construction--total employment remaining constant--led to a significant transfer of purchasing power from expatriates to Africans:

1. Expatriate employees in Public Works
    and Construction:

        1959   :   1,020
        1962   :   788

2. Difference in percent of total 1959 employment:

        about 1.5 to 2   (232 jobs)

3. Percent of wage-bill accruing to African
    employees:

        1959   :   53
        1962-63   :   about 66

4. Difference in percent of 1959 wage-bill:

        + about 24.5

This example shows how Africanization increased African purchasing power in the past.

    The impact of higher wages on production costs would not
be identical for all Senegalese industries; industries which
have high "expatriate-intensity" at present would find it much
easier to offset higher labor costs by Africanization than
those which already have high "indigenous labor-intensity."

    Available data on "expatriate-intensity"[12] makes it
possible to differentiate Senegalese industries. It is
assumed that Africanization at the managerial level is out of
the question; this excludes 2.6 percent of the labor force
from Africanization. It leaves 5.5 percent (expatriate foremen, lower technicians and clerical staff) of the labor force
for Africanization. In the event of a 20 percent wage increase, 740 jobs would have to be Africanized to keep the
wage-bill constant, representing 2.25 percent of total labor
force; in the event of a 25 percent wage increase, 920 jobs
would have to be Africanized to keep the wage-bill constant,
representing 2.8 percent of total labor force. If these
values are added to the "floor" to Africanization (managerial
posts, representing 2.6 percent of labor force), it appears
that firms that have an "expatriate-intensity" (percentage of
expatriate manpower on total employment) of over 5.4 percent
are likely to be able to offset a 25 percent wage rise through
Africanization at the foreman and secretarial level; firms

that have an "expatriate-intensity" of over 4.85 percent are likely to be able to offset a 20 percent wage rise through Africanization.

Firms can be ranged into three groups, according to their present "expatriate-intensity": (i) In a first group are firms which have a low "expatriate-intensity" (less than 2.6 percent); these have already Africanized most nonmanagerial jobs and would be adversely affected by any rise in African wages; (ii) in a second group are firms which have an "expatriate-intensity" comprised of between 2.7 and 5.4 percent; these could compensate part of the additional labor costs by Africanizing, but would probably be unable to offset them entirely that way; (iii) in a third group are firms most likely to be able to offset a 25 percent wage increase through Africanization at the nonmanagerial level; these have an "expatriate-intensity" of over 5.4 percent.

TABLE 58

"Expatriate-Intensity"

	Approximate "expatr.-int."
	%
Group 1 Low "expatriate-intensity" (under 2.6%)	
Transport	2.0
Most Textile Firms	2.2
Group 2 Medium "expatriate-intensity" (2.6% to 5.4%)	
Other Textile Firms	3.0
Salt Extraction and Processing	3.2
Miscellaneous Industries (biscuits, sweets, bedware)	3.3
Matches	3.7
Soft Drinks, Biscuits	4.4

(cont'd)

Table 58 (cont'd)

Group 3   High "expatriate-intensity"
                    (over 5.4%)

Beer and Soft Drinks	5.5
Tobaccoware	6.0
Public Works and Construction	6.0 +
Footwear	6.3
Food Industries (other than already mentioned)	8.0 +
Cement	8.2
Agricultural Machinery Manufacturing	8.8
Groundnut-oil Industry	7.5 - 10.0
Energy and Waterworks	10.0
Flour Milling Industry	8.0 - 13.2
Mining Industry	17.0
Chemical Industries	20.0 +

Source: Ministère du Travail, Statistiques de la Sécurité
          Sociale (Dakar: roneoed, 1964); RIT Sénégal 1958
          and following years (Dakar: Labor Inspectorate,
          1959 ff.).

     The only industries to be seriously threatened by a rise
of 20 or 25 percent in African wages are textile and transport.
The former has already achieved a very high degree of Africanization and enjoys high tariff protection; there is plenty of
room in the textile industry for increasing the productivity
of African manpower through adequate training. The transport
industry belongs to the public sector and could be excluded
from wage increases for the private sector.

     The striking feature of Senegalese industry is that the
great majority of industrial enterprises fall into the third
group: They would be in a position to offset a 25 percent
increase in African wages by Africanizing some supervisory and
clerical jobs.

                    *   *   *

     The likelihood of a policy of higher wages resulting in
actual Africanization depends mainly on political pressure by
the government. Competition is great in neither of the industries mentioned; many of them could continue operating with
their present "expatriate-intensity" after a rise in wages, by
reducing profits or increasing retail prices.

                    *   *   *

It has been found that young Senegalese react positively to economic incentive in the choice of a job. School-leavers from vocational schools were interviewed two or three years after leaving school.[13] Justifications given by former pupils who changed from the sector for which they had been trained to another one (usually from industry to commerce or administration) focus on wages; wage statistics confirm that former pupils change sector only when wages are higher than in industry; the price system effectively influences the choice of a job.

The fact that most transfers from the sector pupils were trained for to another one were from industry into commerce or administration, suggests that an over-all minimum wage system discourages school-leavers (particularly the more gifted ones) from entering industrial employment. Industrial work is notoriously harder than commercial or administrative work; as long as administration and commerce offer equally well- or better-paid jobs than industry, school-leavers are likely to behave as they do at present: They will continue to be discouraged from entering industry which they consider as a poor substitute for clerical work--they will continue trying to become office clerks, shop attendants or "assistant primary school teachers." Studies of Senegalese wages mention several striking examples of distortion of the price system in favor of nonmanual jobs:

Typical Examples of Wages in Senegal (1965)* [14]

African shop attendant in Dakar (Woolworth-type
     department store)   :   144 cfa per hour
                                                      = 25,000 per month

Skilled worker in manufacturing
     industry (VIIth wage-grade)   :   134,25 cfa per hour
                                                      = 23,250 per month

Assistant primary-school teacher
     (first year)   :   18,000 cfa per month

Skilled worker in manufacturing
     industry (VIth wage-grade)   :   18,200 cfa per month

*   assuming 40-hour week.

Productivity of industrial labor would be favorably affected by a modification in the minimum wage system in as far as it would direct a larger proportion of able pupils

leaving vocational training schools into industry. So far,
only less gifted pupils contemplate taking up manual jobs;
this is one of the reasons for which Senegalese industry still
relies on recently urbanized labor for meeting its requirements. A breakdown of minimum wages into two rates--basically,
one for industry and one for services--might enable the government to discriminate temporarily in favor of industry.

Until now, the government could not act in a discriminatory way on industrial--as opposed to other--wages. Its over-
all minimum wage-rate system was initially introduced in
France. In the latter country, a stage of development has
been achieved where there is no need for radical structural
changes, but rather for marginal modifications: Thus, the
distribution of the working population between agriculture,
commerce, administration and industry will remain fairly
stable in the foreseeable future, with only minor modifications. In developing countries requirements are utterly
different, and what is sought by governments is precisely radical structural changes, a modification between the relative
importance of different sectors of the economy. A policy of
industrialization might benefit from the institution of sectoral wage rates.

Will the minimum be operative? In theory it is conceivable that competition for labor might lead commercial
employers and the administration to increase their employees'
wages as industrial wages rise. This would offset attempts
to redistribute high quality labor. However, in the present
situation, effective wages are strongly influenced by the
government and such pessimistic perspectives can safely be
ruled out; moreover, it is doubtful whether the commercial
sector--which shows signs of regression since the end of the
colonial period--where wages represent a very high proportion
of total costs, would contemplate increasing its wage-bill.
There is an excess of supply over demand for low- and medium
skilled labor in Senegal: There is no reason to believe that
wages in commerce and administration would follow industrial
wages if the over-all minimum wage system were replaced by a
sectoral system, and industrial wages raised above other
rates.

*   *   *

Replacing less than 1,000 expatriates by Africans would
make it possible for most industries to increase African wages
by 25 percent without influencing production costs. Gains
from Africanization are so considerable, given the present
wage structure, that additional costs due to (i) temporary

productivity-differentials between Africans and expatriates
and (ii) setting up adequate training programs would not
counterbalance them. The Senegalese government could, with
the help of the ILO, improve the quality of its own manpower-
training institutions so as to alleviate the financial burden
of Africanization in private industry thereby lessening risks
of unemployment in the short run resulting from increases in
industrial wages.

Effects on the Product Market

Africanization and higher industrial wages for African
employees would result in shifting a considerable fraction of
income from the hands of expatriates into those of African
consumers. In the case of a 20 percent increase in African
wages (and Africanization of about 740 jobs), 11.6 percent of
the wage-bill would be transferred from expatriates to Senegalese; in the case of a 25 percent increase (and Africanization of about 920 jobs), 14.5 percent of the wage-bill would
shift.

Most expatriates regard Senegalese products as "inferior"
and have a strong preference for imported consumer goods;
their propensity to spend on imported goods is much higher
than that of the local population. Economic accounts for 1959[15]
indicate what proportion of expenditure on various goods is
spent on domestic productions and on imports; they give an
idea of the likely effect of shifting a fraction of the wage-
bill from expatriates to Africans on expenditure and on the
balance of trade:

TABLE 59

Final Consumption of Households (1959)

Products	African Consumption (in billion cfa)	European Consumption (in billion cfa)	Share of expenditure spent on:	
			Domestic Production by Africans	Imports by Expatriates
			%	%
Fats & Oils	2.52	0.20	96.5	75.0
Grains & Flour	7.97	0.18	54.0	83.0
Sugar, Sweets, Drinks	2.38	1.00	58.0	91.0
Meat & Tinned Food	4.81	1.57	93.5	30.0
Chemicals	0.57	0.10	23.0	100.0
Woodware & Furniture	0.74	0.24	100.0	17.0
Textile & Leatherware	7.69	2.40	68.5	100.0
Tobacco & Matches	1.08	0.07	100.0	100.0

Source: La Planification en Afrique Noire (Paris: Ministère
de la Coopération, 1964), Vol. V, Tables 27 and 28.

Africanization would undoubtedly increase demand for
domestic industrial goods and might ease Senegal's balance of
trade difficulties by reducing imports, depending on the
import content of domestic manufactures on which no data are
available, and on possible changes in African workers' marginal
propensity to import.

The propensity to save of expatriates is much higher than
that of African employees who hardly manage to save any fraction of their income at all. Expatriate savings are almost
all transferred to Europe.[16] In so far as a shift in purchasing power from expatriates to Africans would reduce transfers
of personal savings abroad, it would further increase the
volume of domestic demand (the wage-bill remaining constant).

*   *   *

What would be the effects of higher wages on demand for
specific widely consumed goods by industrial workers? Interviews with industrial workers make it possible to analyze relationships between income and expenditure on certain goods.
Although it is unsafe to try to establish income elasticities
of demand on the basis of data available, trends can be de-
tected. It is assumed that there is a parallel between reactions of industrial workers to changes in income, and the
behavior of workers belonging to different income-groups at
one point of time (1964-65). Detailed breakdown of relationships is given in Appendix H.

Workers are ranged into three income-groups: (i) "Lower
income-group": Basic wage of less than 16,000 cfa francs per
month, (ii) "medium income-group": Between 16,000 and 25,000
cfa per month, (iii) "higher income-group": Over 25,000 cfa
francs.

An upward shift of all African wages in industry by 25
percent would involve transferring a large fraction of the
labor force from the "lower" into the "medium" income-group; a
relatively small fraction of the industrial labor force would
be transferred from the "medium" into the "higher" income-
group.

Data suggest some trends in a field in which no previous
research has been done. It seems that the probable effect of
increased incomes for African industrial workers on demand
would vary according to income-group and product:

Probable Reactions to Higher Wages

1.   Strong increase in demand for lower income-group

> Clothing
> Sugar
> Housing (housebuilding)

2.   Increase in demand mainly for medium income-group

> Rice
> Groundnut oil

3.   Increase in demand in all cases

> Clothing
> Sugar

This suggests that Senegal's main industries (food, textile and housebuilding) would benefit from a change in the
wage pattern in favor of African workers; consumption of
groundnut oil would probably increase for the better-off
workers (earning around 20,000 cfa francs at present). The
effects of higher income on expenditure on imported goods,
other than rice (which will eventually be met by domestic
production), are not known; but the larger part of the workers' expenditure goes on domestic goods and services.

INDUSTRIAL WAGES AND THE EXTENDED FAMILY

The Urban Part of the Problem[17]

The main objection to the efficacy of influencing demand
by increasing industrial wages is based on the belief shared
by most industrial employers that income effects predominate
over substitution effects with the African labor force. When
income rises, workers are faced with a choice between maintaining their previous consumer pattern and standard of living
while enjoying more leisure and working shorter hours--"income effect"--and giving up leisure (the relative price of
which rises as wages increase) and working longer hours--"substitution effect." The two effects work in opposite directions; if workers reduce their effort as a consequence of
higher wages, the favorable effect on demand does not appear.

Employers generally believe that the main effect of higher incomes for African workers is to induce "marginal" relatives from the land to migrate into town, adding to the industrial workers' burden. The weight of traditional family solidarities offsets the main spring of the wage policy envisaged--
a positive response of demand to higher wages. If this argument is correct, then increasing the wage-bill for Africans
would not necessarily increase the workers' income per head
because of additional migration.

Some employers imply that there is a deterministic relationship between the level of wages and the size of the family
living at the workers' homes; others, without departing from
this view, add that the amount of money sent by industrial
workers to the home villages increases as wages rise and that
the standard of living of workers would remain at a constant
level if wages rose.

This argument can be dealt with first. There is abso-
lutely no evidence that the flow of money transferred by
industrial workers to relatives in the country is related to
income in a positive way.[18] If anything, evidence suggests

that younger workers tend to send larger amounts of money home
than older ones.

On the other hand, there is reason to believe that the
first and basic argument expressed by industrial employers is
not without foundation. Leaving out young workers living at
their own fathers' homes who are not in charge of a family
themselves, the coefficient of correlation between (i) total
wage, and (ii) number of people maintained at the worker's
home is positive; for 170 workers, the coefficient was found
to be + 0.3862. It is possible to calculate the association:

$$\frac{\text{Sum of } (Y \cdot F)}{\text{Sum of } (Y^2)}$$ where Y is income and F the number of

people maintained at the worker's home. This might be interpreted as an "income elasticity of 'demand for a larger family'" or marginal propensity to increase the size of the
extended family as income rises. The value found was
+ 0.3192.

A diagram shows that, although there undoubtedly exists a
relationship between income and size of extended family, this
relationship is by no means as close as Senegal's industrialists believe it to be:

FIGURE 10

Relationship Between Income and Extended Family

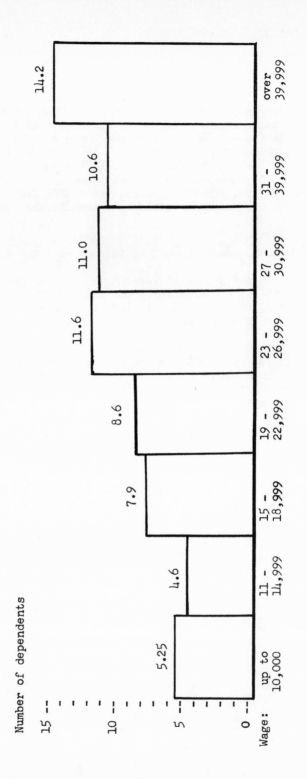

Source: Interviews.

220

There is no increase in the number of dependents maintained at
the worker's home up to about 15,000 cfa per month wage (including social wages). There is an increase between about
15,000 cfa and 25,000 cfa; then there is a "plateau" up to
about 40,000 cfa, Above that level, the number of dependents
increases sharply.

The size of the extended family seems to be related to
age as well as to income. In very broad terms, a relationship can be shown between the size of the extended family and
the worker's age:

TABLE 60

Worker's Age and Extended Family

(coverage: 181 workers)

Number of Dependents	Under 31	31 to 40	Over 40
less than 6	63%	21.5%	17.0%
6 to 9	26%	35.0%	22.5%
10 and more	11%	43.5%	60.5%
Total	100%	100 %	100 %

Source: Interviews: W 15.

The influence of age on the size of the extended family
may be stronger than that of wage: Young workers with high
incomes support smaller families than old workers with low
wages.[19] This is hardly surprising since the nucleus of the
extended family consists of the workers' wives and children.

Ownership of a home also plays a role in attracting relatives from the country. About one-third of all workers interviewed lived in their house (or were engaged in the process of
paying for it); of these, 70 percent support 10 people or
more. Among nonhouseowners, proportions are different: 44
percent of them support less than 6 people; 33 percent 6 to 9
people; only 23 percent support 10 people or more.

Since previous data showed that the purchase of a house
is one of the first results of increased income, this very

attraction may endanger the success of a policy of higher
wages, by indirectly increasing the size of the extended
family. A modification of public health laws on housing--
limiting the number of persons allowed to dwell in rooms of
certain sizes--might provide a protection against the inflow
of relatives "from the bush" responding to the development of
housebuilding.

Tribal factors may also play a role in influencing the
size of the extended family; it seems that the Lebu and the
Toucouleur have larger families to maintain than the Wolof and
Serer. The Lebu are the original inhabitants of the Cap Vert
area and do not have to migrate long distances to go and live
with wage-earning relatives. This may explain why their
extended families are larger than average. The Toucouleur are
a traditionally migrating people from the border of Mauritania.[20] Both Lebu and Toucouleur come from rural areas that
are only about half as prosperous as the groundnut basin in
which the Wolof and Serer live. Further sociological research
is needed here that reaches beyond the scope of this study.

Although there undoubtedly exists a relationship between
income and number of dependents fed at the workers' homes,
other factors play a role as well in influencing the size of
the extended family. Emphasis laid on several explanatory
factors aimed at throwing doubt on the assumption that there
exists a simple deterministic relationship between any one
factor and the influence of the extended family on economic
policies.

But it is not possible to have a full picture of the
economics of extended families so long as the analysis remains
confined to the urban side of the problem.

The Family System at Work

This section attempts to go further in analyzing the
mechanism of migration which has so crucial an influence on
economic analysis.

The extended family can be broken down into (i) the
"nuclear family," consisting of the workers' wives and children, and (ii) the "nonnuclear family" (NNF) including relatives other than the workers' wives and children who are
permanently maintained at the workers' homes. The number of
wives varies according to age and income; but this is true
both in urban and in rural areas, and does not necessarily
affect comparisons between income levels in town and in the
country.

It seems that the size of the workers' nonnuclear families is related to the relative prosperity of rural areas from which workers originate. In his thesis, Claude Adam estimated the per capita income of Senegal's rural population.[21] Since the thesis was written, neither productivity per man nor crop prices have changed significantly.

TABLE 61

Income per Head in the Agricultural Sector
(Monthly)

Area	Main Tribes	Income (cfa francs)
Groundnut area:	Wolof and Serer (about 1.7 million)	2,050
Senegal River:	Toucouleur (about 350,000)	1,200
Cap Vert:	Lebu (40,000)	1,260

Source: Claude Adam, L'Equilibre Vivrier au Sénégal (Montpellier, Doctorate Thesis, Faculty of Law, 1964), Vol. I., p. 67.

The average per capita income of workers included in our sample (i.e., income/extended family) is 2,075 cfa francs per month. There is a relationship between (i) the per head income-differential between the workers' area of origin and their present place of work, and (ii) the size of the nonnuclear family; the coefficient of correlation between these two variables was found to be - 0.89. Workers from poorer areas are more likely to attract a large number of "relatives" than those coming from more prosperous regions.

*   *   *

Similarly, it appears that transfers of money by industrial workers to relatives "in the bush" may keep the size of the nonnuclear family down by reducing the income-differential between village and industrial center in favor of the former. Nonnuclear families of workers who regularly transfer a fraction of their wages to their relatives on the land are smaller than those of workers who do not "bribe their relatives away":

Average size of nonnuclear family

Workers who do send money regularly: 3.09 persons

Workers who do not send money regularly: 4.65 persons

These transfers can also be viewed as part of a traditional system of social security; workers who wish to retire
in their home villages once they have reached pensionable age,
send money more often than those who wish to retire in town;
transfers constitute savings that ensure that workers will be
maintained in their home villages after retiring:

TABLE 62

Transfers and Retirement

	Workers sending money home regularly	Other workers
Workers wishing to retire in village:	60%	40%
Workers wishing to retire in town:	19%	81%

Source: Interviews: W 20, W 64.

Transfers of money to relatives also vary according to the
ethnical group; the Serer and Toucouleur workers in the sample
sent larger sums of money home than the Lebu and Wolof: (W 4,
W 64)

Average Transfers
(per month in cfa)

Wolof workers	292
Serer workers	950
Toucouleur workers	818
Lebu workers	115

Nonnuclear family

Wolof workers	3.98 persons
Serer workers	2.48 persons
Toucouleur workers	4.87 persons
Lebu workers	5.88 persons

There is a coefficient of correlation of - 0.68 between the amount of money sent home regularly by industrial workers and the size of their nonnuclear families.

*   *   *

An interpretation of this data is that urbanization is related to economic factors and that Senegalese farmers perceive economic opportunities in spite of their illiteracy. There is a tendency towards equating rural and urban income per head through traditional "extended family solidarities."

*   *   *

The question that remains to be answered is why, if there is no great discrepancy between income per head on the land and in industrial centers, should peasants continue to migrate to town? Is there an economic reason for migration?

A partial answer can be found in a "fallacy of composition" illustrating Samuelson's allegation according to which "each individual naturally tends to look only at the immediate effects upon him of an economic event,"[22] and where an action that appears advantageous to an individual is not advantageous if a large number of people do the same.

Young farmers focus their attention on comparing their present personal income with the expected income which they would have in town.

Two cases must be examined by the farmers: (i) In case they succeed in finding a job, their income is expected to be much higher than on the land; (ii) but young farmers also count with the possibility of not being able to find a job, or at least not immediately; in this event, they know that they can live at a relative's expense, so that their income per head would not be inferior to their present income on the land. The main consideration about migration is that, given the Senegalese tendency towards equating income per head within the framework of extended family solidarities, in no case would the farmer's income after migration be lower than on the land; it is expected to be higher or, at worst, equal.

Young migrants are not immediately concerned with the extended family's impact on their own income: Even if they have to send a substantial fraction of their wage home, the remainder is still higher than their income before migration. It is only once young men have found a stable job, have

married and have had children, that the extended family becomes a real threat to their standard of living: Once workers
have a house, relatives come to live with them--temporarily or
permanently--with almost total certainty. After a few years,
the income-differential per head is offset; however, the effort required in industrial employment (in terms of hours
worked per year) remains higher than that required on the land.

Objectively, migration is economically advantageous to
individual farmers if (a) they find a job in town, and (b)
during the initial period of employment, before they settle
for good and relatives start "moving in."

*   *   *

As long as it is possible for farmers to leave the agricultural sector without reducing food consumption per head for
the population as a whole (i.e., as long as the supply elasticity of export products of the economy remains positive),
migration to town may continue, spurred by the anticipation of
permanently higher incomes, at no economic risk. In fact,
this anticipation is fallacious in the longer run because of
the tendency to equate income per head in town with that in
the village. However, once wage-earners carry the responsibility of maintaining a substantial fraction of their extended
family, it is too late for them to return to less-well-paid
occupations.

A hypothetical model of decision-making can be shown to
represent the stages of migration:

Hypothetical Model: Migration decision-making

Phase 1. Individual farmer compares his present income with
          current industrial wage rates;

Phase 2. Individual farmer receives the assurance that he can
          "come and stay with a relative" in town even if he fails
          to find a job, and that migration will not affect his
          income adversely;

Phase 3. Individual farmer goes to town and starts living at
          a relative's expense, looking for a job; this means that
          his income has not substantially varied, but that the
          "effort-price of income"[23] has decreased when compared
          with what it was in the village;

FIGURE 11

Hypothetical Model = Migration, Effort and Income per Head

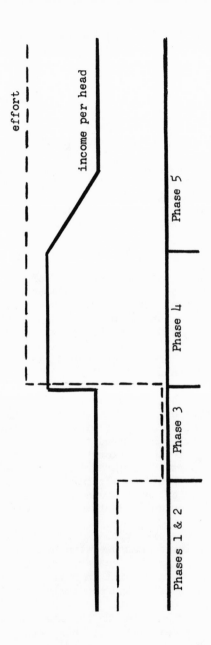

Phase 4. A job is found (usually by relative trying to rid
     himself of migrant); despite having to send a fraction of
     his wage home, the worker enjoys a higher income than he
     used to on the land;

Phase 5. Relatives start "moving in" after the worker has
     shown that his job is stable and has "settled for good"
     (possibly marriage and birth of children induce rela-
     tives to come); the initial income-differential is
     eventually offset by weight of extended family; once
     it is offset, the worker is socially entitled to stop
     the inflow and to refuse feeding additional relatives;
     the effort required remains constant; it is higher than
     what it used to be on the land--but the "effort-price of
     income" increases as income per head decreases;

Phase 6. See Phase 1.

The only profitable periods for the migrant are phase 4 and
part of phase 5; phase 4 does not last for a very long time
(the propensity of workers to marry is high). Migration
implies a long-term loss because income remains constant in
the long run while the "effort-price of income" increases.

     This social phenomenon has consequences for economic
analysis and policy.

     Although some association seems to exist between income
and size of extended family, a policy of higher industrial
wages aimed at increasing demand for industrial goods is not
necessarily condemned to failure. However, in so far as increases in the workers' extended family lower urban income per
head, instead of obtaining a change in the pattern of consumption one would obtain merely a geographical shift in demand
from agricultural areas to urban ones; moreover, agricultural
production would decline as urban unemployment grew.

     Therefore emphasis of a policy of industrial growth
should lay on manpower training and Africanization rather than
on raising real wages for industrial workers. Africanization
would--the wage-bill in real terms remaining constant--create
demand for domestic productions by increasing the propensity
to spend on domestic goods of the population of Senegal's
cities as a whole and by diverting sums at present transferred
abroad (expatriate personal savings) to domestic consumption.

     The government of Senegal might influence resource allo-
cation on the factor market in a way favorable to industry by

replacing the over-all minimum wage-rate system inherited from
France by a system of multiple rates (industry versus services); nonindustrial wages could remain frozen for a period
of time sufficient to have favorable effects on the quality of
recruitment in industry. Industrial wages could be maintained
at a constant real level, which would act as a factor of dis-
sociation between industrial and nonindustrial wages.

The gains from Africanization might be reflected in
price-reductions on the product market. These would have an
impact on the consumer population as a whole and not merely
on urban wage-earners. Reducing the retail price of goods
sold in the villages (canned food, cloth, building materials,
etc.) would increase the real incomes of farmers and might push
the frontier of the money economy further back by making it
attractive for marginal consumers to increase their output of
cash versus food crop. There is not enough information on
consumer patterns in agriculture for any meaningful quantitative appraisal to be given, but there is no doubt that Senegalese industry would benefit greatly if farmers could eventually abandon their role of "marginal consumers" of manufactured goods; the "marginal" character of rural consumption
of industrial goods is certainly not unrelated to the
extremely high prices for manufactured goods in Senegal.

Evidence suggests that policies increasing agricultural
productivity and income might reduce the rate of migration to
town. Such policies might have a strong effect on the rate of
urban unemployment if they focused on the poorer areas (Senegal River, for example).

Leaving the domestic framework, we must now replace
Senegal into the broader perspective of a post-colonial
situation.

Notes to Chapter 12

1. P. N. Rosenstein-Rodan, "Problems of Industrialization in
    Eastern and South Eastern Europe," Economic Journal (June-
    September, 1943).

2. Allyn Young, "Increasing Return and Economic Progress,"
    Economic Journal (December, 1928).

3. R. Nurkse, "Balanced Growth and Specialization" in Equi-
    librium and Growth in the World Economy (Cambridge, Mass:

Harvard University Press, 1961). Quoted in A. Mathur, "Balanced versus Unbalanced Growth--A Reconciliatory View," Oxford Economic Papers (July, 1966).

4. Hla Myint, The Economics of the Developing Countries (London: Hutchinson, 1965), p. 130.

5. R. Nurkse, Problems of Capital Formation in Underdeveloped Countries (Oxford: Blackwell, 1953). See Paul Streeten, "Unbalanced Growth: A Reply," Oxford Economic Papers (March, 1963).

6. E. S. Mason, "Monopolistic Competition and the Growth Process in Less Developed Countries: Chamberlin and the Schumpeterian Dimension," in Monopolistic Competition Theory: Studies in Impact, R. E. Kuenne ed. (New York: John Wiley & Sons, Inc., 1967), p. 86.

7. V. V. Bhatt, "Some Notes on Balanced and Unbalanced Growth," Economic Journal (March, 1965), p. 97.

8. R. Nurkse, "Balanced Growth and Specialization," op. cit., p. 248.

9. Ibid., pp. 279-280. See V. V. Bhatt, "Theories of Balanced and Unbalanced Growth: A Critical Appraisal," Kyklos, Vol. 4, 1964.

10. V. V. Bhatt, "Some Notes ..." op. cit., p. 89.

11. H. W. Singer, "Balanced Growth in Economic Development," in International Development: Growth and Change (New York: McGraw-Hill, 1964), p. 46.

12. Ministère du Travail, Statistiques de la Sécurité Sociale (Dakar: roneoed, 1964); RIT Senegal, 1958, and following years (Dakar: Labor Inspectorate, 1959 ff.).

13. Enquêtes Relatives à la Situation des Anciens Elèves des Etablissements d'Enseignement Technique (Dakar: Centre National d'Orientation Professionnelle, 1963 and 1964).

14. Charles F. Brun and Georges Vermot-Gauchy, "La Question des Salaires au Sénégal," Afrique Documents (Supplement No. 2, 1965).

15. La Planification en Afrique Noire, Vol. V (Paris: Ministère de la Coopération, 1964), Tables 27 and 28.

16. Based on interviews with bank managers, Dakar, 1964.

17. Much of this section relies on workers' interviews.

18. Relationship between Basic Wage and Transfers of Money
     Home:

Money sent home: (cfa)	none	up to 1,000	more	total
Wage: under 16,000	57.5%	19%	23.5%	100%
16-25,000	61.5%	21%	17.5%	100%
more	85.0%	nil	15.0%	100%

     coverage: 183 workers.

19. Isolating young workers (under 31) earning more than
     16,000 cfa per month and older workers (over 40) earning
     less than 16,000 cfa per month, we can compare the res-
     pective sizes of extended families:

Extended family:	1-5 people	6-9 people	over 9 people	total
younger workers	50%	40.0%	10.0%	100%
older workers	26%	30.5%	43.5%	100%

     coverage: 43 workers.

20. Ministère de la Coopération, La Moyenne Vallée du Sénégal
     (Paris: PUF, 1962); this work shows the result of
     several years of socio-economic team work in the poorer
     areas of Senegal.

21. Claude Adam, L'Equilibre Vivrier au Sénégal (Montpellier,
     Doctorate Thesis, Faculty of Law, 1964), Vol. I., p. 67.

22. P. A. Samuelson, Economics (New York: McGraw-Hill, 1955),
     p. 6.

23. Phase 3. "Effort" is measured in days'-work per year
     (about 120 in agriculture); the concept of "effort-price
     of income" is borrowed from Elliot Berg, in Q.J.E. August,
     1961, op. cit.

CHAPTER **13** POLITICAL ECONOMY OF
POST-COLONIALISM
IN SENEGAL

It is clear that much of Senegal's economic future depends on the possibility for the government to incluence policies of private (mostly foreign) industrial firms. Now that it has been seen how industrial labor policies and economic development policies have been inadequate, it is necessary to broaden the picture and to place economic problems of industrial labor into a political perspective: Senegal's economy depends on foreign countries (mainly on France) for capital formation, know-how, monetary stability and balance of trade equilibrium. Senegal, as a member of the Franc zone, is not free to determine its own policy in the economic realm which is so overwhelmingly dominated by foreign enterprise. The crucial question to be asked is not: "What should the government do in order to achieve its aims in industrial policies?", but "what can the government do?" Constraints and advantages of the Franc zone system influence economic analysis policies very deeply. They will be analyzed in a first section. The question of the actual freedom of maneuver and bargaining power of the Senegalese government --faced with foreign capital, technical knowledge, etc.--will be posed as a way of assessing changes of effective industrial policies to be implemented in the next few years.

THE CONSTRAINTS OF THE FRANC ZONE
SYSTEM AND ECONOMIC GROWTH

The Franc zone constitutes a closed "liberal" system; it can be called "liberal" in that it involves freedom of transfer of men and capital within its boundaries; it is "closed" because it discriminates against nonmember-countries.

The former colonial power exerts economic domination over tropical African member-states of the zone (including Madagascar). French firms produce a very large share of GNP in the "peripheral" member-states and political agreements restrict the local governments' freedom to plan their economies.

A 1961 Report to the Economic and Social Council (Paris) shows the distribution of French private investment in overseas countries in 1959. It shows that Senegal occupies a relatively insignificant part in the system. Algeria is not included in the table; about half of French private investment overseas was in Algeria.[1] Of the remaining part, 60 percent was located in Morocco and Tunisia, 30 percent in tropical Africa. Senegal's share of French private investment was about 5 percent, of which one-half in commerce and one-half in industry. The Senegalese industrial sector represents about 1.25 percent of the French capital stock invested overseas.

TABLE 63

French Capital Stock Overseas, Excluding Algeria (1959)

Country	Percent
Morocco	50.9
West Africa	13.9
Tunisia	10.9
Madagascar	7.3
Vietnam (S)	6.6
Equatorial Africa	5.1
Cameroon	3.1
Cambodia	1.4
Togo	0.8
Laos	negligible
Total	100.0

Source: Overseas Department, CNPF, Paris.

It appears that "The French West African economy was an integral part and a minor part at that, of the over-all economy of the ... Franc zone and as such was subject to decisions made in Paris. These decisions affected both the governmental and private sectors."[2] A fortiori the Senegalese economy fits in as a small part of a vast system. The corollary of bloodless decolonization has been that France effectively secured protection of its economic interests overseas, perpetuating the highly centralized structure of the zone. Banks, shipping companies, insurance companies, public works firms all operate on a world-wide scale; policy decisions

concerning any part of the system are weighted in the light
of policies and interests of the companies as a whole.

*   *   *

The French government signed detailed agreements with
13 African states (Senegal, Mauritania, Ivory Coast, Dahomey,
Niger, Upper Volta, Togo, Central African Republic, Gabon,
Tchad, Congo (Brazzaville), Cameroon and Madagascar). These
agreements influence economic, monetary and financial policies of the "peripheral" countries.

A preferential regime has been established between
France and her former African dependencies. It is based on
(i) free circulation of goods and exemption from customs
duties--except for specific "infant industries" protected
with France's consent; (ii) quota and guaranteed prices for
export produces--as far as these are compatible with EEC
provisions.

Monetary agreements perpetuate the colonial pattern of
international trade: The African states' receipts and expenditure in foreign exchange are centralized in Paris. Each
state has a right to withdraw from an account with the Fonds
de Stabilisation des Changes of the zone. Currency reserves
are kept with the Fonds. Participation in the zone also entails the existence of an account with the French Treasury
for each African state; unlimited amounts of Francs can be
exchanged through this account for local currency and vice
versa. This solves the African states' balance of trade
problems since deficits constitute a burden to the common
reserves of the Franc zone and do not affect local currencies. The extent up to which countries can draw on this
account depends on the readiness of the French government to
provide them with funds.

The rate of exchange between French Francs and African
currencies is fixed. No national devaluation is possible
without France's previous agreement. France has wide control over banking and credit overseas: Freedom of capital
transfers (to and from France) is the rule; in return,
France commits herself to guarantee full convertibility to
African currencies, at the prevailing rate of exchange.

It is implicitly but clearly understood that French aid
to African states depends on the observance of the rules of
the zone. Aid consists of capital investment, technical
assistance--France's over-all expenditure in technical assistance is second only to that of the USA--purchases of primary

products under conditions favorable to African economies, and subsidies balancing current expenditure of African govern- ments when needed. Agreements on strategic goods give France priority of exploitation and purchase for oil products and derivates, uranium, etc., in these African states. Estab- lishment agreements ensure that citizens of any member- country enjoy the same civil rights as the citizens of any other member-country, when in the territory of the latter. Circu- lation of persons is free. With a view to coordinating poli- cies on general matters (in economic, monetary and financial questions as well as in foreign affairs. France and her partners agreed to consult each other periodically at the highest level. The same applies to educational policies.[3]

Artificial conditions for economic development are thus created. African countries are relieved of some of their problems (balance of trade adjustments, balanced public budg- ets, etc.). French private investments are heavily protected against foreign competition and from intervention by African governments. Attempts to evaluate respective gains and loss- es for African countries and France have not been conclusive. Some distortions affecting industrial labor must be pointed out.

One of the paradoxes of the Senegalese economy (and of several other Franc zone countries) can be solved when placed into the context of Franc zone agreements. In these coun- tries there is (a) a shortage of agricultural labor leading to inelastic food supply, and (b) a large pool of urban un- employment. In normal circumstances, any country that cannot produce enough food for the growing mass of urban unemployed must face grave tensions: Either there is widespread mal- nutrition or, if food is imported, and export earnings do not increase, reserves of currency decline and balance of trade problems may arise.

Franc zone agreements relieve African member-states of such tensions. Young farmers leave their villages and mi- grate to town; since employment is stable, urban unemploy- ment grows. Agricultural production decreases as a result of migration.

It is because France backs Senegal's balance of trade deficit that large quantities of food can be imported in the face of stagnating productivity per man in agriculture.

The possibility of a fall in cash crop prices in line with EEC agreements aiming at ending French subsidies of African cash crop (notably groundnuts) must be viewed in the

light of rural migration. Should peasants respond to lower
cash crop prices by migrating in greater numbers to town, it
is most likely that Senegal's balance of trade situation will
deteriorate even further. Senegal will, in that way, increase, if anything, her dependence on French aid for balancing her balance of trade (in the absence of migrant labor
from neighboring countries to help Senegal's agriculture).

    In this perspective, Franc zone agreements increase sup-
ply elasticity of labor of the country as a whole, and--since
there is little or no industrial growth--they increase urban
unemployment, encouraging traditional extended family solidarities to act as a leveling instrument for incomes per
head. As long as food can be imported without increased exports earnings, there are few reasons for which young Senegalese should remain in agriculture.

                    *   *   *

    A second effect of Franc zone agreements on growth is
that capital is free to flow out of Senegal. Because of the
narrowness of the domestic market, marginal efficiency of
capital is low in Senegal; lack of investment opportunities
causes capital funds to flow out of the country. There are
indications that industrial profits are high in expatriate
enterprises--the "fast rate of amortization and high rates of
profit"[4] were already noted. Capital outflows constitute a
loss for the domestic economy. Because of secrecy of transfers within the Franc zone, accurate measurements are difficult; a document of the Dakar agency of the Banque Centrale
des Etats de l'Afrique de l'Ouest, the central bank of the
monetary union of West Africa, is interesting in this regard:
It gives evidence of massive outflows of capital from Senegal:

TABLE 64

Net Movement of Funds
Between Senegal and the Rest of the World

(In billion cfa francs)

1961	- 2.6
1962	- 7.0
1963	-13.6
1964 (6 months)	- 5.3*

*The latter figure includes receipts from sales of 1963-64
groundnuts, which means that the yearly capital inflow
outflow balance for 1964 is in all probability of the same
order of magnitude as in 1963.

Source: BCEAO Agence de Dakar, Rapport Mensuel, October
         1964.

It is interesting to relate balance of capital flows to
French economic aid. In 1963, French aid in capital investment amounted to 2.2 billion cfa francs; groundnut price
subsidies amounted to about 5 billion cfa francs.[5] These
sums exclude France's participation in constructing Dakar
University and wages for French technical assistants. It is
extremely difficult to appraise the over-all magnitude of
French aid because of lack of comprehensive documents. From
1965 onwards, EEC agreements stopped France from continuing
subsidizing groundnut prices directly.

Senegal's balance of payments suggests that outflows of
factor income payments exceed inflows of capital on account
of aid and private investment. Thus, while Senegal has balance of trade difficulties, it also is a net exporter of income (mainly profits of expatriate firms) to France. In this
way, French business firms in Africa help France ease her own
balance of payments difficulties. The relationship between
aid and factor income payments is very hard to specify, but
it seems (notably on the basis of the Guinean experience)
that (a) close political ties between African countries and
France usually go together with (b) aid and (c) absence of
restrictions on factor income payments abroad on the part of
African countries; conversely, there is no case where one
or two of these factors exist and not the third. Whatever

the rationale behind French aid--motives are extremely involved and complex--it does less than compensate, in the
short run, outflows of factor income payments in the case of
Senegal.

*   *   *

By forward and backward linkages as well as through financial flows, the induced effects of industrial activity in
Senegal are transmitted to France rather than felt in Africa.
In a study by Professor François Perroux's institute in
Dakar, it is expressly stated that "profits ... leave the
country ... and induced effects are exerted on the economy
from which capital originates."[6]

*   *   *

The Franc zone framework perpetuates pre-independence
ties with France which create artificial conditions for
economic growth, notably by facilitating migration from the
agricultural sector to town and by rendering massive outflows of capital possible.

The underlying problem of industrial development on a
national basis is manifestly a political one: It is to a
large extent that of the relationship between African governments and expatriate firms, that generate a large fraction of
GNP on African territory.

The question which arises is that of the relationship
between expatriate firms and the government. What are the
powers of the government over these firms?

THE GOVERNMENTS' DEPENDENCE IN MATTERS OF INDUSTRIAL POLICY

Larger industrial firms operating in French-speaking
Africa belong to international financial groups; these control enterprises throughout the world. They have "their own
rules, their own objectives and their own time-horizons for
economic development";[7] these are in no way necessarily
spontaneously compatible with government plans in the countries in which they operate. They need not even coincide
with such basic objectives as maximizing investment, employment and output in any particular plant.

Within the Franc zone, decisions concerning different
sister-plants located in different countries are taken at
headquarters--usually in Paris--on the basis of a marginal
calculation: Maximizing the over-all economic advantage of

an industrial concern may involve reducing output and employment in one plant and shifting production to another one;
when new industrial firms are established in the Ivory Coast,
in Cameroon, etc., these investments affect already existing
industries in other Franc zone countries adversely. Fear of
political change involving a breakdown of the Franc zone
system (e.g., national tariff barriers being set up in the
future) and the will of traditional investors to retain their
favorable trading position--even if production does not pay
off, the latter is thought of as a necessary condition for a
firm to sell its product in African countries--lead French
firms to invest in different parts of the zone rather than
expanding already existing plants. Concern for spreading
political risk between several countries is often so strong
that factories operate below capacity for years, until economic growth broadens the market.

     This is particularly harmful to the Senegalese economy.
When new plants are being established in former client-
countries of Senegal, the latter's share in total production
declines. As the first French colony in tropical Africa to
industrialize--with the whole market of tropical French
Africa in mind--Senegal is particularly hard hit by industrialization in other parts of the Franc zone.

                    *   *   *

     For several reasons, the government of Senegal's in-
fluence on decisions taken in Paris, on which the rate of
industrial investment, of industrial employment and of development depend, is limited. The possibility of France reducing aid restricts the government's freedom to exert strong
pressure on private industry. Indeed, the scope of possible
measures by which the government could influence the private
sector--notably the industrial sector--in view of greater
participation to national development is very limited.

     Nationalization and expropriation are ruled out by lack
of indigenous managers and higher technicians, indeed one of
the symptoms of economic underdevelopment. The possibility
of the government acquiring shares of the capital of expatriate firms is limited by lack of available funds and by reluctance on the part of expatriate owners to give away control
over their firms to local governments.

     In a way, in limiting its influence in the private sec-
tor, the government of Senegal responds to rewards "for good
behavior" as outlined by M. Bronfenbrenner: "The expectation

of rewards for good behaviour, in the form of future foreign
loans and investments, seems already much more efficacious
in forestalling expropriation than is the fear of punishment
or the bolstering of 'friendly' governments by military aid.
When a country stands to lose more in future aid by confis-
cating private capital within its control than it stands to
gain from the value of the capital at stake, it usually ex-
ercises a seemly caution and restraint in dealing with private interests affiliated with sources of potential largesse.
But the hope or the promise of reward must be substantial,
plausible, and contemporary."[8]

Although there might be a theoretical case for financing
long-term development through expropriation, there are severe
limiting factors in the case of Senegal: In the short run,
Senegal and the other Franc area countries in Africa do not
have a sufficient number of technicians to run industry in
the event of expropriation; it cannot be supposed that expatriate personnel would remain on duty; also, these countries are dependent on (a) trade connections with advanced
economies for importing necessary semi-finished inputs for
industry and for marketing industrial exports--it is questionable whether these connections would survive expropriation, since commercial and industrial interests in the advanced countries are closely interwoven; (b) nonfinancial
aid in the form of inflow of know-how, technical assistance,
etc. There, too, one may doubt whether these inflows would
continue after confiscation; it seems likely that the
technological gap between the confiscated industries severed
from these flows, and competing industries in other countries would widen in time, unless know-how can somehow be
"bought" against political pressure from advanced countries.

Even in matters of tax policy, freedom of the Senegalese government is very limited indeed. According to the
government, the upward limit of company taxation has been
reached in Senegal since 1962-63;[9] it is generally believed
by government officials that additional taxation might deter
further inflows of private capital into Senegal and divert
them to other countries instead. The basic attitude of the
government is to wait for more capital to be invested rather
than to use the tax mechanism to channel more of the present
industrial resources into the National Development Plan.

Measures of price control instituted in 1942 on the
basis of war legislation were revived in 1964 in the framework of economic development policies.[10] These measures were
taken with the consent of the Chamber of Commerce and Industry; indeed, the government consulted French manufacturers

on what rates to apply and their advice was followed. Price
control is aimed against imported goods in competition with
local ones; it also fits into the government's policy to
favor African enterprise in trading and to reduce the share
of trade held by the Syro-Lebanese. The price-control machinery has been used so far against the latter rather than
indiscriminately; in fact, Syro-Lebanese traders are recognized to be more experienced and more efficient than most indigenous ones. Whatever use is made of war legislation on
prices, the situation is totally different now from what it
was in 1942: At that time there was demand-inflation and
black market; today high prices are mainly effects of imperfections in the structure of the market. It is questionable
whether the government can contain the present rise of retail
prices by enforcing war legislation. According to employers'
interviews, none of the expatriate industrialists concerned
was adversely affected by price control.

A further way in which the Senegalese government is influenced in economic policy-making is the presence of many
hundreds of French technical assistants in most realms of
public administration. French businessmen are also usually
consulted by the government before any significant step in
economic policy is taken. The number of Senegalese trained
in economic analysis is far too small at present--and will
presumably remain so at least during the next five years--for
the present situation of "technical" dependence to change
rapidly. It has already been noted that over 90 percent of
secondary school teachers are French. Perhaps most striking
for a country advocating "African socialism" is the foreign
presence in the commission in charge of working out Senegal's
Second National Plan:

TABLE 65

Composition of the Planning Commission

	Senegalese Members	French Members
"Vertical" Commissions (each in charge of a sector of activity)		
Agriculture	15	17
Energy, Mining, Industry	16	16
Hydraulics	9	14
Commerce, Tourism	13	9
Public Health, Social Affairs	20	7
Infrastructure, Transport, Construction and Town Planning	17	16
Education, Manpower Training and Information	23	9
"Horizontal" Commissions (each in charge of a type of problem)		
Finance	15	16
Structure of Development	14	7
Aménagement du territoire	11	12
Regionalization of Planning	19	5
Studies and Research	3	20
Synthesis	26	17+
Total	199	165+
In percent	54.5%	45.5%

Note: The same person may occur more than once; members of
         commissions are counted as such, not as individuals.
Source: Chambre de Commerce de Dakar.

Of the Presidents and Speakers of the 13 commissions, 14
are Senegalese and 12 expatriates; in all commissions but
one, either the Speaker or the President is French.

*   *   *

Unofficial pressure is exerted on the administration
when government policy does not correspond to objectives on
which the private sector had agreed. The First National Plan

included provisions for the industrial sector of Senegal's economy. They did not correspond to the plans of foreign firms and were consequently not implemented, except in oil research (largely financed by French public funds).

The disparity between the National Plan and the plans of private firms is best shown in a table:

TABLE 66

Plan and Realization of Plan

(In billion cfa)

	Plan's Objective	Actual Realization	Percent
Gross capital formation in Industry			
1961	4.2	0.75	18.0
1962	8.2	1.61	19.6
1963	8.2	(less than	
1964	6.4	(1962	
Gross capital formation in Mining and Oil Research			
1961	1.5	1.73	115
1962	1.5	0.96	64
1963	1.5	(less than	
1964	1.5	(1962	

(Net investment amounted to 15-20% of gross capital formation)*

Increase in industrial employment 1961-1964

	10,000	nil	nil

*ISEA found that net investment constituted only 14% of gross investment in Senegal in 1959, a year which was found to be typical.

Source: Ministère du Plan, Plan Quadriennal de Développement 1961-1964 (Dakar: roneoed, 1961), pp. 108-110; Comptes Economiques du Sénégal 1959-1962 (Dakar: Services de la Statistique, 1964).

Plans of private firms were so much at divergence with
the National Plan, that a "revised plan" had to be worked out
in 1963-64. The Second National Plan reduced the share of
investment to be financed by the private sector.

It is quite clear that some private firms "are powerful
in all respects, possibly more so than national states--they
can exert 'counter-planning' against national development
plans. This fundamental obstacle is far more important than
mere technical difficulties of development planning."[11]

If industrial policies involving coordination between
the government and the private sector are to succeed, a systematic exchange of information on respective plans and in-
tentions must be organized. Despite emphasis laid by spokes-
men of "African socialism" on dialogue between various parts
of the economy, no such coordination has yet been established: Outside the public sector, the government is unable
to anticipate and to plan matters such as educational policy,
investment programs, etc., with any means of ascertaining
their compatibility with the private firms' own plans.

Discrepancies between (i) big public investments in
infrastructure (financed by foreign aid) and almost negligible net investment in directly productive sectors, and
between (ii) government policies of manpower training and
great reluctance to Africanize in the private sector, are
most harmful economically, socially and politically. Establishing a permanent institutional framework for liaison between the administration and expatriate firms, preferably at
the highest level--representatives of foreign headquarters
of private firms--appears to be necessary if any national
plan is to prove workable; this could be done by indicative
agreements on investment, production targets, employment,
taxation, etc., between the parties. The present type of
dialogue between various Ministries and representatives of
the local Chamber of Commerce is vague and politically in-
effective.

Unless African governments and international firms
operating in their territories recognize the need for coordination of plans (implying that governments should act in
such a way as to be taken seriously enough by expatriate
concerns, for the latter to commit themselves for several
years), the colonial pattern will continue to be the rule:
Expatriate firms will not necessarily contribute through
their own labor policies and their investment plans to
creating more favorable conditions for government policy
being successfully implemented.

*   *   *

To use the wage-determination machinery for forcing
expatriate firms to Africanize is a poor substitute for dialogue among equals; the transformation that is necessary,
on the part of expatriate employers, is not so much a quantitative one as a qualitative one: What is needed is for
them to depart from prejudice and attitudes dating back to
the colonial period--to reappraise their ideas on African
labor, notably on its potential, and to realize that to a
large extent future productivity of African labor is their
own responsibility. But faute de mieux, given the present
balance of power between the government and private industry, the wage-determination machinery might be used to
achieve a gradual transformation of industry through Africanization. However, a great deal of political pressure may
have to be exercised on private firms, for such policy to
achieve its end.

The likelihood of the government exercising such pressure depends, in turn, on the degree to which it might affect
the political relationship between the French and the Senegalese governments. The margin of freedom of African governments ultimately depends on their position vis-à-vis the
former colonial power. Internationalization of foreign trade
(at present about 85 percent of Senegal's exports go to
France, 72 percent of her imports come from France) and of
aid--especially in technical assistance--are two ways by
which a new international economic relationship might be
established. This would facilitate a rearrangement of Franco-
African political relations by giving African governments
more power over private industry.

It seems that within the present political set-up there
is little African governments can do to implement policies
in the private sector; it seems that to a large extent
greater political freedom of the government towards international firms depends on greater political and economic independence vis-à-vis the former colonial power. Unless greater
political independence is gained, urban unemployment will in
all likelihood continue to increase, thus increasing economic
dependence towards aid-giving countries (mainly France), private plans will continue not necessarily to be compatible
with national plans, employers will be unlikely to adopt more
labor-intensive methods of production and to train greater
numbers of Africans than hitherto. Unless the government
succeeds in increasing agricultural productivity, trends of
GDP and industrial output will continue to vary--as they do

now--mainly according to purely fortuitous elements such as
the climate.

*   *   *

Alternative policies for industrial labor may increase employment and industrial output, mainly through adequate Africanization. While it is theoretically in the power of the Senegalese government to implement such policies, the government
is practically not in a position to do so, because of dependence
on the former colonial power. A modification in the political
situation of Senegal and of the Franc zone framework may well be
a prerequisite to enforcing government policies for industrial
labor that may increase employment and industrial production
effectively.

Notes to Chapter 13

1. Information communicated by the Overseas Division of the
    CNPF, Rue Pierre Ier. de Serbie, Paris 8.

2. W. J. Foltz, From French West Africa to the Mali Federa-
    tion (New Haven, Conn.: Yale University Press, 1965),
    pp. 38-39.

3. See Les Accords de Coopération entre la France et les
    Etats Africains et Malgache (Paris: La Documentation
    Française, 1964). This study includes an analysis of the
    main features of agreements concluded between France and
    her former dependencies in tropical Africa.

4. CINAM, "Rapport sur les Perspectives de Développement au
    Sénégal," Rapport Général sur l'Industrialisation
    (Paris: CINAM, 1960), Chapter 11-7-12.

5. Information obtained from the French Aid Mission in Dakar.

6. ISEA, Etude d'une Firme dans une Jeune Nation Insuffisam-
    ment Développée (Dakar: ISEA, 1963), p. 65.

7. François Perroux, "Grande Firme et Petite Nation," in
    Rapport Jeanneney (Paris: La Documentation Française,
    1963), Annexes, p. 58.

8. M. Bronfenbrenner, "The Appeal of Confiscation in Economic
    Development," Economic Development and Cultural Change,
    Vol. III, No. 3 (Chicago: April, 1955).

9. This belief is firmly anchored in the minds of Sene-
    galese officials. It rests on a macro-economic ap-
    proach that ignores the dualistic structure of the econ-
    omy and private capital outflows. As an example:
    "Fiscal pressure being near 21% of GDP a ceiling which
    one does not want to exceed" (Speech to Parliament of a
    higher civil servant, in Marchés Tropicaux, May 30, 1964
    Paris). A somewhat more meaningful ratio might be
    based on GNP, instead of GDP figures, that do not ex-
    clude factor income payments abroad.

10. Arrêté of May 11, 1942, instituting a regulation on trade
    and prices in AOF; arrêté of May 20, 1949, setting maxi-
    mum retail prices in AOF; decree of March 8, 1961, on
    retail and wholesale prices based on an arrêté-général
    of September 30, 1954; decree of September 21, 1961,
    reorganizing departments for price-control of the Min-
    istry of Commerce, Industry and Crafts; decree of June
    14, 1962, instituting regional economic control inspec-
    torates; arrêté of September 11, 1962, organizing
    details for implementing the previous decree.

11. François Perroux, Les Techniques Quantitatives de la
    Planification (Paris: PUF, 1965), p. 28.

CHAPTER **14** CONCLUSIONS

Imperfections in the Senegalese labor market are so pronounced that the relevance of a concept such as "market equilibrium with imperfections" becomes very questionable. The
Senegalese case clearly shows how very deeply social factors
should influence economic analysis; economic choices are
complicated by factors such as colonial institutions and
policy-making, the post-colonial economic dependence on
France, the family system, and the political role of trade
unions. Policies based on a strictly economic analysis of
problems of industrial development are likely to fail in
achieving their end.

Government and trade-union policies for industrial labor
aim at maximizing industrial employment in the short run;
they have maintained wages at a constant nominal level since
1961 and advocate the use of labor-intensive methods of production. Why did these policies fail to succeed in raising
industrial employment? Reasons for failure can be placed in
two groups: (a) Inconsistent policies; (b) inadequate or
oversimplified analysis of underlying factors by government
and trade unions.

It is not difficult to find inconsistencies in policies
for industrial labor; labor legislation slows down Africanization (i.e., expansion of Senegalese industrial employment)
by making it expensive for employers to recruit female labor
and by placing greater legal obstacles in the way of employers wishing to dismiss older rather than younger employees;
remediary provisions of labor legislation defeat (although
with limited effects) the government's wage freeze by spreading economic gains to inefficient industries. Likewise, educational policies of the government do not efficiently contribute to reducing the present shortage of skilled and
supervisory Senegalese labor: Vocational schools do not turn
out enough Senegalese willing to take up industrial employment and sufficiently qualified to satisfy industrial requirements. This also slows down the growth of Senegalese

248

industrial employment. Finally, government wage policies
do not contribute to increasing Senegalese employment. They
prove inadequate because they do not discriminate between
industrial and tertiary employment in minimum wage-determination
and therefore do little or nothing to prevent school-
leavers from taking up tertiary employment rather than manual
jobs--even though they may have been trained for the latter.
More important for future employment prospects, the government's policy of crystallizing pre-independence relative
wages (at the request of trade unions) may make it too expensive for future industrial employers to hire skilled and
supervisory Senegalese in preference to French labor.

It has been shown throughout this book that Senegalese
policy-makers have failed to achieve their objectives in
labor legislation, education and wage-determination by continuing to use an institutional framework created during the
colonial period when "assimilation" to France was the main
concern; provisions designed for metropolitan France do not
fit easily into Senegalese society and economy: The family
system, dualistic structure of employment, low level of indigenous productivity, and great poverty of the economy as a
whole are not to be found in France. Trade unions also ig-
nored underlying facts of the Senegalese economy; their policies aimed at maximizing the number of hours worked, their
credit policies, and their lack of concern for workers' education depress productivity and increase employers' bargaining power, while at the same time these policies are designed
to increase employment.

Self-defeating policies and policies that fail to
achieve their aim are usually due either to inadequate analysis of underlying factors or to rigidities in the institutional framework which perpetuate assimilationist policies
that may have been relevant before independence but are now
largely deprived of usefulness.

Wrong conclusions often result from oversimplified
analysis. Government policy is largely based on the belief
that wage-earners constitute an "over-privileged" group compared with peasants; this belief, based on Western-type income comparisons justifies, in the eyes of "African socialists," a general wage freeze for "wage earners." It is
somewhat dangerous to lump civil servants and industrial
workers together in a concept such as "wage earners" in an
economy where industrial workers are almost certainly more
productive than employees in commerce and administration.
But even disregarding this (intentional) confusion, evidence
suggests that there is no wide gap--in terms of income per

head, which is the criterion used by policy-makers--between
rural and urban Senegalese. The family system tends to
equate incomes per head throughout the country; industrial
workers support up to 25 "relatives" on their wages and/or
send money regularly to relatives who remain in the villages.

The family system complicates economic policies on the
supply side. Although it has been suggested that the supply
curve of labor is positively inclined within the region of
existing wages, there is no doubt that the family system acts
as a disincentive to industrial workers. It also contributes
to the workers' indebtedness that keeps down productivity by
creating an atmosphere of uninvolvement in the plant.

The post-colonial situation also complicates economic
policies: (a) Senegal has an expatriate population of about
50,000 and most industrial ventures are owned and managed by
Frenchmen. The multiracial structure of employment is one
of the major forces that keep down Senegalese employment in
industry. Pre-colonial prejudice has not yet disappeared in
many expatriates--this slows down the pace of Africanization.
In a sheltered economy with little or no competition on the
domestic market, the multiracial structure of employment can
remain, as it does, at pre-independence levels in industry,
or at best change only very slowly. (b) The post-colonial
situation also implies that the bulk of existing legislation
was created at a time when France was there to finance the
cost of running assimilationist institutions. Colonial
policy-making in France during the Fourth Republic was socially rather than economically minded and not always the
work of the most competent experts. It concentrated power
in the hands of the colonial administration--being distrust-
ful of colonial employers--and was extremely detailed and
comprehensive. This made legislation both inadequate after
1960 and very difficult to change for a government that does
not wish to break away completely from French traditions.

Above all, it is because of the impact of socio-political
factors on economic life that government and trade unions
failed to achieve their aim--the increase of industrial employment for Senegalese in the short term. By keeping workers poor, the family system makes it difficult for any program of "balanced growth" to succeed within Senegalese industry. Similarly, increases in the workers' income would attract more and more "marginal" relatives to town and, instead
of a change in consumption patterns, there would merely be a
geographical shift in demand from the rural areas to town
and a decline in agricultural output. Therefore, programs of
industrial development should emphasize training and

Africanization rather than creating additional demand through
wage increases. It has been shown throughout most parts of
this book that Africanization might represent a very substantial saving in labor costs to Senegalese industry.

Perhaps the most important effect of social and political factors on economic activity is the preference for capital-intensive factor-proportions in Senegalese industry, despite the existence of surplus labor. Analysis of factor-
proportions in terms of homogeneous factors proves unsuited to
the case of former French colonies in tropical Africa. Actual determinants of factor-proportions appear to be: (i) Extreme scarcity of certain types of labor; (ii) high cost of
labor due to persistence of "assimilationist" wage-determination; (iii) need for expatriate labor that brings total labor costs to levels differing only slightly from those prevailing in Europe; (iv) standardization requiring machine-
paced operations that tend to be more mechanized than operator-paced ones--this trend will be even more marked if Senegal's industry is to compete more in international trade;
(v) monopoly positions and tariff protection which do not encourage managerial initiative and significant departures from
traditional policies. Above all, the dualistic structure of
the capital market discriminates in favor of nonindigenous
firms that have access to cheap capital in Europe, capital
which remains inaccessible to small indigenous firms.

Demonstrably, there is still room for modifying present
factor-proportions, notably for ancillary operations in existing plants and in the case of new industrial plants. Why,
then, does the government, that wishes to increase industrial
employment in the short run, not act in a way which effects
this? The government does have constitutional powers to act
effectively: It could influence factor-proportions by more
specialized manpower-training schemes, by sectoral wage rates,
by changes in labor legislation. It could also lower tariff
barriers and encourage indigenous business (once adequate
training facilities have been set up for training African
managers), by various means such as broadening the scope of
development banks and requesting aid from international
institutions such as the ILO.

An answer is that political factors influence economic
policy; the government of Senegal--as well as those of most
former French colonies of tropical Africa--is bound by agreements with France. In exchange for a stable currency, a
great deal of economic, financial and technical aid, and for
French investment in Senegal, the Senegalese government accepted a "special relationship" that has great disadvantages:

In particular, there is an unspoken but effective agreement
that French business should be interfered with as little as
possible by the government. Capital funds flow freely into
and out of Senegal; Senegal has balance of trade difficulties, and exports capital to France. The freedom of the
government to influence industrial policies in the private
sector is very limited indeed. Industry remains largely a
foreign sphere in the eyes of Senegalese policy-makers;
these are heavily influenced in many ways (French technical
assistance, Chamber of Commerce, French government, cultural
ties, etc.) not to depart radically from pre-independence
attitudes towards private industry. Only a very deep modification in the relationship between government and industry
(which may not be feasible unless an equally deep modification takes place between the Senegalese and the French governments) might make it possible for the Senegalese government to achieve its aim: Maximizing industrial employment
and output in the near future. As long as no new relationship between government and expatriate firms develops, it
might be realistic for national planners to exclude industry
from their plans and to focus on agricultural development;
the government does not have a significant influence on decisions to invest, to recruit, and to train. There is not
sufficient coordination between national plans and plans of
private firms.

This political weakness is one of the essential features
of the Franc zone system in West Africa. Another point that
has been stressed is the fact that urban unemployment is
exacerbated by agreements between France and her overseas
partners. Since currency resources of France and her African
partners are pooled in Paris (so that France's balance of
payments, in fact, includes that of her former overseas possessions in tropical Africa), France so far helped African
countries out of their balance of trade difficulties. This
makes it possible for African countries to import food in
excess of their own import-capacity, so that there is little
or no pressure on farmers to remain on the land and to grow
their own food (or export cash crop). It is far from certain
whether, even in the absence of this type of French aid,
farmers would remain on the land; but the government would
then have better arguments to put forward to encourage farmers to remain in their villages; people would see that migration to town might mean a decline in food consumption.

*   *   *

Social and political factors rather than the intrinsic complexity of economic problems hinder the government from taking measures that would effectively raise industrial employment and output. The family system, the colonial past, and present international agreements all influence economic life profoundly. Policies in developing countries that fail to take noneconomic factors into account are not likely to achieve their ends.

*   *   *   *   *

APPENDIXES

APPENDIX   A   THE STRUCTURE OF THE
EMPLOYERS' ASSOCIATIONS
IN AOF

Two pressure groups protected the interests of French
investors and employers of AOF in France. The Comité
Central de la France d'Outre-Mer (former Comité de l'Empire)
was a "nonindustrial organization."[1] However, the list of
its members shows that French economic interests in the
overseas territories were well represented with the Comité.
The Comité acted, according to its constitution,[2] by "in-
terventions and demands with public institutions and ...
administration." It acted as a pressure group for large industrial and commercial firms with the Ministry for Overseas
France.

The French employers' associations <u>stricto sensu</u> were
organized along the same lines as the trade unions. The
Conseil National du Patronat Français (CNPF) comprises the
representatives of vertical industrial federations and of
horizontal regional unions. Colonial interests were dealt
with by a Comité d'Etudes et de Liaison du Patronat de
l'Union Française (later "pour l'Outre-Mer") (CELPUF/CELPOM).
In 1960 this body was transformed into a Commission des In-
vestisseurs a l'Extérieur.

The main function of the CELPUF was acting as legal adviser to local employers' associations of the colonies. Its
first role was especially important in coordinating the positions of employers bargaining collective agreements with the
local trade unions. Although the CELPUF had no direct authority over the local associations, it was able to influence
their policies in matters of agreed wage rates, wage-
differentials and working conditions, as an adviser.

West African interests were represented in metropolitan
France at a lower level by a number of organizations. The
most influential of these were the employers' associations
of the commercial sector, notably the Fédération Nationale
des Syndicats des Commerçants de l'Ouest Africain (FENASYCOA)
with its regional headquarters at Paris, Bordeaux and

Marseille. The industrial employers' associations were less
centralized than the commercial ones. The Union Intersyndicale des Industries d'Outre-Mer had none of the influence of
its commercial counterpart. This is due to the greater concentration and centralization of commercial firms when compared with industrial ones, in the overseas territories. One
effect of this difference is that bargaining collective
agreements took a much longer time for the commercial than
for the industrial sector. In the case of the former negotiations, constant contact with the metropolitan employers'
associations was necessary.

In Africa, employers' associations were grouped by industry. The interests of commercial employers of AOF are
represented with the Syndicat des Commerçants Importateurs
et Exportateurs de l'Ouest Africain (SCYMPEX) which has its
seat in Dakar. Industrial employers are grouped within the
Union Intersyndicale d'Entreprises et d'Industries (de l'AOF)
(UNISYNDI) also based at Dakar. Being less dependent on
metropolitan centers of decision than the commercial employers' association, UNISYNDI was better able to adapt its political change.

Coordination between the Dakar headquarters of these employers' associations and the local offices in the other capitals of French-speaking West Africa was maintained after
independence (directly and via the Chambers of Commerce).
The main reason for continuing to operate on an international
scale is that many commercial and industrial firms operate in
several countries, while their headquarters are based at
Dakar or Paris.

The relatively marginal position of the Senegalese industrial sector in relation to the whole Franc area explains
how little influence the CNPF in fact exerted on the local
industrial employers' associations during the colonial period. The centers of power were the Paris, Bordeaux and Marseille offices of the commercial employers' association, and
the Dakar headquarters of the industrial employers' association.

Diagram of Employers' Associations (1957)

Local Organizations   Metropolitan Organizations

         SCYMPEX   FENASYCOA ── C   C
        (commerce)   (Paris)   E
                                                  L   N
         UNISYNDI   Union Intersyndicale P
        (industry)   des Industries   U   P
                                   d'Outre-Mer ──┘ F
                                                      F

Notes to Appendix A

1. Constitution, Art. 1.

2. Ibid., Art. 2.

B

A CASE OF SUCCESSFUL
AFRICANIZATION IN
SENEGAL

Interview with the personnel manager of a phosphate
mining and processing company:

The enterprise started from scratch in late 1958. Recruitment was made in the local villages, near the
mining site (about 50 miles North of Dakar). This
corresponds to recommendations by the Senegalese administration. A minority of skilled workers were
recruited in Dakar.

Manpower training was started on a large scale.
From 1958 to 1963 school teachers dispensed general education to the workers. A program of alphabetization was established and implemented over 4
years. Of the 150 workers who followed it, about
60 were promoted after having completed it. The
age group 30-40 years had the greatest proportion
of failures. The younger workers did better.

After 1963 there was a change in policy. The firm
ceased to recruit unskilled workers. Despite pressures from the administration to hire any Senegalese applicants, the company restricted recruitment
to holders of a CEP (having successfully completed
primary school). Since 1960 there are many CEP
holders looking for employment. Technical training
of CEP holders takes place within the firm.

For the higher skills the firm recruits CAP holders.
The main difficulty is the mentality of "spoilt
children" prevailing among technical school-leavers.
This results, among other things, in a lack of
discipline.

Technical training is decentralized. It is given
by expatriate foremen especially recruited in France
for this purpose:

Heads of Departments
train expatriate and Senegalese foremen;

Foremen
train workers.

Special emphasis is laid on training young Senegalese in order to convert them into highly skilled and supervisory workers.

An attempt to Africanize the department responsible for maintenance of the plant (one of the largest of its kind in Africa using capital-intensive complex techniques or processing for taking advantage of the outstanding quality of the raw material) failed. Lack of technical know-how and of initiative on the part of the newly promoted Senegalese forced the firm to re-hire expatriates.

The risks of bad handling of the equipment are enormous. The essential machine in the mine is a drag-line (one of the largest in the world). The cost of this machine is US $2.4 million. A stoppage of production (due to poor maintenance, etc.) costs US $200,000 per hour. In 1964, the firm had not yet amortized its investment costs. The technical optimum had not yet been reached; and in 1963 the cost of producing one ton of phosphate was equal to 200 percent of the retail price (retail price = about US $13 per ton).

The capital of the firm is French, American (USA) and Senegalese (minority share). Management is French and American.

The Process of Africanization

1. Over-all Perspective

	1961	1962	1963	1964 (Mch.)
Management and Foremen				
Manpower:	12	80	98	113
Percent Africans	1.5	7.5	16.0	19.5
Increment	+6	+8.5	+3.5	
Highly Skilled Workers				
Manpower:	152	130	143	196
Percent Africans	41.5	54.0	64.0	83.5
Increment	+12.5	+10	+19.5	

2. Staff in November 1964

	Expatriates	Africans
Management	24	2
Foremen	71	25
Highly Skilled Workers and Salaried Staff:		
a) Salaried Staff	26	-
b) Seventh wage-grade	15	11
c) Sixth wage-grade	-	72
d) Fifth wage-grade	-	120
Skilled Workers		238
Unskilled workers		129
Total	136*	597

*Includes 4 foremen and 26 office employees recruited in Senegal.

3. Detailed case-study of Africanization

T = total manpower; A = African manpower; R = ratio A/T (in percent)

Wage-grades	October 1961			October 1962			October 1963			March 1964		
	T	A	R	T	A	R	T	A	R	T	A	R
Management	15	1	7	23	1	4	26	2	8	22	2	9
Foremen:												
M5	1	-	0	1	1	50	-	-	-	1	-	0
M4	7	-	0	7	-	0	12	-	-	10	-	0
M3	5	-	0	9	-	0	2	-	-	10	1	10
M2	11	-	0	8	-	0	16	3	19	21	4	20
M1	33	-	0	32	4	13	42	11	26	49	15	30
Highly skilled:												
7	30	4	13	48	4	8	44	7	16	34	10	30
6	82	29	35	38	22	60	11	26	63	61	52	85
5	40	40	100	44	44	100	58	58	100	101	101	100
Medium skilled and Unskilled (All Africans)												
Total	480*	330	69	393	259	66	511	377	74	612	488	79

*Includes temporary personnel for constructing the plant.

After a very short period, it becomes increasingly difficult to find marginal candidates for training and promotion. The few gifted workers are easily found out and
trained. External sources of manpower must then be used.

The success of the program depends on being able to
create involvement in the job with the African labor force.
Frequent meetings of managers, staff and foremen help to
achieve this.

One index of successful integration is the evolution of
work injuries:

1961	115
1962	144
1963	74
1964	41 (ten months)

Cadres and foremen spend about one-seventh of their working
time training Africans.

The relevance of this case of successful partial Africanization to other industrial firms depends on their economic horizon. It is possible to enforce similar policies in
firms which can anticipate 20 to 25 years of satisfactory
output levels. Unless this is so, the cost of Africanizing
may exceed the profitability of the operation. This shows
the important role of political factors in manpower training.
Insecurity and lack of coordination between the government's
national plan and the plans of industrial firms are detrimental to both parties.

APPENDIX C WORKERS' STATEMENTS
ON TRADE UNIONS

I. <u>Workers</u> (W 39, W 42, W 43, W 46, W 49, W 50)

1. The unions care about their own interests. They do not
   even know of the workers' existence.

2. Nowadays, the unions disregard the standard of living of
   the workers. This is why they are unable to help. Per-
   sonally, with my income of 12,000 cfa francs per month,
   I spend almost twice as much as I earn. I am caught in
   a vicious circle of which it seems difficult to get out.

3. The unions do nothing. But nothing! They have got
   offices and cars. That is all.

4. This is my third union, because the others haven't done
   anything for me.

5. The unions must understand the situation of the workers
   in order to do something about it. In Senegal there is
   general discontent. The wage-grades are stuck, employers act as they like, life becomes expensive. We work
   day after day and earn barely what we need in order to
   settle our debts for food. When will this system end?

6. I do the same as everyone: Become a member of a union
   without any reason; since everyone is in it one has got
   to join. But the union doesn't make sense. Since I
   started work here, I was never promoted. The unions
   ignore us.

7. Yes, the unions are using us as robots for the time
   being, in order to have their own income. This is why
   I do not want to waste 600 francs for dues.

8. The unions changed a lot. In the first place, the
   honesty and the spirit of union officials are now cor-
   rupted. Before, they were really fighting in a

disinterested way and with force. But now, they are
really weak with the employers.

9. I prefer to give my 600 francs to the mosque, rather
    than for a union card for a union which does not even
    know that workers exist.

10. There are two tendencies in the UNTS (the governmental
    trade union) ... but a majority of workers is always
    deceived in the sense that a union official comes for
    collecting dues, and afterwards, we don't ever see him
    again.

11. The object of the union is to defend our interests and
    also to educate the workers so that they become con-
    scious of their role ... without favoring the employers
    ... as the unions do now. I earn 20,000 francs in the
    seventh grade. In other firms, they make more ...

12. I shall decide whether to vote for UNTS or for UST
    according to my promotion.

13. In the old days, the unions had their <u>raison d'être</u>.
    But now, being in a young Nation, we cannot afford to
    join the unionists in making war on the employers; for
    the more annoyed they become, the less they will come
    and invest here; there would be growing unemployment
    ... and moreover, the unionists are profiteers ...

Economic Information on the 13 Workers

Worker	Wage-grade	Age-group	Literacy	Basic Wage (cfa francs per month)	Persons to Maintain
1	3rd	21-30	+	12,000	1
2	4th	41-50	+	12,425	14
3	4th	21-30	−	15,000	6
4	3rd	21-30	+	12,000	1
5	foreman	31-40	+	26,000	8
6	foreman	41-50	−	21,500	10
7	foreman	41-50	+	48,000	11
8	4th	21-30	+	12,400	8
9	3rd	21-30	−	12,000	5
10	6th	31-40	−	23,000	13
11	7th	over 50	+	20,000	9
12	5th	31-40	−	20,500	4
13	7th	31-40	+	35,000	9

II. Shop Delegates

1. The unions' leaders are all eager to improve their own
    position. There is no regular contact between unions
    and workers. Unionists do not even care for the work-
    ers, because they follow aims of their own. They are
    all corrupted, which makes it impossible for them to say
    "no" to a boss.

2. We regret the lack of contacts between the union and
    ourselves and the absence of congresses during which we
    could express our opinions freely, so as to eliminate
    corrupt leaders who are imposed upon us by the govern-
    ment.

3. The leaders have no time ... they fight for political
    posts in order to make a lot of money; this makes them
    corruptible and enables employers to trample them for
    the time being. Employers have bought the leaders who
    cannot move. Otherwise the bosses will remind them of
    the money they gave them.

4. We cannot afford any strikes ... They would slow down
    progress. The violence of pre-independence times can-
    not continue because it would discourage foreign in-
    vestors from coming to Senegal. But it seems ... that
    this is no sufficient reason for mixing up cooperation
    and weakness. It is desirable that the government
    understand this situation, for people are unhappy.
    Prices are rising and wages not ... For these reasons,
    people are discouraged with the unions. Only the top
    leaders are satisfied but they forget that if they are
    satisfied, they owe it to the rank and file's exist-
    ence.

5. Whatever the union, there are hardly any honest new
    members for now people are discouraged because of the
    inertia of the unions, and their lack of contact with
    the workers.

6. Nowadays the only reason we join a union is to deceive
    our employers. They are under the illusion that we are
    protected. But in fact the unions are busy with other
    things than protecting us. The leaders do not have any
    time for this ...

7. Unions are there, nowadays, as masks vis-à-vis employ-
    ers who believe that they should not commit offences
    against labor legislation, by fear of being sued by

the unions.   But nothing of this kind would happen
to them ...

8.   Here, the unionized workers split into two groups.   The
     satisfied ones join the UNTS and the dissatisfied ones
     the Cartel.   For it seems that the Cartel has better
     contacts with the workers than other unions.

     The general feeling among workers and shop delegates is
that, because of the uninvolvement of union leaders in industrial matters, and of the government's policy of favoring
foreign investment, employers have much stronger bargaining
power than during the colonial period.

APPENDIX D COLLECTIVE AGREEMENTS
IN FORCE

Collective agreements signed under the provisions of the nondiscriminatory Labor Codes of 1952 and 1961 applicable to the whole of Senegal.

Date	Industry	Scope
7/ 6/1956	Construction and Public Works	AOF
11/16/1956	Commerce	AOF
10/ 8/1957	Mechanical Engineering	AOF
12/16/1957	Auxiliary Transport Employees	AOF
4/25/1958	Banking	AOF
5/17/1958	Textile Industries	AOF
7/ 4/1958	Fats and Oils Industries	AOF
7/12/1958	Chemical Industries	AOF
7/19/1958	Food Industries	AOF
3/28/1958	Pension Scheme*	AOF
5/23/1959	Electrical Energy	Senegal
12/17/1959	Public Road Transport	Mali Federation
4/14/1960	Mining	Mali Federation
9/28/1960	Printing	Senegal
1/10/1963	Clothing Industries	Senegal
Under consideration	Insurance	Senegal

* The Pension Scheme for AOF was worked out by bilateral
  bodies and was given the legal status of a collective
  agreement.

i.   Pattern of expenditure of the African population of Dakar (1960-1961) compared with the official standard budget used by the government for evaluating the cost of living of unskilled workers.

Income per head in cfa francs (monthly)

Expenditure in per mille:	Under 3,000	3,000-4,999	5,000-8,999
Food	702	623	535
Tobacco and Cola	28	25	23
Other daily expenses	93	80	64
Clothing	30	67	100
Durables	10	17	32
Rent	39	45	59
Services	19	39	60
Transportation	34	32	29
Miscellaneous	45	72	98

Source: Situation Economique du Sénégal (1962), p.75.

Engel's Law is confirmed by the results of the survey: Food expenditure decreases in relative terms as income rises; Tobacco, cola nuts, transportation seem to be prime necessity items -- their proportion in total expenditure decreases slightly as income rises; all other items (except "other daily exp.") increase their share as income rises and can be regarded as less essential expenditure. It seems that the expenditure on rent has been underestimated.

Expenditure and Official Standard Budget

	A. Observed values	B. Official values
Food, Cola and Tobacco	730	423
Durables	10	48
Rent	39	192
Clothing	30	90
Other expenditure	191	247

The main difference is that in food expenditure; this does not appear to have been weighted heavily enough in computing the administrative standard budget on which the minimum wage is (theoretically) based. In fact, about 70% of the poorer workers' income is spent on food; this is particularly important since food prices increased more rapidly in the past than other prices.

ii. Evolution of prices according to the government's computations for the standard budget.

The standard budget is computed on an annual basis; it does not constitute an index of cost of living, but is one of the few reliable sources of information available.

Figures are worked out by the government's statistical services; they differ from similar statistics worked out by trade union and employers' associations' representatives to the consultative commissions; these statistics are internal administrative documents which have not been published since 1958.

Prices of goods other than food have not been as carefully observed since independence as those of food. This explains partly the underevaluation of rises in prices and the apparently greater stability of nonfood prices.

Taking September 1957 as a basis (= 100), the evolution
of yearly expenditure takes the following course:

Date	Food expenditure	Nonfood expenditure	Total yrly. expenditure
September 1957	100	100	100
April 1958	91.5	103	100.5
February 1959			101.5
April 1959			103
September 1959			110
November 1960	105.5		115
March 1961	105.7		114
December 1961 -			
January 1962	120		125
April 1962	102	127	117
September 1962	136		131
December 1962	128		129
March 1963	118	127	123
June 1963	116		121
September 1963	136		132
December 1963	133		131
March 1964	132	128	130
June 1964	140	128	133
September 1964	153	129	139

Excluding seasonal variations several trends appear:
Since independence, food prices have risen faster than nonfood prices; this may be due in part to inaccurate observation.   The sharp rise in the cost of food cannot be denied,
and is supported by other sources of information.   Food prices
were higher in 1963 than in 1962, and in 1964 than in 1963:

	Food Expenditure Index	(Workers' budget estimate - 9 months of each year, 1957 = 100)
1962	120	
1963	124 (+ 3%)	
1964	142 (+ 14%)	

Relating the standard budget to the national minimum
wage rate gives a picture of the evaluation of real income:

	Minimum Wage*	Indexes	Food Expenditure	Total Expenditure **
1957	31.67	100	100	100 (12 months)
1958	36.58	116	91.5	100.5 (12 months)
1959	40.0	126		104.5
1960	40.0	126	105.5	115.0 (November)
1961	41.67	132	112.8	119.5
1962	44.0	139	120	124
1963	44.0	139	124	125
1964	44.0	139	142	134

* Yearly average in cfa francs.
** For 9 months (Jan.-Sept.) except for 1957, 1958 and 1960.

This makes it possible to follow the variation in the following ratios:

(a) minimum Wage Rate/Food Expenditure.
(b) minimum Wage Rate/Total Expenditure.

Year	Real Wages Ratio (a)	Ratio (b)
1957	100	100
1958	126	110
1959	no data	120
1960	119	109
1961	117	110
1962	116	112
1963	112	111
1964	98	104

These indexes represent the minimum wage deflated by expenditure (in Ratio (a) Food Expenditure only; in Ratio (b) Total Expenditure) for unskilled workers. The discrepancy between the two series is most probably due to inaccurate observation, since independence, of nonfood prices, by government services. However, food prices appear (in comparison with other indexes) to have been observed fairly accurately throughout the relevant period. Since food expenditure represents the most important part of the poorer workers' expenditure, Ratio (a) is more representative than Ratio (b) of the evolution of real wages for them.

Average expenditure of industrial workers interviewed (cfa francs per month):

Rent	2,200
Rice	2,650
Groundnut Oil	1,850
Sugar	700
Milk (tinned)	660
Soap	490
Clothing	1,880
	10,430

Daily Food Expenditure:　about 235 cfa francs = 7,150 cfa francs per month.

Daily Transport Expenditure　(Dakar workers only):　about 20 cfa.

Total Food	about 13,000 cfa per month
Rent	2,200
Clothing	1,880
Total	about 17,100
Average income	about 20,000

Structure of Expenditure:

Food	about 65.0%
Rent	about 11.0%
Clothing	about 9.4%
Other	about 14.6%

APPENDIX   **G**   INTERVIEWS AND
ANSWERS

Scheduled interviews were carried out in 1964 and 1965
with industrial employers and industrial workers in Senegal.
Interview results are used in this study mainly as supporting material complementing information available from other
sources. As such, the features of the samples do not have a
critical influence on the argument of the study: Nowhere
have interview results been used in isolation.

The main reason for lack of scholarly work on Senegalese
industry is the difficulty experienced in gathering information
at the plant-level. Most industrial firms are owned and managed by French nationals, and the presence of French authority
in this limited but essential part of Senegalese economy often
gives rise to tensions between management and labor force.
Although employers established a modus vivendi with government, and (recently) with government trade unions, a potential
danger remains of a confusion, by the African labor force, of
industrial grievances and anti-French feelings. This political
difficulty accounts for reluctance shown by many employers to
allow themselves and, a fortiori, their labor force, to be
interviewed. Traditional discretion of French industrialists
must be added to the politically motivated reserve. These
factors account for most imperfections in the samples.

However, it appears that trends brought out by interviews are in accordance with other sources of information.
The only ambition of this study is to try to detect trends,
without entering into a detailed breakdown of the answers
given to the questionnaire. Results are interpreted in the
light of these reservations, and serve above all to supplement
information obtained from other sources.

Two sets of questions were used: One for industrial
employers, and one for industrial workers. Most questions, in
both sets of interviews, were open-ended. Both series of
interviews were oral. What are the main features of the samples chosen?

275

1. Industrial Employers

The management of 25 firms (26 plants) were successfully approached for interviews.

Of the plants covered 80.8 percent are located in the Cap Vert area (Dakar and surroundings). Statistics available for mining, energy and manufacturing show that 86.5 percent of all firms in these sectors are located in the Cap Vert area. Our sample meets the criterion of location. (This figure and all further figures used in this appendix are found in "Deuxième Plan de Développement Economique et Social, Dakar, 1965, pp. 292 ff). The only reliable recent statistics available on the structure on industry and industrial employment concern firms of 50 employees and more. It seems that smaller firms only represent 9.8 percent of total industrial employment, and that the average employment of small firms is 18.8, suggesting "small-scale industry," maintenance shops, etc., rather than industrial plants. The average size of plants interviewed is 350 employees (as compared to 222 for all firms of 50 employees or more). Thus, the sample is biased in favor of relatively large units of production.

The following list shows the firms interviewed:

Name of Firm	Industry	Employment	Source
SOFRA TP	Public Works	500	M
SOCOCIM	Cement	291	M
SHELL	Oil	350	M, P.
CSPT	Calcium Phosphates	730	P, E.
LESIEUR AFRIQUE	Groundnut Oil	1,135	P, E.
V.Q. PETERSEN	Groundnut Oil	514	E
ICOTAF (3 plants)	Textiles	840	E
SOCOSAC	Textiles	305	M
BATA	Shoeware	1,000	M
GMD	Flour Mill	250	M
SENTENAC	Flour Mill	135	M, E.
MEDINA	Biscuits, Beds	270	E
WEBHE	Biscuits and Soft Drinks	160	M
SOBOA	Beer and Soft Drinks	330	M, E.
CSSS	Salt	400	M
CAPA	Sugar	150	M
SISCOMA	Agricultural Equipment	370	M
AIR LIQUIDE	Pressed gas	54	M
SOFRIGAL	Tuna Refrigeration	144	M
MTOA	Tobaccoware	165	M

CAFAL	Matches	137	M
RTS	Urban Transport	896	M, P.
RCF	Railways	4,350	P, F.
SODEC	Groundnut Oil	700	M

(Note: Source means person(s) interviewed; M stands for man-
aging director, P stands for personnel manager, and E stands
for senior executive).

Comparison for the manufacturing sector between the structure of the sample and that of the population shows that the
sample is fairly representative, both in terms of number of
firms for each industry and in terms of employment:

Manufacturing Industries

	Percent of firms		Employment by sectors	
	Sample	Population	Sample	Population
Food Industry	27.3	24.1	16.8	23.2
Groundnut Oil	13.6	13.0	30.5	24.2
Textile and Footwear	22.7	24.1	27.9	28.5
Other Manufacturing	36.4	38.8	24.8	24.1
Total	100.0	100.0	100.0	100.0

In the mining sector, the main enterprise operating in
Senegal was interviewed; it employs 52.9 percent of the mining
sector's employment. In transportation the two firms interviewed cover 38.1 percent of that sector's employment. The
public works and construction sector is under-represented in
the sample because that sector relies a great deal upon seasonal and casual employment, and because conditions there are
not representative of industrial work; the firm interviewed
covers 4.2 percent of employment in that sector. To sum up,
the following table shows the relationship between sample and
total population:

Employment

	Sample	Population	Sample as percent of Population
Mining	730	1,381	52.9
Transportation	5,246	13,760	38.1
Public Works and Construction	500	12,000	4.2
Manufacturing	7,700	11,481	67.1
Total	14,176	38,622	36.7

II. Workers' Interviews

Interviews were carried out orally with 188 industrial workers of 13 firms (average: 14.5 worker per firm). In 11 out of 13 firms, 15 workers were interviewed.

The firms in which interviewed workers were employed cover the following fractions of total employment in each sector:

Public Works and Construction	4.17 percent
Transportation	31.30 percent
Manufacturing	37.90 percent

No mining firm granted permission to interview workers.

Workers interviewed represented the following percentage of total employment in their respective firms:

Public works and Construction	2.90 percent
Manufacturing	3.70 percent
Transportation	0.33 percent
All firms	2.55 percent

(or slightly over 1 worker in 50)

The choice of firms was determined largely by willingness of managers to allow interviews to be carried out in their plants; it is not possible to evaluate the effect of this constraint on the results of the survey. The following firms accepted to have interviews carried out:

SOFRA TP	GMD
SOCOCIM	SENTENAC
SHELL	SOBOA
LESIEUR AFRIQUE	CAPA
ICOTAF	SISCOMA
SOCOSAC	SOFRIGAL
	RCF

The sample includes 1 public works firm, 1 transportation firm (railways), 4 plants in the food industry, 1 groundnut oil firm, 2 textile firms, 1 cement plant, 1 oil plant, 1 agricultural implements firm and 1 tuna refrigeration plant.

Seventy-six percent of workers were interviewed in Dakar, thus roughly reflecting the geographical distribution of industrial labor in Senegal (81 percent of industrial labor is employed in Dakar).

Within industrial plants, the choice of workers depended on two main criteria: The workers' age and their professional qualification. However, unwillingness on the part of certain employers to let certain workers leave their job for three-quarters of an hour for being interviewed limited the degree of precision of stratification. Likewise, the fact that many workers did not know their own age with precision led us to be satisfied with "broad" age-groups. The result obtained is indicated below:

Age-groups	Percent of workers interviewed
Young ("under 31")	29.
Medium ("31 to 40")	38.
Older ("over 40")	33.

In the opinion of the plant's management, this structure is not too far off the mark as far as reflecting the age-structure of employment is concerned.

Skills	Percent of workers interviewed
Unskilled and Medium-skilled (wage-grades I to IV)	50.0
Skilled (Wage-grades V to VII)	37.5
Supervisory	12.5

The sample appears to be slightly biased in favor of
supervisory labor (the national average share of supervisory
labor is about 7.3 percent of the labor force). The effect
of this bias is felt in economic data: Average incomes are
on the high side. This does not, however, affect the argument that is central in the discussion of policies: The
impact of the extended family on per head incomes to the
extent that a relationship exists between income and the
size of the extended family.

The ratio of skilled to unskilled workers appears, in
the light of statements by managers, to reflect the situation in Senegalese manufacturing industry.

The independence of the interviewer from the firm and
the government was made clear to the interviewees. Interviews
were carried out in the native tongue of the workers or, when
workers understood that language, in French.

APPENDIX **H** INTERVIEW
SCHEDULES

Interview Schedules

    I.   Employers' Interviews
   II.   Workers' Interviews (noneconomic questions)
  III. Workers' Interviews (economic questions)
   IV. Correlation

I. Employers' Interviews

      (i)   number of questions
     (ii)   question and possible answers
   (iii)   percentage of answers
    (iv)   coverage
     (v)   percentage of employees covered including
           transport
    (vi)   percentage of employees covered excluding
           transport (i.e., manufacturing industry and
           public works)

(i)	(ii)	(iii)	(iv)	(v)	(vi)
1.	**Location of Firm**				
	Dakar	80.8	14,176		
	Rest of Senegal	19.2	workers		
2.	**Employment of Firm**				
	0 to 99	8.0	14,176		
	100 to 199	21.0	workers		
	200 to 499	33.0			
	500 and more	38.0			

281

3. Nationality of Capital

100% French	66.66	14,176 workers	41.4	67.3
Entirely Foreign but not 100% French	12.33		11.0	17.9
Including Senegalese	21.0		47.6	14.8

4. Dependence on Foreign
    Headquarters for Labor

Entire freedom	62.5	14,176 workers	76.3	62.4
Dependence for expatriates	25.0		17.3	27.5
Dependence for wage-adjustments	12.5		6.4	10.1

5. Period of Starting
    Business

Before World War II	30.0	14,176 workers
1940-44	12.5	
1945-57	37.5	
After 1957	20.0	

6. Exports in Percent of
    Output

Nil	19.0	8.3
0 - 25%	33.0	36.2
26 - 50%	14.0	5.7
51 - 75%	9.5	15.5
76 - 99%	19.0	23.3
100%	5.5	9.0

7. Non-Franc zone Export in
    Percent of Exports, if
    any

Nil	50.0	39.6
1 - 25%	25.0	30.6
26 - 50%	nil	nil
51 - 75%	8.33	5.0
76 - 99%	8.33	14.7
100%	8.33	10.1

8. Senegalese Inputs in Per-
    cent of Total Input
    excluding Labor

Nil	39.5		35.4
1 - 25%	22.0		12.9
26 - 50%	5.5		19.6
51 - 75%	nil		nil
76 - 99%	11.0		13.7
100%	22.0		18.4

9. Market Trend since 1957

Decline	13.0	37.2	6.1
Stagnation or slow progress	57.0	32.7	49.0
Rise	4.0	5.6	8.3
Protected markets (groundnut products)	13.0	17.9	26.7
State controlled	13.0	6.6	9.9

10. Domestic Competition

Monopoly	52.0	67.3
Coordinated oligopoly	22.0	12.3
Competition	26.0	20.4

11. Firm's Share of Domestic
    Market

Under 10%	nil	nil
10 - 24%	7.0	13.0
25 - 49%	7.0	5.8
50 - 74%	7.0	4.5
75 - 99%	29.0	20.9
100%	50.0	55.8

12. Product Price Deter-
    mination   21 firms

Groundnut agreement	14.0
World market	5.0
Market	47.5
State price-control	33.5

13. Percentage of Capacity
       Used

Over 90%	nil		nil
76 - 90%	31.0		26.2
51 - 75%	50.0		62.4
0 - 50%	19.0		11.4

14. Investment Time-horizon

No investment planned	24.0		21.6
Year to year	9.5		9.7
Three to five years	42.5		35.7
Over five years	24.0		33.0

15. Major Concern of
       Management   22
                                          firms

Market	72.5
Technical problems	9.0
Other	4.5
No particular problem	14.0

16. Trend of Employment
       since 1957

Slowly decreasing	9.0	3.1	5.1
Decreasing, then stable	30.0	53.3	33.8
Stable	39.0	20.5	34.0
Slowly expanding	13.0	10.8	17.9
Rising rapidly	9.0	12.3	9.2

17. Did Firm Recruit since
       Two Years

Yes	41.5	60.0	44.8
No	37.5	30.9	40.0
No reply	21.0	9.1	15.2

18. Major Causes Affecting
       Level of Employment
       in Firm?

Market	52.5	51.6	57.3
Technical change	31.5	31.1	34.6
Other	16.0	17.3	8.1

19. **Where Do You Recruit?**   23
                                                firms

    All over Senegal   56.5
    Dakar   43.5

20. **Skills Needed**   23
                                                firms

    None   8.7
    Unskilled workers   8.7
    Skilled workers   55.6
    Primary-school-
      leavers   13.0
    Other   13.0

21. **Method of Selection**
    for Labor

One-month trial	58.0	26.3	45.9
Tests for foremen			
and skilled labor	21.0	26.5	33.5
Tests for everyone	21.0	47.2	20.6

22. **Manpower-Training**
    Scheme?

Yes	42.0	63.4	51.9
No	58.0	36.6	48.1

23. **Do You Have a Choice**
    between Different
    Capital/Labor Ratios?

No	91.0	95.5	93.0
Yes (conceivably)	9.0	4.5	7.0

24. **Systematic Promotion**
    Policy

Yes (periodical			
revision)	31.5	52.9	25.9
No (case by case)	68.5	47.1	74.1

25. **Turnover (African**
    Labor)

    Stability, no com-
      plaints   100.0

Unstability, com-
plaints   nil

26. Evolution of Turnover
    (African Labor)

     No evolution   80.0   78.4   75.5
     More stability now   20.0   21.6   24.5
     Less stability now   nil   nil   nil

27. Is Absenteeism a Problem?   8,930
                                     workers

     No (is low)   63.5   67.3
     Yes   36.5   32.7

28. Evolution of Absenteeism

     No evolution   41.0   49.8
     Less absenteeism now 50.0   33.0
     More absenteeism now   9.0   17.2

29. Problems of Caste and Tribe?   16
                                     firms

     No problems   62.5
     Some problems   25.0
     Important problems   6.25
     Does not know   6.25

30. Does the Organization of
    Teams Post Tribal Prob-
    lems?   17
                                     firms

     No   88.0
     Yes   12.0

31. Do You Face Problems of
    Supervision and Auth-
    ority?   14,176
                                     workers

     No grave problems   50.0   37.4
     Yes, between
       Africans   50.0   62.6

32. Major Problem with African   22
    Labor Force?   firms

     Qualifications   45.0
     Moral qualities   36.0
     Authority   9.5
     No major problem   9.5

33. Expatriate Labor Force in
    Percent of Total Labor
    Force

3% or less	31.0	58.9	32.7
4 - 6%	31.0	20.3	33.3
7 - 9%	25.5	13.9	22.7
10 - 15%	nil	nil	nil
Over 15%	12.5	6.9	11.3

34. Percentage of Expatriate
    Foremen

Nil	15.0	19.8	22.6
1 - 20%	10.0	43.9	5.0
21 - 30%	10.0	6.1	12.1
31 - 40%	15.0	9.4	18.8
41 - 50%	15.0	4.5	9.0
51 - 75%	10.0	1.3	2.5
Over 75%	25.0	15.0	30.0

35. Ratio: Cost of Expatriate
    Labor/African Labor

150 to 200%	23.0	20.8
200 to 300%	39.0	8.1
300 to 400%	15.0	28.0
400 to 500%	23.0	43.1
over 500%	nil	nil

36. Has There Ever Been an   14,176
    Expatriate on Strike?   workers

No	100.0
Yes	nil

37. Ratio: Productivity of
    Expatriate Labor/
    African Labor

Depends on mechan- ization	53.0	51.2
No comparison possi- ble	17.0	17.9
100 to 200%	12.0	10.1
200%	6.0	12.9
300%	nil	nil
Over 300%	12.0	7.9

38. Methods Used for Apprais-
    ing Productivity   9,126

        Physical criteria   27.0   30.0
        Foremen's appraisal   73.0   70.0

39. Turnover of Expatriate
    Labor Changes since
    World War II

        No change   66.66   74.0
        Faster turnover   33.33   26.0
        Slower turnover   nil   nil

40. Average Age of Ex-
    patriates

        Under 30   8.5   3.5
        31-40   83.0   89.5
        41-50   8.5   7.0
        Over 50   nil   nil

41. Can the Firm Work without
    Its African Labor Force?

        Yes, normally   nil   nil
        Yes, at slow pace   22.5   21.0
        No   77.5   79.0

42. Is Your Firm Bound by
    Collective Agreements?

        Yes   95.7   97.2
        No   4.3   2.8

43. Plant-level Agreement   9,826
                                               workers
        Yes   35.0   51.6
        No   65.0   48.4

44. African Employment
    Contracts

        Mostly oral   54.5   46.4   51.5
        Mostly written   32.0   36.8   29.9
        Written only for
          higher wage-grades   13.5   16.8   18.6

45. Wage-Determination   9,126
                                           workers

     Collective agree-
       ments   56.5   68.0
     Administrative rates   4.5
     Above agreed rates   21.5   12.0
     Plant-level agreement   17.5   20.0

46. Does the Wage-grade Legis-   18
       lation Create Problems in   firms
       the Firm?

     No   61.0
     Yes   22.0
     Firm's own wage-
       grades   17.0

47. Wage-revision Policy

     According to change
       in national rate   27.0   19.1   30.8
     Case-by-case review   36.5   25.3   30.3
     Systematic review   36.5   55.6   38.9

48. Wage-policy Coordination

     Through employers'
       associations   57.0   46.9   51.7
     Through other agree-
       ment   19.0   14.8   16.4
     No explicit co-
       ordination   24.0   38.3   31.9

49. Credit Policy   13,246
                                           workers
     No problem of credit   nil
     No credit policy   17.0   9.8
     Unsuccessful attempts
       at containing credit   19.0   10.8
     Credit causes psycho-
       logical disincentive   57.0   66.5
     Credit causes admin-
       istrative problems   26.0   12.9

50. Periodicity of Wage-   22
       payment   firms

50. (cont'd)

     14 days   68.5
     Monthly with fort-
        nightly account   27.0
     Monthly   4.5

51. Effective Working Hours   13,176
     per Week   workers

Under 40 hours	9.0		6.2
40-42 hours	18.0		28.6
43-45 hours	9.0		2.1
46-48 hours	60.0		62.4
Over 48 hours	4.0		0.7

52. Do You Pay Out Premiums   20
     and/or Gratuities?   firms

     Yes   75.0
     No   25.0

53. If Any, How Much per   12
     Year?   firms

     Less than 1 week's
       wages   12.5
     1-2 weeks' wages   33.0
     3-4 weeks' wages   42.0
     Over 4 weeks' wages   12.5

54. Does your Firm Have a
     System of Monetary   14,176
     Incentives?   workers

     Premiums   46.0   59.6
     No   54.0   30.4

55. According to Your Ex-
     perience, Are Premiums
     Effective Means of In-   7,147
     creasing Productivity?   workers

     Yes   31.0   35.5
     No   62.0   54.3
     Neutral statement   7.0   10.2

56. <u>How Many Trade Unions</u>   11,746
    <u>in Your Firm</u>?   workers

        One   62.0   67.5
        Several   33.0   31.3
        Does not know   5.0   1.2

57. <u>Judgement of Workers'</u>
    <u>Involvement in</u>   9,826
    <u>Unionism</u>   workers

        Workers "follow the
          mass"   61.0   61.7
        Little interest   13.0   13.6
        Some interest   26.0   24.7

58. <u>Past Industrial Relations</u>   14,176
                                          workers
        Calm relationship
          with unions   58.0   73.8   62.3
        Strikes, without
          violence   29.5   17.2   24.8
        Strikes and physical
          violence   12.5   9.0   12.9

59. <u>Judgement on Unionism</u>   13,476
    <u>in Senegal</u>   workers

        Satisfactory   35.0   33.33
        Mediocrity creates
          problems   65.0   66.66

60. <u>Membership of Employers'</u>
    <u>Association</u>

        Yes   76.0   83.7
        No   24.0   16.3

61. <u>Main Attraction of</u>
    <u>Employers' Assn. for</u>
    <u>You</u>?

        Economic information 31.5   18.8
        Economic coordina-
          tion   25.0   31.6
        Legal advice   25.0   35.4
        Contracts with govern-
          ment   12.5   7.5
        Recruitment problems 6.0   6.7

62. Permanent and Exclusive
     Personnel Manager in   13,621
     Firm?   workers

         No   52.0   27.0   39.2
         Yes (expatriate) 26.0   27.0   39.2
         Yes (African)   22.0   46.0   21.6

63. Time Spent by Top-manage-   21
     ment on Labor Problems   firms

         Little time (no com-
           plaint)   33.0
         Medium (6-10 hours/
           week)   24.0
         More than 10 hours/
           week, complaints 43.0

64. Are You Satisfied with the
     Structures for Human   8,835
     Relations in Your Firm?   workers

         Yes   66.66   74.0
         No   19.0   19.7
         Neutral comment   14.33   6.3

65. Policy towards Grievances   22
                                     firms

         "Always prepared to
           talk"   45.0
         Hierarchy must be
           respected   55.0

66. Appraisal of Shop Dele-   14,176
     gates   workers

         Low intellectual
           level   29.0
         Very low intel.level 21.0
         Positive appraisal 33.5
         "Depends on person" 16.5

67. Most Frequent Grievances   14,176
                                 workers
         Wages   29.0   35.8   24.8
         Credit   29.0   21.5   38.3
         Promotion, wage-
           grades   20.0   31.6   17.3

67. (cont'd)

Fringe Benefits	12.0		5.9	10.5
Other	10.0		5.2	9.1

68. <u>Changes in Grievances</u>
    <u>since Independence?</u>   11,672
                                            workers

No change	53.0		30.3	48.3
Less grievances	29.0		49.5	19.6
New kinds of				
grievances	12.0		14.1	22.5
More grievances	6.0		6.1	9.6

69. <u>Relationship to Shop</u>   20
    <u>Delegates</u>   firms

"Emotional-paternal"	85.0
Legalistic	10.0
Matter-of-fact	5.0

70. <u>Judgement on Relationship</u>
    <u>between Shop Delegates</u>   18
    <u>and Workers</u>   firms

Emphasis on authority	44.5
Complaints about mix-	
ing-up union's and	
firm's hierarchy	22.5
Palavers	16.5
Other	11.0
Does not know	5.5

71. <u>Was the Legal Protection</u>
    <u>of Shop Delegates ever</u>   16
    <u>a Problem?</u>   firms

Yes	75.0
No	25.0

72. <u>Appraisal of Labor Code</u>   21
                                            firms

O.K.	66.66
Too close to French	
model	14.33
Other criticisms	19.0

73. Frequency of Labor In-
    spectorate Visits after
    Independence versus
    Before

Less frequent	19.0	32.8	23.5
Much less frequent	19.0	20.5	23.3
No visit since Ind.	62.0	46.7	53.2

74. Extra-economic Institutions

Food cooperatives	11 firms
Housing material	7 firms
Other	5 firms
None	6 firms

75. Judgements on African
    Workers' Attitude   4,838
    towards Their Jobs   workers

No involvement	41.5	28.0
Foremen more invol- ved than workers	41.5	46.0
Satisfactory invol- vement	17.0	26.0

76. Judgement on African
    Workers' Attitude
    towards Machines   3,782
                                        workers

Favorable	nil	
Unfavorable, pessi- mistic	80.0	77.0
Unfavorable, opti- mistic	20.0	23.0

77. Forecast on Adaptation of
    African Labor Sorce to   6,278
    Technical Environment   workers

Moderate long-term optimism	54.0	49.0
Optimism	38.5	46.5
Frank pessimism	7.5	4.5

II. Workers' Interviews: Noneconomic Questions

      (i)   number of question
     (ii)   question and possible answers
    (iii) percentage of answers
    (iv) coverage (total sample comprises 188)

Unless there is a mention "does not know" or "no reply,"
workers who fall into either of these categories are not
included in the coverage.

(i)	(ii)	(iii)	(iv)
1.	Age		187
	10-30	29.0	
	31-40	38.0	
	Over 40	33.0	
2.	Place of Birth		181
	Dakar	6.6	
	Other city	44.2	
	Village	49.2	
3.	Place of Employment		188
	Dakar area	76.0	
	Rest of Senegal	24.0	
4.	Ethnical Group		179
	Wolof	39.1	
	Lebu	14.5	
	Toucouleur	12.8	
	Serer	15.0	
	Bambara	5.6	
	Diola	::	
	Other	11.7	
5.	Occupation of Father		184
	Agriculture and fishing	73.5	
	White collar (excl. administration)	12.5	
	Worker (including transport)	8.0	
	Public employee	4.0	
	Other	2.0	

6. Occupation of Paternal Grandfather   184

        Agriculture and Fishing   94.0
        White collar (excl. administration)   4.0
        Worker (including transport)   1.5
        Public employee   nil
        Other   :::

7. Have You Ever Attended School?   185

            Yes   45.5
            No   54.5

8. Did You Obtain a Certificate?   185

            No   89.7
            CEP   6.5
            CAP (vocational)   3.8

9. For How Long Did You Attend School?   73

        One year   ::
        Two years   10.0
        Three years   10.0
        Four years   20.5
        Five years   15.0
        Six years   17.8
        Seven years   5.4
        Eight years   5.4
        Nine years   5.4
        Ten years   7.0

10. For How Many Years Have You Been Living
        in Dakar?   110

        Up to five years   17.2
        Six to ten years   27.2
        Eleven to fifteen years   22.7
        Sixteen to twenty years   18.1
        Twenty to twenty-five years   7.2
        Twenty-six to thirty years   4.0
        Over thirty years   ::

11. How Frequently Do You Visit Your
        Village?   110

        Once yearly   44.5
        Less than once a year   16.4

11. (cont'd)

Never	7.5
3 to 4 times a year	5.0
5 to 11 times a year	7.5
Over once monthly but less than once weekly	14.4
Once weekly and more frequently	: :

12. <u>Did You Serve in the French Army?</u>   185

Yes	34.5
No	65.5

13. <u>How Many Wives Do You Have?</u>   188

None	13.8
One	61.2
Two	21.3
More than two	3.7

14. <u>Number of Children</u>   188

0	40 workers	21.3
1	25	13.3
2	24	13.0
3	18	
4	20	10.6
5	21	
6	9	
7	10	
8	8	
9	4	
10	2	
11	2	
12	3	
13	1	
14	1	

15. <u>How Many People Are Fed at Your Home on Your Sole Wage?</u>   187

0	16 workers
1	nil
2	1
3	10
4	13
5	20

15. (cont'd)

6	9 workers
7	15
8	17
9	12
10	18
11	14
12	5
13	10
14	4
15	6
16	2
17	2
18	5
19	1
20	2
21	1
22	nil
23	2
24	nil
25	1
...	
30	1

16. How Many of Children Go to School?   172

0	52.3
1	18.0
2	15.0
3	7.0
4	3.0
Over 4	::

17. What Career Would You Prefer Your
     Children to Choose Ideally?   84

Law or medicine	36.5
Teaching	16.0
Technical job (engineer, etc.)	14.4
Public service	6.9
Industrial workers	5.3
Fatalistic attitude	15.4
Other	5.5

18. Can You Read French?   184

Yes	42.9
No	57.1

19. Can You Write in French?   184

         Yes   39.1
         No   60.9

20. When You Are Old, Do You Prefer To
       Retire in Town or in a Village?   186

         In town   62.3
         In a village   35.5
         Indifferent   2.2

21. Motivation for Question 20   172

         Family reasons   54.6
         Habit and agreement   26.1
         Economic reasons   18.3

22. Do You Listen to the Radio?   177

         Yes (regularly)   60.7
         No   39.5

23. Does Your Job Involve Authority Over
       Other Employees?   188

         No   77.7
         Yes   22.3

24. Wage-grade   188

         I to IV   50.0
         V to VII   37.5
         M   12.5

25. Previous Occupation   153

         Agriculture and fishing   38.2
         Industry   45.0
         Commerce and other services   16.8

26. Reasons for Changing Occupation in
       the Past   113

         Remuneration   72.5
         Dismissal   21.6
         Joining the family   3.9
         Bad crop   ::
         Other   ::

27. Industrial Training   185

        On the job   67.5
        Apprenticeship   20.5
        Technical school   12.0

28. Did You Perform Your Military Service
    in a Function Related to Your Job?   68

        Yes   4.5
        No   95.5

29. Seniority in the Present Firm   185

        5 years or less   40.5
        6 to 10 years   27.0
        11 to 15 years   18.4
        16 to 20 years   12.4
        Over 20 years   ::

30. By How Many Wage-grades Have You Moved
    up Since You Entered This Firm?   172

        0   34.8
        1   19.2
        2   18.6
        3   12.8
        4   4.7
        5 and more   9.9

31. How Did You Find Your Present Job?   173

        With the help of a relative
          employed in this firm   39.3
        By myself   56.6
        Administrative examination
          (railways)   4.1

32. Do You Prefer Working Under a Senegalese
    or an Expatriate Foreman?   115

        Senegalese   34.9
        Expatriate   15.6
        Indifferent   49.5

33. <u>Motivation for Question 32</u>   55

     Less particular, more human respect 27.3
     Understanding of native language   23.6
     Other   49.1

34. <u>Do You Like Your Present Job?</u>   180

     Yes   46.2
     Very much   50.5
     No   3.3

35. <u>Motivation for Question 34</u>   180

     Economic motives   39.0
     Habit   13.2
     Vocation, taste for the job   22.5
     Not satisfied   7.7
     Does not know   13.7
     Other   ::

36. <u>Would You Change Firms if You Were</u>
    <u>Offered Another Job with a Higher</u>
    <u>Wage?</u>   128

     Yes   60.9
     No   34.4
     Does not know   4.7

37. <u>For How Much More Would You Change?</u>   53

     Less than 1,000 per month   58.4
     1,000 to 1,500 per month   24.5
     1,501 to 2,000 per month   3.9
     Over 2,000 per month   13.2

38. <u>Do You Have Any Plans for Your Job?</u>   140

     No   83.7
     Wishes to follow training course   12.1
     Follows course   4.2

39. <u>Are You a Member of a Trade Union?</u>   187

     Yes   72.8
     No   27.2

40. <u>Do You Hold a Trade-Union Card?</u>   180

      Yes   70.0
      No   30.0

41. <u>How Much is the Yearly Union Fee?</u>   180

      All workers except railways: 600
      Railway workers: 1,200

42. <u>Which Union Do You Belong To?</u>   135

      UNTS (governmental)   61.3
      Cartel (nonpolitical)   17.1
      UST (nongovernmental)   11.9
      Does not know   9.7

43. <u>Since When Have You Been a Member?</u>   104

      Less than 5 years   29.8
      6 to 10 years   35.5
      11 to 15 years   18.2
      16 to 20 years   12.5
      Over twenty years   ::

44. <u>Motivation for Choice of Union</u>   104

      Quality of shop delegate   11.5
      Follows the majority in the firm   41.3
      Specific qualities of union   16.3
      Political motivation   16.3
      No choice   3.0
      Does not know   9.6
      Others   2.0

45. <u>Opinion of Unions</u>   147

      Member, no opinion   48.4
      Not member   19.9
      Member, criticism   31.7

46. <u>What Are Unions There For?</u>   175

      Protection against bosses and
       defense of interests   71.3
      Emphasis on labor disputes   10.0
      Emphasis on advancement   9.0
      Other   9.7

47. What Does the Union Do?   60

      They do their job all right   25.2
      Criticism of gap between leaders
        and workers   36.8
      Don't do anything   21.2
      Other criticisms   13.6
      Other   3.2

48. Why Did You Choose the Shop Delegate
     You Voted For?   128

      Single list or followed the mass   77.3
      Competence   7.0
      Moral qualities   14.8
      Other   ::

49. Judgement on Own Union (including
     ex-members)   160

      Positive appraisal   33.7
      Negative appraisal   25.6
      Weighted view pointing out positive
        as well as negative points   33.1
      Does not know   7.6

50. Criticisms against Own Union   98

      Gap between leaders and workers   59.5
      Corruption   21.0
      Excessive political involvement   6.3
      Lack of unity   5.8
      Other   ::

51. Favorable Aspects of Union   95

      Shop delegate's job   77.8
      Political motives   9.0
      Other   13.2

52. Would You Contemplate Becoming Shop
     Delegate?   170

      Yes   11.2
      No   86.5
      Does not know   2.3

53. <u>If Not (Question 52), Why?</u>   121

        Lack of education   43.0
        Drawbacks of the function   40.0
        Fear of the boss   7.4
        Other   9.6

54. <u>Who Initiates Strikes?</u>   149

        Shop delegates   15.8
        The unions (officials)   52.3
        The workers   9.0
        Employers   3.3
        There are no more strikes   16.7
        The government   ::
        Other   ::

55. <u>Did You Participate in Former Strikes?</u>   173

        Always followed   52.0
        Never followed (includes young
          workers who never experienced a
          strike)   42.8
        It depends   5.2

56. <u>To Whom Do You Submit Claims Concerning
     Your Work?</u>   176

        Foreman   40.0
        Shop delegate   51.4
        It depends   6.3
        Does not know   2.3

57. <u>Do You Obey Orders by Your Shop Delegate?</u>   139

        Always   85.0
        Never   3.6
        Sometimes   11.4

58. <u>Have You Noticed a Change in the Unions
     Since Independence?</u>   150

        No change, unions always O.K.   17.6
        No change, no appraisal   15.7
        Slowing-down of activity   32.3
        Widening gap between leaders
          and workers   8.8
        No promotion since independence   7.8
        No change, unions always bad   8.9
        Other criticisms   ::

59. <u>Have You Brought a Case to a Labor Court?</u>   166

       Never   92.1
       Yes, successfully   5.5
       Yes, unsuccessfully   1.8
       Yes, no result yet   0.6

60. <u>Are You a Member of a Political Party?</u>   126

       No   38.8
       UPS   58.0
       PRA-S   3.2

III.   <u>Workers' Interview: Economic Questions</u>

      (i)   number of question
     (ii)   question and possible answers
    (iii)   number of workers
     (iv)   percentage of answers
      (v)   coverage

(i)	(ii)	(iii)	(iv)	(v)
61.	Basic Wage (monthly) (in cfa francs)			188
	6,000 - 6,999	1		
	7-7,999	-		
	8-8,999	14		
	9-9,999	8		
	10-10,999	2		
	11-11,999	8		
	12-12,999	23		
	13-13,999	8		
	14-14,999	8		
	15-15,999	14		
	16-16,999	8		
	17-17,999	4		
	18-18,999	9		
	19-19,999	2		
	20-20,999	6		
	21-21,999	12		
	22-22,999	6		
	23-23,999	2		
	24-24,999	4		
	25-25,999	10		

61. (cont'd)

26-26,999	1
27-27,999	1
28-28,999	4
29-29,999	1
30-30,999	4
31-31,999	1
32-32,999	2
33-33,999	1
34-34,999	3
35-35,999	3
36-36,999	1
37-37,999	1
38-38,999	1
39-39,999	1
42-42,999	1
45-45,999	1
46-46,999	1
48-48,999	1
50-50,999	1

over 50,000   9

62. <u>For How Many Children Do You Receive
     Family Allowances?</u>   170

0	29.4
1	12.3
2	9.4
3	8.2
4	10.0
5	12.9
6	6.5
7	4.7
8	1.2
9	1.8
10	1.8
11	::
12	::
13	::

63. <u>Do You Have Any Nonwage Income?</u>   182

No	79.5
Wife works (petty occupation)	2.2
Petty work outside working hours	17.0
Other	::

64. How Much Money Do You Regularly Send
    to Relatives at Home?   182

    No regular transfers   66.1
    500 francs or less per month   5.0
    500 to 1,000 francs   9.9
    1,000 to 1,500 francs   6.6
    1,500 to 2,000 francs   5.5
    Over 2,000 francs   7.5

65. Cost of School   188

    State school or no children
      at school   94.1
    Koranic school, less than
      1,000 francs   1.7
    Koranic school, 1,001 to 1,500 francs   2.1
    Koranic school, over 1,500 francs   2.1

66. How Many Debts? (total amount divided
    by number of months time-limit for
    repayment)   184

    None   58.6
    Less than 5,000 francs   31.1
    5,000 to 10,000 francs   7.6
    Over 10,000 francs   2.7

67. To Whom Do You Owe Money?   75

    Firm   92.0
    Bank   2.7
    Friend   4.0
    Other   1.3

68. For What Reasons Did You Borrow?   80

    Religious feast   53.8
    Family celebrations   5.0
    Construction loan   12.5
    Hire-purchase   12.5
    Rice, tax   10.0
    Medicine   ::
    Other   6.2

69. <u>Does Anyone Owe You Money, and How Much</u>?   134

        No   92.3
        Less than 5,000 francs   4.0
        5 to 10,000 francs   3.0
        Over 10,000 francs   0.7

70. <u>How Much Tax Do You Pay</u>? (yearly total
        converted into monthly rate)   173

        None   21.4
        Less than 500 francs   57.2
        501 to 1,000 francs   18.5
        Over 1,000 francs   2.9

71. <u>How Much Rent Do You Pay</u>?   188

        None   33.3
        Less than 1,000 francs   3.3
        1,000 to 1,499 francs   16.9
        1,500 to 1,999 francs   13.8
        2,000 to 2,999 francs   16.1
        3,000 and more   13.8

72. <u>Do You Own a Vehicle</u>?   183

        No   80.8
        Bicycle   1.2
        Moped or motor-cycle   13.0
        Car   5.0

73. <u>Amount of Rice per Month</u>   112

        Less than 50 kilo   3.6
        50 kilo   18.0
        51 to 99 kilo   29.7
        100 kilo   38.8
        101 to 150 kilo   8.1
        Over 150 kilo   1.8

74. <u>Amount of Groundnut oil per Month</u>   100

        Less than 6 litres   2.0
        6 to 10 litres   15.0
        11 to 15 litres   22.0
        16 to 20 litres   41.0
        Over 20 litres   20.0

75. <u>Amount of Sugar per Month</u>   86

      Less than 6 kilo   27.2
      6 to 10 kilo   50.3
      11 to 15 kilo   16.6
      16 to 20 kilo   4.7
      Over 20 kilo   1.2

76. <u>Amount of Milk per Month</u>   57
      (100 gramme tins)
      Less than 5 tins   19.5
      6 to 10 tins   45.5
      11 to 15 tins   12.3
      16 to 20 tins   6.3
      21 tins and more   16.1

77. <u>Clothing Expenditure</u>   152

      Less than 501 francs   10.5
      501 to 1,000   27.0
      1,001 to 1,500   23.1
      1,501 to 2,000   7.9
      2,001 to 2,500   14.0
      2,501 to 3,000   3.0
      3,001 to 3,500   ::
      3,501 to 4,000   ::
      4,001 to 4,500   3.5
      4,501 to 5,000   3.0
      Over 5,000   5.0

78. <u>Do You Have a Radio?</u>   188

      Yes   52.0
      No   48.0

79. <u>Do You Own Your House?</u>   168

      Yes (including hire-purchase)   32.2
      No   67.8

80. <u>Other Durables in Sample</u>   188

      4 sewing machines
      2 refrigerators

IV. Correlation

a = horizontal axis

b = vertical axis

1. a = percentage of expatriate supervision (Question E 34)
    b = ratio: cost of expatriate/African labor (Question
                E 35)

	1	2	3	4	5	6	7	
1								
2			1		1			
3		1			1		1	
4						1	1	(number of firms)
5			1			1	2	

2. a = percentage of expatriate manpower on total employment
        (Question E 33)
    b = ratio: cost of expatriate/African labor (Question E
        35)

	1	2	3	4	5	
1						
2		1	1	1		
3		2	1	1		
4			1	1		(number of firms)
5		1		1	1	

3. a = market trend since 1957 (Question E 9)
    b = recruitment in last two years (Question E 17)

	1	2	3
1	3 firms 4,887 workers	5 firms 1,799 workers	nil
2	nil	4 firms 795 workers	1 firm 730 workers

CODE

Correlation 1:   a = 1: nil, 2: 1 to 20%, 3: 21 to 30%,
                     4: 31 to 40%, 5: 41 to 50%, 6: 51 to 75%,
                     7: over 75%

                 b = 2: 150 to 200%, 3: 200 to 300%,
                     4: 300 to 400%, 5: 400 to 500%

Correlation 2:   a = 1: 3% and less, 2: 4 to 6%, 3: 7 to 9%,
                     4: 10% and more

                 b = as in Correlation 1.

Correlation 3:   a = 1: decline, 2: stagnation or slow progress,
                     3: rise

                 b = 1: no recruitment, 2: recruitment

| RELATIONSHIPS BETWEEN
WORKERS' WAGE, EXPENDITURE
AND SIZE OF EXTENDED FAMILY

1. Relationships between wage and expenditure

I = percent of workers, among those earning less than
16,000 cfa francs
II = percent of workers, among those earning between
16,000 and 25,000 cfa francs
III = percent of workers, among those earning more than
25,000 cfa francs

A. Rice

	0-50 kilo	51-99 kilo	100 kilo and +	total
I	30.	35.	35.	100
II	20.	31.	49.	100
III	12.	15.	73.	100

coverage: 112 workers

B. Groundnut Oil

	0-15 litres	16-20 litres	over 20 litres	
I	49.	44.	7.	100
II	41.	41.	18.	100
III	22.	39.	39.	100

coverage: 100 workers

C. Sugar

	under 5 kilo	6-10 kilo	over 10 kilo	
I	41.	47.	12.	100
II	25.	59.	16.	100
III	14.	41.	45.	100

coverage: 86 workers

D. Clothing   Total
        0-1,000 cfa   1,001-2,000 cfa   over 2,000 cfa

	0-1,000 cfa	1,001-2,000 cfa	over 2,000 cfa	Total
I	57.	33.	10.	100
II	32.	44.	24.	100
III	11.	17.	72.	100

coverage: 147 workers

E. Housing   do not
    workers who   own a house   own house

	own a house	do not own house	
I	14.	86.	100
II	44.	56.	100
III	55.	45.	100

coverage: 168 workers

2. Relationship between wage and size of extended family

A. People supported:

	1-5	6-9	10 and +	
I	47.	28.	25.	100
II	24.	36.	40.	100
III	17.	20.5	62.5	100

coverage: 186 workers

B. Same relationship, excluding workers living without
    dependents:

	1-5	6-9	10 and +	
I	36.	33.5	30.5	100
II	20.5	38.	41.5	100
III	16.5	21.	62.5	100

coverage: 170 workers

3. Relationship between workers' age and size of extended
    family

People supported:

	1-5	6-9	10 and +	
less than 31 yrs.	63.	26.	11.	100
31-40	21.5	35.	43.5	100
over 40	17.	22.5	60.5	100

coverage: 181 workers

BIBLIOGRAPHY

BIBLIOGRAPHY

I. Primary Sources

Assemblee de l'Union Française. Rapport d'Information sur les
    Conditions d'Application du Code du Travail Outre-Mer en
    AOF, No. 55. Paris: 1954.

Banque Centrale des Etats de l'Afrique de l'Ouest. Rapport
    Mensuel. Dakar: 1964.

Caisse de Compensation. Rapport d'Activite 1962-1963. Dakar:
    1964.

International Labor Organization. Records of Proceedings,
    Second African Regional Conference. Geneva: 1964.

La Documentation Française. Annuaire Economique de la France,
    1965. Paris: 1966.

Ministère des Finances. Budget Général 1963-1964. Dakar:
    1964.

Ministère du Plan. Plan Quadriennal de Développement 1961-
    1964. Dakar: 1961.

_____. Deuxieme Plan de Développement Economique et
    Social. Dakar: 1965.

Ministère du Travail. Correspondence between Ministry of
    Labor and Labor Inspectorate. Dakar.

_____. Rapport de Synthèse sur les Travaux de la Com-
    mission sur le Chômage. Dakar: 1959.

_____. Rapports d'Inspection du Travail: AOF, 1946, 1947,
    1948, 1951; Sénégal-Mauritanie, 1951; Sénégal, 1938,
    1950, 1956, 1958, 1959, 1960, 1961; Dakar, 1943, 1944,
    1945, 1958; Cap Vert, 1960, 1961, 1962; Sud Sénégal,
    1951, 1952-53, 1954, 1956, 1957. Dakar.

_____. Salaires 1963-1964 et Evolution des Salaires depuis
    1937. Dakar: 1964.

_____. Statistiques de la Sécurité Sociale. Dakar: 1964.

Services de la Statistique. AOF 1957. Dakar: 1958.

_____. Annuaires Statistiques de l'AOF. Dakar: 1949, 1951,
    1957.

317

_____. Bulletin Statistique et Economique Mensuel.
(Periodical). Dakar: from 1963.

_____. Comptes Economiques du Sénégal 1959-1962. Dakar:
1964.

_____. Répertoire des Villages. Dakar: 1964.

_____. Situation Economique du Sénégal. Dakar: 1962,
1963, 1964, 1965.

Union Progressiste Senegalaise. Rapport du Ministere des
Finances au Conseil National. Dakar: 1964.

_____. Rapport sur l'Orientation Syndicale de l'UPS.
Dakar: 1963.

                    II. Secondary Sources

Adam, Claude. L'Equilibre Vivrier au Sénégal, Thèse de Doctorat en Droit. Montpellier: 1964 (roneoed).

Africa. (Periodical). Dakar: 1963-1964.

Afrique Documents. (Periodical). Dakar and Paris.

Afrique Nouvelle. (Periodical). Dakar: 1947-1965.

Bagchi, A. K. "The Choice of Optimum Technique," Economic
Journal. London: September, 1962.

Balogh, Thomas. "The Problem of Education in Africa," The
Centennial Review of the Michigan University, Vol. VI,
No. 4. 1962.

Barbier, Jean. L'Economie de l'Arachide au Sénégal, Thèse de
Doctorat en Droit. Lille: 1960 (roneoed).

Bauer, P. T. "Regulated Wages in Under-developed Countries,"
in Bradley, Philip D., (ed.), The Public Stake in Union
Power. Charlottesville: University of Virginia Press,
1959.

_____, and B. S. Yamey. The Economics of Under-developed
Countries. Cambridge: Cambridge University Press, 1959.

BCEAO. Rapports Annuels. Paris: 1959 to 1965.

Berg, E. J. "Backward-sloping Labor Supply Functions in Dual
    Economies--The African Case," Quarterly Journal of
    Economics. Cambridge, Mass.: August, 1961.

_____. "The Economic Basis of Political Choice in French
    West Africa," The American Political Science Review, Vol.
    LIV. Madison, Wisc.: June, 1960.

_____. "French West Africa," in Galenson, Walter, (ed.),
    Labor and Economic Development. New York: John Wiley and
    Sons, Inc., 1959.

_____. "Real Income Trends in West Africa 1939-1960," in
    Herskovits, M. J., and M. Harwitz, (eds.), Economic Transi-
    tion in Africa. New York: Routledge and Kegan Paul, 1964.

Bettelheim, Charles. Some Basic Planning Problems. London:
    Asia Publishing House, 1961.

_____. Studies in the Theory of Planning. London: Asia
    Publishing House, 1959.

Bhatt, V. V. "Some Notes on Balanced and Unbalanced Growth,"
    Economic Journal. London: March, 1965.

_____. "Theories of Balanced and Unbalanced Growth: A
    Critical Appraisal," Kyklos. Basel: 1964.

Boeke, J. H. Economics and Economic Policy of Dual Societies
    as Exemplified by Indonesia. New York: Institute of
    Pacific Relations, 1953.

Bouthier, Mirielle. "La Diversification des Cultures et ses
    Problèmes au Sénégal," Tiers Monde, Vol. VI, No. 24.
    Paris: 1965.

Bronfenbrenner, M. "The Appeal of Confiscation in Economic
    Development," Economic Development and Cultural Change.
    Chicago: April, 1955.

Brun, Charles F. Droit du Travail. Dakar: Clairafrique, 1962.

_____, and Georges Vermot-Gauchy. "La Question des Salaires
    au Sénégal," Afrique Documents, Suppl. No. 2. Dakar: 1965.

_____. Salaires 1961-1962. Dakar: Clairafrique, 1962.

Buchanan, N. S. International Investment and Domestic Welfare.
    New York: H. Holt and Co., 1945.

Centre National d'Orientation Professionnelle. Enquêtes
    Relatives à la Situation des Anciens Elèves des Etablisse-
    ments d'Enseignement Technique. Dakar: 1963 and 1964
    (roneoed).

Chambre de Commerce de Dakar. Bulletin. (Periodical). Dakar.

_____. "Réglementation Relative à l'Importation des Mar-
    chandises au Sénégal." Dakar: August, 1964 (roneoed).

Chambre de Commerce de Kaolack. Bulletin. (Periodical).
    Kaolack.

CINAM. "Rapport sur les Perspectives de Développement au
    Senegal," Rapport Général sur l'Industrialisation. Paris:
    1960.

Clark, C. and M. Haswell. The Economics of Subsistence Agri-
    culture. London: Macmillan, 1964.

COGERAF. Etude Monographique de Trente et Un Pays Africains.
    Paris: COGERAF, 1964.

_____. Rapport sur les Structures des Administrations Cen-
    trales de la République du Sénégal. Paris: COGERAF, 1960.

Coleman, James S. and Carl G. Rosberg, Jr. Political Parties
    and National Integration in Tropical Africa. Berkeley:
    University of California Press, 1964.

Davies, Ioan. African Trade Unions. London: Penguin African
    Library, 1966.

Deschamps, Hubert. Le Sénégal et la Gambie. Paris: PUF,
    1964.

Dobb, Maurice. "A Note on the Discussion of the Problem of
    Choice between Alternative Investment Projects," Soviet
    Studies, Vol II, No. 3. Oxford: January, 1951.

_____. "A Note on the So-called Degree of Capital-Intensity
    of Investment in Underdeveloped Countries," Economie
    Appliquée, No. 3. Paris: July, 1954.

_____. "Second Thoughts on Capital-Intensity," Review of
    Economic Studies, Vol. XXIV. Cambridge, England.

La Documentation Française. <u>Les Accords de Coopération entre la France et les Etats Africains et Malgache</u>. Paris: 1964.

Eckhaus, R. S. "The Factor-Proportions Problem in Underdeveloped Areas," <u>American Economic Review</u>. Menasha, Wisc.: September, 1965.

Enke, Stephen. <u>Economics for Development</u>. Englewood Cliffs, N. J.: Prentice-Hall, 1963.

Fei, J. C. H. and G. Ranis. "Unlimited Supply of Labour and the Concept of Balanced Growth," <u>Pakistan Development Review</u>, Vol. I, No. 3. Karachi.

Foltz, W. J. <u>From French West Africa to the Mali Federation</u>. New Haven, Conn.: Yale University Press, 1965.

_____. "Social Structure and Political Behaviour of Senegalese Elites." New Haven, Conn.: Yale University Press, 1964 (roneoed).

Galenson, W. and H. Leibenstein. "Investment Criteria, Productivity and Economic Development," <u>Quarterly Journal of Economics</u>. Cambridge, Mass.: August, 1955.

Gamble, David P. <u>The Wolof of Senegambia</u>. London: International African Institute, 1957.

Gonidec, Pierre F. "L'Evolution du Syndicalisme en Afrique Noire," <u>Penant</u>. Paris: 1962.

Griffin, Keith B. "Reflections on Latin American Development," <u>Oxford Economic Papers</u>. Oxford: Oxford University Press, 1966.

Harbison, Frederick H. "Egypt," in Galenson, Walter, (ed.), <u>Labor and Economic Development</u>. New York: John Wiley and Sons, Inc., 1959.

Hauser, André. "L'Absentéisme et la Mobilité des Travailleurs des Industries Manufacturières de la Région de Dakar." Dakar: University of Dakar, undated (roneoed).

_____. "Les Industries de Transformation de la Région de Dakar et leur Main d'Oeuvre." Dakar: University of Dakar, 1958 (roneoed).

Herskovits, M. I. and M. Harwitz. <u>Economic Transition in Africa</u>. New York: Routledge and Kegan Paul, 1964.

Higgins, Benjamin. "The Dualistic Theory of Underdeveloped
    Areas," Economic Development and Cultural Change.
    Chicago: January, 1956.

Hirschman, A. O. The Strategy of Economic Development. New
    Haven, Conn.: Yale University Press, 1958.

IBRD. World Bank Atlas of Per Capita Product and Population.
    Washington, D. C.: 1966.

ISEA. Etude d'une Firme dans une Jeune Nation Insuffisamment
    Développée. Dakar: 1963 (roneoed).

_____. Inventaire des Etablissements Industriels du Séné-
    gal. Dakar: 1963 (roneoed).

Kahn, A. E. "Investment Criteria in Development Programs,"
    Quarterly Journal of Economics. Cambridge, Mass.: 1951.

Kirsch, Martin. Memento de Droit du Travail Outre-Mer.
    Paris: 1965.

Kuenne, Robert E. Monopolistic Competition Theory: Studies in
    Impact. New York: John Wiley and Sons, Inc., 1967.

Leduc, Gaston. "Les Prix et leur Formation dans les Economies
    Africaines," Cahiers de l'ISEA, Suppl. No. 145. Paris:
    1964.

Lewis, W. A. "Economic Development with Unlimited Supplies of
    Labor," The Manchester School. London: May, 1954.

Lord, R. F. Economic Aspects of Mechanized Farming at
    Nachingwea in Tanganyika. London: HMS Office, 1963.

Marchés Tropicaux et Mediterraneens. (Periodical). Paris.

Marshall, Alfred. Principles. London: Macmillan, 1961.

Mas, J. B. Le Rôle de l'Arachide dans la Croissance Economique
    du Sénégal. Dakar: Services de la Statistique, 1964.

Mason, E. S. "Monopolistic Competition and the Growth Process
    in Less Developed Countries: Chamberlin and the Schum-
    peterian Dimension," in Kuenne, Robert E., (ed.), Monop-
    olistic Competition Theory: Studies in Impact. New York:
    John Wiley and Sons, Inc., 1967.

Masse, Marcel. A Study of Manufacturing in Senegal, B.Phil.
    Thesis. Oxford: 1966.

Mathur, A. "Balanced versus Unbalanced Growth--A Reconcilia-
     tory View," Oxford Economic Papers. Oxford: Oxford
     University Press, 1966.

Mazumdar, Dipak. "Underemployment in Agriculture and the In-
     dustrial Wage-Rate," Economica. London: November, 1959.

Meek, R. L. "Ideal and Reality in the Choice between Alter-
     native Techniques," Oxford Economic Papers. Oxford:
     Oxford University Press, November, 1964.

Meier, Gerald M. Leading Issues in Development Economics.
     Oxford: Oxford University Press, 1964.

Meynaud, Jean and Anissé Salah-Bey. Le Syndicalisme Africain.
     Paris: Payot, 1963.

Ministère de la Coopération. La Moyenne Vallée du Sénégal.
     Paris: PUF, 1962.

_____. La Planification en Afrique Noire. Paris: 1964.

_____. République du Sénégal--Economie et Plan de
     Développement. Paris: 1964.

Mission d'Aide et de Coopération. Notes sur la Coopération
     Française au Sénégal. Dakar: 1964 (roneoed).

Le Monde. (Daily). Paris: Oct. 21, 1964 and Dec. 12-13, 1965.

Moore, W. E. Industrialization and Labor. Ithaca, N. Y.:
     Cornell University Press, 1951.

_____. "Labor Attitudes Towards Industrialization in Under-
     developed Countries," American Economic Review. Menasha,
     Wisc.: May, 1955.

Myint, Hla. The Economics of the Developing Countries. London:
     Hutchinson, 1965.

Nurkse, R. Equilibrium and Growth in the World Economy. Cam-
     bridge, Mass.: Harvard University Press, 1961.

_____. Problems of Capital Formation in Underdeveloped
     Countries. Oxford: Blackwell, 1953.

Perroux, Francois. "Grande Firme et Petite Nation," in Rapport
     Jeanneney, Annexes. Paris: La Documentation Française,
     1963.

_____. Les Techniques Quantitatives de la Planification.
    Paris: PUF, 1965.

Pfeffermann, Guy. "Trade Unions and Politics in French West
    Africa during the Fourth Republic," African Affairs.
    London: July, 1967.

Phelps Brown, E. H. The Economics of Labor. New Haven: Yale
    University Press, 1962.

Polak, J. J. "Balance of Payments Problems of Countries Re-
    constructing with the Help of Foreign Loans," in Ellis,
    H. S. and L. A. Metzler (eds.), Readings in the Theory of
    International Trade. Philadelphia: Blakiston, 1949.

Ranis, G. "Production Functions, Market Imperfections and
    Economic Development," Economic Journal. London: June,
    1962.

Rosenstein-Rodan, P. N. "Problems of Industrialization in
    Eastern and South Eastern Europe," Economic Journal.
    London: June-September, 1943.

Samuelson, Paul A. Economics. New York: McGraw-Hill, 1955.

Schultz, T. "The Role of Government in Promoting Economic
    Growth," in Eicher and Witt, (eds.), Agriculture in Eco-
    nomic Development. New York: McGraw-Hill, 1964.

SCYMPEX. "Régime des Importation dans la Republique du Séné-
    gal." Dakar: 1964 (roneoed).

Sen, A. K. Choice of Techniques. Oxford: Blackwell, 1960.

Senghor, Leopold S. On African Socialism. London: Pall Mall
    Press, 1963.

Singer, H. W. International Development: Growth and Change.
    New York: McGraw-Hill, 1964.

Streeten, Paul. "Unbalanced Growth: A Reply," Oxford Econom-
    ic Papers. Oxford: Oxford University Press, 1963.

Travaux et Professions d'Outre-Mer. (Periodical). Paris.

Turner, H. A. Wage Trends, Wage Policies and Collective Bar-
    gaining: The Problems for Underdeveloped Countries.
    Cambridge: Cambridge University Press, 1965.

Weatherford, W. D., Jr. "Pakistan," in Galenson, Walter, (ed.),
    Labor in Developing Economies. Berkeley: University of
    California Press, 1962.

Young, Allyn. "Increasing Return and Economic Progress,"
    Economic Journal. London: December, 1928.